Youth and History

Youth and History

Tradition and Change in European Age Relations,
1770–Present

Expanded Student Edition

JOHN R. GILLIS

Livingston College
Rutgers, The State University
New Brunswick, New Jersey

ACADEMIC PRESS, INC.
Harcourt Brace Jovanovich, Publishers
Orlando   San Diego   New York
Austin   Boston   London   Sydney
Tokyo   Toronto

Cover illustrations: (top): *The Greenwich Hospital School, 1855* (Permission of the National Maritime Museum, London); (bottom): A selection from Honoré-Victorin Daumier's "Alarms and Alarmists" series (1848) from Plate 40, "The Dangerous Children," published in Howard P. Vincent, *Daumier and His World* (Evanston, Ill.: Northwestern University Press, 1968).

Appreciation is expressed for permission to reprint selections from Chapter VII of *Bohemian vs. Bourgeois: French Society and the French Man of Letters in the Nineteenth Century*, by Cesar Graña, ⓒ 1964 by Basic Books, Inc., Publishers, New York.

ACADEMIC PRESS, INC.
Orlando, Florida 32887

United Kingdom Edition published by
ACADEMIC PRESS, INC. (LONDON) LTD.
24/28 Oval Road, London NW1 7DX

Library of Congress Cataloging in Publication Data

Gillis, John R.
    Youth and history.

    (Studies in social discontinuity)
    Bibliography: p.
    Includes index.
    1. Youth--Europe--History.   2. Adolescence.   I. Title.
II. Series.
HQ796.G514 1981   305.2'3'09   81-7919
ISBN 0-12-785264-6   AACR2

PRINTED IN THE UNITED STATES OF AMERICA

87 88 89   9 8 7 6 5 4 3 2

In Memory of Randall Gillis

Contents

Preface

This book is dedicated to the proposition that youth makes its own history, a history linked with and yet analytically separable from that of the family, the school, and other adult institutions with which it is usually associated. For more than 80 years now, ever since the child study movement began in Europe and America, youth has been the object of investigation by psychologists, sociologists, and, most recently, historians. Yet, up to now, research has dealt less with youth's own response to change and more with the educational, penal, and welfare institutions that are supposed to be the agents of its transformation.[1] Youth's own role in creating the social and cultural forms that we associate with the part of the life cycle that spans childhood and adulthood remains obscure; and so, too, do the "traditions of youth," David Matza's term for the patterns of behavior and styles of thought that have characterized the age group over long periods of time and which demonstrate the historicity of youth and its value systems. "Tradition" is a particularly useful term precisely because it suggests that any explanation of youthful behavior at a given point in time must take into account not only social and economic structures but the previous historical experience of the age group, as an independent variable with a dynamic of its own.[2]

The very fact that many of the traditions of youth that we treat as contemporary—student radicalism, bohemianism, gang behavior, delinquency—can be traced back at least 200 years provides incentive

---

[1] For a review of four recent books on the history of American youth that fall into this category, see Gillis, "Youth and History."

[2] Matza, "Subterranean Traditions."

to the historian interested in questions of continuity as well as change. But it is also the opportunity to probe the causes of various forms and values and to try to account for their rise and fall in terms of certain key demographic and economic variables that provides motivation for this kind of study. To identify the origins of the modern traditions of youth requires that the history of the age group be related to that of broader societal structures and values. These shape the situations to which young people respond as they assess their passage to adulthood; and as these change, so too do the traditions that youth creates and sustains in its own interests. Parental expectations, economic opportunities, conditions of education and leisure—all these affect the way youth plots its social, economic, and cultural strategies. As the history of the past two centuries amply demonstrates, demographic and economic conditions have been primary factors in shaping the historical phases through which the traditions of youth have passed since the eighteenth century. As mortality and fertility rates have changed, and the conditions of industrialization and urbanization have altered, young persons have been confronted with a series of different situations affecting the duration and character of that segment of the life cycle which bridges childhood and adulthood. Because the same factors have simultaneously affected the perceptions and reactions of adults, we are dealing here with a history that operates on two distinct levels, however. On one hand, there are those expectations of youthful behavior that are established by adults in the home, the school, and the workplace. On the other, there are the youth groups themselves, sustained by their own independent traditions, acting from habits and values that are sometimes closely aligned with adult interests, at other times in opposition to them.

If the history of youth is to be written, it must focus on that interface where the expectations of the young and those of their elders interact in a dynamic manner. The task is further complicated, however, by the fact that at any point in time the demographic and economic experiences of differently situated class and status groups are also so varied. Differences in the life cycles both between and within major social classes have contributed substantially to the dynamics of European age relations since the eighteenth century. Chapters 2 and 3 explore the emergence of separate working-class and middle-class traditions of youth; Chapter 4 traces the conflict between these traditions, as it was institutionalized in the academic and extracurricular cultures of the early twentieth century.

Social history cannot be separated from institutional history, but the latter must not be allowed to obscure the existence of those autonomous traditions of youth that are associated with class, ethnicity, and locality. A purely functional approach should also be avoided, for it, too, ignores the age group's sense of connectedness with its own past and thus vastly underestimates the historical sources of moral and social authority that, quite apart from adult sanctions, shape youthful behavior. Restoring youth to its own history is a complicated task, not only because we must deal with different levels of historical reality—the personal, the group, the societal—but because each of the major phases in the history of youth since 1770 has produced a unique layer of tradition which continues to affect the present.[3] The historian must operate much like an archeologist as he attempts to discover the different strata of behavior and connect each to its historical orgins; and he must also use the tools of the demographer and sociologist in explaining how changing social conditions have caused these traditions to shift over time. Yet, none of these methods is complete in and of itself if the feelings and perceptions of those involved, the young themselves, are not given a primary place in the historical investigation. For, however important the historical context may be, it is the consciousness of the young, determined in part by the past experiences of their age group, that has determined the direction of change.

Clearly, any history of a largely anonymous group like youth requires methods different from those ordinarily employed. Because it was important to capture the voices and faces of the young, as well as those of the adults who claim to speak in their name, I have chosen to work on two levels, the national and the local, in order to research the whole spectrum of society. Two university towns with similar characteristics, Oxford and Göttingen, were the locations of intensive research during the year 1969–1970. This was combined with work on a national scale in both England and Germany, for the purpose of isolating those *general* trends that span cultural boundaries. The findings presented in this volume reflect more intensive use of English materials, if only because the kinds of demographic and economic materials I wished to use are more abundant there than in Germany. The history of German youth, particularly the middle class, differs in important ways from that of its English counterpart, but, on the whole, similarities in the timing and sequence of youth groups and cultures in the two countries support the notion that the history of youth in Europe has everywhere moved along the broad lines laid down by economic and demographic modernization.

---

[3] A model for the psychohistory of youth, a dimension which is excluded in this study, is discussed in Keniston, "Psychological Development."

"Modernization," as it is used here, is not to be equated with "progress." I use it only as a convenient covering term for the general direction of change that has been occurring since the middle of the eighteenth century, of which the history of youth is an integral part. The major turning points of youth's history have coincided with the important economic and demographic transformations of the past 200 years, transformations that have strongly affected every major social institution, including the family. I have attempted here to use the fruits of the demographers' labors, supplemented by my own social research, to establish the conditions under which children have come into the world, how these children have been treated once part of a family, and how they have coped with those social and economic situations imposed on them by birth into a particular class or status group. The conditions confronting the young have varied enormously in accordance with such things as family size and class situation. The more closely their history is interwoven with both economic and demographic factors, the more concrete and understandable it becomes.

I have also attempted here to explore the ways the traditions of youth have interacted with the political history of the past two centuries. Abstracted too much from this more conventional type of narrative, social history is always in danger of losing its significance and interest. It has not been my intention to open up yet another specialized field of inquiry, but rather to demonstrate the integral nature of the historical process. Readers will have to judge the success of this effort by the degree to which this volume's treated matter contributes to their understanding of their own fields. My hope is that social scientists will find insight into the origins and evolution of an age group about whose contemporary structures and functions they are relatively well-informed, but whose historical dynamics they have almost entirely neglected.[4] As for my fellow historians, I offer the approach used here as a possible starting point for further investigation of other age groups, including the middle-aged and the elderly, whose past is, at this point, at least as obscure as that of the younger age groups. And, as this study is concerned mainly with the traditions of masculine youth, there is obviously work to be done on the traditions of their feminine counterparts.

---

[4] Most of the literature in the social sciences remains essentially ahistorical in its approach, valuable for its structural-functional analysis of the young at various points in time but ignoring almost entirely the dynamics of continuity and change. For example, Eisenstadt, *Generation to Generation*; Parsons; Kingsley Davis; and Gottlieb *et al.*

Acknowledgments

The research for this work, completed in Oxford and Göttingen during the academic year 1969–1970, was made possible by the Rollins Bicentennial Preceptorship Fund of Princeton University. I am particularly thankful to the Fellows of St. Antony's College and their Dean, Theodore Zeldin, for making the months in Oxford such enjoyable ones. Their hospitality was matched by that of the officials of the Bodleian Library and the City of Oxford Library. Special permission to use unpublished records was generously granted by the Clerk to the City Justices, the Education Department, and the Town Clerk, Keeper of the Oxford City Muniments. Nuffield College opened the G. D. H. Cole Papers to me, and I was helped greatly by the generosity of individuals in charge of the archives of various private organizations, including Mr. George Springall and Mr. W. R. Willis of the Scouts, Mr. DelNevo of the Y.M.C.A., and Dr. Willis Bund, Dean of Balliol College. Mr. Thomas Dunn allowed me to use the log books of St. Barnabas School, while Mr. F. S. Green graciously shared his memories of a career in Oxford youth work, providing me with unpublished material in his possession.

The officials of the Göttingen *Stadtarchiv* were no less helpful than their Oxford counterparts; and Dr. Hans Wolf, Director of the *Wandervogel* archive at Burg Ludwigstein, was most energetic in his assistance. Frau Luebbecke of Reckershausen made our stay in the valley of the Leine a delightful as well as profitable experience.

I regret I cannot mention all those who have listened at one time or another to my rambling commentaries on social history. However, I would like to express my special thanks to Charles Tilly, Joseph Kett, Edward Shorter, James McLachlan, Dorothy Ross, John E. Talbott,

Peter Stearns, and Richard Andrews. I am indebted to those members of the Institute for Advanced Study, Princeton University, Rutgers University, and the Davis Seminar who have discussed parts of this work in seminars over the past three years. Those who participated in the Conference on the History of Youth, held at Princeton in April, 1971, also provided constructive criticisms, as did the members of the Social History Group at Rutgers. Last but not least in this bill of gratitudes are the students of Livingston College, who responded with tolerance and insight as this book unfolded in lecture and seminar. It is my hope that they find something of themselves in these pages.

Youth and History

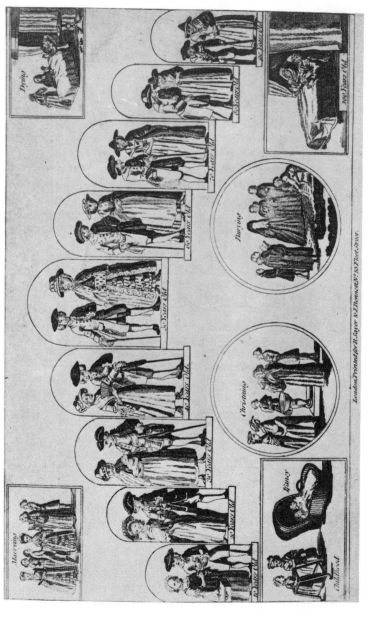

"Ages of Man," ca. 1733, a print representing the life cycle as it was perceived in the early eighteenth century. Copyright by The Warburg Institute, University of London. Reproduced by permission of The Warburg Institute.

1

Like a Family and a Fraternity: Youth in Preindustrial Europe

By the standards of today's biologically exacting vocabulary, the language of age in preindustrial Europe is hopelessly vague. Even as late as the eighteenth century, the French and German words *garçon* and *Knabe* referred to boys as young as 6 and as old as 30 or 40. In part, such confusions stemmed from the fact that such terms also denoted status or function, *garçon* meaning "servant" as well as "boy." Even today, "lad" and "boy" still carry traces of this original double meaning; and among Irish peasants it is still common to call unmarried, propertyless men "boys," regardless of their age, because this denotes their low status in a community where marriage and inheritance mark one of the most important social boundaries. The same holds for the American South, where the low status of blacks is regularly reinforced by reference to them as "boys" or "girls," whatever their real ages may be.[1]

Philippe Ariès has argued from this linguistic evidence that preindustrial Europe made no distinction between childhood and other preadult phases of life. There was, he says, "an ambiguity between childhood and adolescence on the one hand and the category known as youth on the other. People had no idea of what we call adolescence, and the idea was a long time in taking shape."[2] Noting that the Latin terms *puer* (child) and *adolescens* were used interchangeably until the eighteenth century, and arguing that youth was wholly

---

[1] Ariès, pp. 25–29; Arensberg and Kimball, p. 55.
[2] Ariès, p. 29.

2

identified with what we would now call "young adulthood," he concludes that Europeans recognized no intermediate stage that would
resemble our current notion of adolescence. "Nobody would have
thought of seeing the end of childhood in puberty. The idea of childhood was bound up with the idea of dependence: the words 'sons,'
'varlets,' and 'boys' were also in the vocabulary of feudal subordination. One would leave childhood only by leaving the state of dependence, or at least the lower degrees of dependence." [3]

But it was precisely in these degrees of dependence that preindustrial society recognized and institutionalized a stage of life that was
different from both childhood and adulthood. What they commonly
called "youth" was a very long transition period, lasting from the
point that the very young child first became somewhat independent
of its family, usually about seven or eight, to the point of complete independence at marriage, ordinarily in the mid- or late twenties. Im-
precise as youth's boundaries were, there being no universally recognized age-grading as in today's society, its sociology was relatively
clear. Beginning at what seems to us to be a very young age, children
began to separate from their families and to go to live in other households. By 14, a great majority would be living in a state of semidependence, either as servants in households, apprentices living in their
masters' homes, or students boarding away from their families. It was
precisely this detachment from family that gave preindustrial youth
its peculiar structure and meaning, as depicted in the idealized life
plan presented in Figure 1.

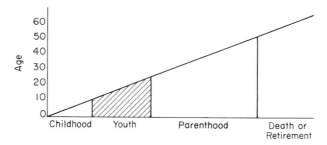

Figure 1 Phases of life in preindustrial society.

Here is a stage of life very different from anything we know as
"youth" or "adolescence" today. Not only was it more drawn out and
differently related to both childhood and adulthood, but the tradi-

[3] Ariès, p. 26.

tions that evolved from the long and often difficult transition from childhood to adulthood were necessarily at variance with modern youth cultures. Youth, as it was experienced both by those passing through that stage of life and by adults, must therefore be understood on its own terms and in the context of the unique demographic and economic conditions that prevailed before the mid-eighteenth century.

I

Evidence of youth as a separate stage of life with its own history and traditions comes to us from a variety of sources, some literary and iconographic, others economic and demographic. Folk traditions inform us of popular ideas concerning age-grading which are not readily accessible through the written record; and even in the festive and leisure activities we find evidence of age divisions. Holidays, such as New Year and Easter, saw boys and girls at play and in performance of games and dances reserved to their age group. In England, village sport pitted young bachelors against older married men, thus underlining both age and status differences. Certain festival occasions were regarded as the property of the young, such as Oxford's November 5th, Guy Fawkes Night, when the ceremonial burning of the Guy was usually followed by a violent town-versus-gown row in which youth was allowed to exhaust its energies. In most of the traditional calendar processions, both sacred and profane, age cohorts were also clearly distinguishable. Dancing, singing, and mumming on holidays provide evidence of age groups of which Ariès was not unaware but which he tended to present as survivals of an earlier pagan society, customs that had lost meaning and function by the seventeenth and eighteenth centuries.[4] From the work of Natalie Davis and others, we now know, however, that the organized role of young men and women in festive occasions was only one manifestation of an institutionalized system of youth groups that existed in many parts of preindustrial

---

[4] Ariès, pp. 76–99; Hole, *English Sports*, pp. 97, 116, 122.

Europe. Furthermore, these groups bear striking resemblance to, and were sometimes complemented by, the activities of various craft and corporate cohorts. Students, journeymen in many of the major trades, and novices in the army, clergy, and bureaucracy all had their own organizations and traditions which distinguished them from children on one hand and married adults on the other.

The definition and composition of village and corporate youth groups varied widely and there was no uniform age of entry, even in schools and universities. This meant that universal age distinctions, such as those imposed in our society by schooling, were lacking in preindustrial Europe. Nevertheless, that society recognized certain *ideal* ages of entry and exit from the semidependence of youth. In Germany, for example, church confirmation—usually occurring about the fourteenth year—was considered a kind of rite of passage into youth, a time for beginning journeyman's status in urban society or joining the village youth group, commonly called the *Brüderschaft*.[5] At the other end of youth, the expectation that young men would enter into marriage and inheritance in their late twenties reflected another established *ideal*. Premature entry into the marriage market was bound to provoke public censure, while remaining unmarried past a certain age made "old maids" of girls and confirmed bachelors of boys.[6]

It is important to note that we are dealing here with popular notions that were prescriptive rather than descriptive. Life itself was commonly thought of as having a certain symmetry, a cycle from birth to death in which the prime of life was reached in the first years of marriage. For the fifteenth-century Florentine, a man's prime, his *gioventute*, ranged from his late twenties to the age 35. But that was a society in which men married later than the preindustrial norm; ordinarily, for males it was in the late twenties and for females the mid-twenties that the peak of the life cycle was reached through marriage.[7] Childhood and youth were commonly viewed as subordinate stages of life, leading up to, but hardly challenging, the supremacy of the young marrieds.[8] It could hardly have been otherwise in a society where half the children born did not survive to the age of 20. The popular conception was that of the survivors, who viewed

---

[5] Wikman, pp. 20–22; Hornstein, pp. 118ff.
[6] Hajnal, pp. 101–146.
[7] Herlihy, p. 1339; Gilbert, pp. 7–32.
[8] See illustration opposite page 1.

with relief their passage through those dangerous early phases and looked upon old age as another time of dependence and trouble. As we shall see, the hierarchy of ages—with childhood, youth, and old age placed in various stages of dependence on young adulthood —was, in fact, a fairly accurate blueprint of preindustrial society's economic, social, and political age structure, as that structure was viewed by those with the social and economic power. They prescribed dependence to childhood, semidependence to youth, and retiring senility to old age because, to a large extent, this was the only way the transmission of culture, property, and skill from generation to generation could be guaranteed.

II

The modern reader is inevitably struck not only by the extraordinary duration of the period defined as "youth," but by the lack of clear distinctions between younger and older members of that age group. We are so used to contrasting the dependence of the teen years (adolescence) with the relative independence of the early twenties (youth) that we are surprised by the lack of differentiation. We associate adolescence with certain tasks of personal growth, including sexual maturation and personality formation, while conferring on the later ages the choice of occupation, courtship, political commitment, and other social responsibilities. Preindustrial Europe did not break down the life cycle in this way, however. Personal, social, and economic tasks of development were concurrently rather than sequentially organized, a fact which accounts for the lack of distinction between adolescence and youth in the society's conception of the normal life cycle.

Prevailing economic, demographic, and biological conditions account for these differences. There was no universal schooling to postpone entry into the world of work, and because social mobility was more limited, choice of occupation was less of a problem. Many a lad followed his father's plow from the age of 7 or 8 without thought to alternatives; but even those for whom some choice was open began their training early, apprenticeships beginning at age 14 or even before. In the less tightly-structured unskilled occupations a boy or girl might move in and out of jobs, but here again there was no pattern that would mark a break between early and later youth. The sons of the aristocracy entered the university at an average age of 15 in seventeenth-century England, spending a variable amount of time there, many not even bothering to graduate. Apparently, the less well-to-do who were able to enter the university followed a very different pattern, arriving, on the average, when more than a year older. They often had to work until their mid-teens, only then having enough money to continue their education at Latin school or university.[9] In any case, education was commonly taken by all strata in bits and pieces, constantly being interrupted by seasonal work and other more important demands on the children's time.[10]

Neither work nor education were as sharply age-graded as we have come to expect; and this accounts, in part, for the lack of distinctions within the long age-span of preindustrial youth. The onset of physical and sexual maturity also might be expected to have marked a break, but it did not, primarily because children were accustomed to assuming adult sex roles very early and the attainment of puberty was not signified by change in dress or by other external manifestations of maturity. For the modern teenager, considerable anxiety often results from physical changes which conflict with a self-image inherited from the largely asexual world of modern childhood. A changing body shape and the development of secondary sex characteristics rather suddenly make obsolete both children's clothing and the special roles prescribed for preadolescents in our society. But prior to the nineteenth century, children were dressed as miniature adults, complete with all the external manifestations of masculinity and femininity. Exposed to the social aspect of adult sexuality earlier than modern children, they had much less difficulty in coping with their own biological changes.[11]

Equally important in explaining the absence of crisis at the onset of puberty is the fact that it and its associated physical growth occurred later and more gradually in preindustrial populations. As recently as the mid-nineteenth century, physical changes that we asso-

---

[9] Stone, "Size and Composition," p. 53; Ariès, p. 225.

[10] Ariès, Chapter 4. For preindustrial America, see Kett.

[11] Hunt, pp. 180–186. On American childrearing in the same period, see Demos, Chapter 9.

ciate with early teen-age were occurring 3 or 4 years later. In Norway in 1850 the average age of menarche was a little over 17 years, as compared to $13\frac{1}{2}$ today.[12] Data for those centuries prior to the nineteenth is less reliable, but there seems little doubt that the ages of both puberty and menarche were at least as high as 16 for the mass of the rural population, perhaps a bit lower in towns. Undoubtedly, the children of the rich matured earlier than the children of the poor, nutrition being a prime factor in the maturation process; but differences between groups only further reduced the importance of puberty as an institutionalized social turning point.[13]

Equally important is the fact that physical growth associated with puberty occurred at a much more gradual rate. According to one mid-sixteenth-century encyclopedia, full physical powers were not attained until the late twenties, sometimes even the early thirties.[14] Additional, more reliable, evidence from medical records indicates that the mid-twenties was the more likely norm; but, in any case, the slower growth rate would help account for why earlier generations of Europeans placed so little emphasis on the uniqueness of the adolescent (teen) years as opposed to the longer stage of life they called "youth." [15]

Puberty rites are ordinarily socially defined anyway. If we look at the position of the teen-aged in the preindustrial social and economic order it becomes apparent why, regardless of the obvious biological differences, the definition of "adolescence" was bound to be different from that of today. In our time, the adolescent is distinguished from older youth primarily by the fact that he or she is coresident with his or her own family. When a young person leaves home, he or she ceases to be looked upon as an adolescent and enters into the category of "youth." Preindustrial society made no such distinction, precisely because children were sent out to live in other households as early as 7 or 8 years. There they lived and worked as servants to the receiving family, sometimes taking up more formal apprenticeships in other households at 13 or 14, but in one way or another living outside their own families for most of their youth. An Italian visi-

---

[12] Tanner, pp. 928–930; Laslett, "Age of Menarche"; Muchow, *Jugend und Zeitgeist*, pp. 83–85; Hajnal, p. 128.
[13] Tanner, p. 929; Hunt, p. 181, footnote 10.
[14] Ariès, p. 21.
[15] Tanner, p. 928.

tor to sixteenth-century England described the practices there as follows:[16]

> The want of affection in the English is strongly manifested towards
> their children; for after having kept them at home till they arrive at
> the age of 7 to 9 at the utmost, they put them out, both males and
> females, to hard service in the houses of other people, binding them
> generally for another 7 to 9 years. And these are called apprentices,
> and during that time they perform all the most menial offices; and
> few are born who are exempted from this fate, for every one, how-
> ever rich he may be, sends away his children into the houses of others,
> whilst he, in return, receives those of strangers into his own.

That this practice derived from a want of affection is, as we shall
see, debatable; and the Italian visitor was wrong in thinking it confined only to England. Informal and formal apprenticeship of children prevailed in all countries until the eighteenth century, giving to
the terms *garçon* and "boy" the double meaning of age and function
that they retained well into the nineteenth.[17] Since all ranks of society had it, there was nothing demeaning in this role. The young
strangers and the natural children of the family were treated much
alike, both subject in the same manner to the authority of the head
of the household. As it was set down in one late sixteenth-century
treatise on household government: "The householder is called *Pater
Familias*, that is, father of a familie, because he should have fatherly
care over his servants, as if they were his children." In turn, the duty
of the little servant toward his master and mistress was "to love them
and be affectionated towards them, as a dutifull child is towards his
father." [18]

Leaving home at an early age, both boys and girls moved from a
state of dependence to one of semidependence that would characterize their existence until the age of marriage. Thus, the ages of 7
or 8 took on a significance for preindustrial parents that they do not
have for us. This was deemed a great turning point in the development of the child. Ready for semidependence, they were dressed as
miniature adults and permitted to use the manners and language of

---

[16] *A Relation or rather a True Account of the Island of England . . . about the
year 1500,* by an Italian, quoted in MacFarlane, p. 206; also Tranter, pp. 276–277.
    [17] Ariès, pp. 26–27.
    [18] John Dod and Robert Cleaver, *Godly Forme of Household Government,* quoted
in Schochet, p. 415; for Germany, see Brunner, pp. 37–44.

adult society. The future Louis XIII was provided with adult garb as early as his fifth birthday, being told at that time: "Monsieur, now your bonnet is removed, you are no longer a child; you begin to become a man." [19]

This stage of becoming was, however, an extraordinarily long, drawn-out process. The young were to remain in a subordinate position until they attained, through marriage or inheritance, the status of heads of households. They were constantly reminded of their semidependence by their inferior economic, social, and legal status in a society in which full rights were reserved mainly to the heads of families and other "masters" of the craft and corporate hierarchies. Even the children of the rich and the powerful were made to feel their inferiority; and until the mid-eighteenth century, Oxford students were still subject to corporal punishment, the symbol of the subordination they shared with servants and apprentices of lower station in life.[20] Moving, at age 14, from the informal apprenticeship to more formal indentures in the trades or professions signified, as did entry into the university, a further step beyond the dependence of childhood, but then only in degree. Until marriage, the role of both males and females continued to be characterized by semidependence, a time spent away from home and family, mainly in the company of strangers.

III

How are we to understand a system of age relations so very different from our own? The Italian suggested a lack of tenderness on the part of parents. Thomas Hobbes did him one better by ascribing selfishness as a motive. Boys were sent to Oxford, he said, "by their parents to save themselves the trouble of governing them at home, during that time wherein children are least governable." [21] Not surprisingly, the parents themselves put forward another reason: They

---

[19] Hunt, p. 180.
[20] Ariès, pp. 252–266.
[21] Quoted in Stone, "Size and Composition," p. 18.

wanted to avoid spoiling their children by sending them away.[22] The fact is that various motives were probably involved, but behind them all were the demographic conditions of the age, the facts of life which, in combination with the economic structure of preindustrial society, determined the definition of youth.

For all but a very thin strata of the privileged elites existence was, as Thomas Hobbes described it, "nasty, brutish, short." High mortality in the first years of life dictated at birth a life expectancy that in the 1690s was 32 years in England and 27.5 years in Breslau, Germany, ranging slightly higher or lower according to local circumstances, and plunging still further at times due to war, famine, or natural disaster. This was to be the case for the mass of the population until well into the nineteenth century; for, even among the English aristocracy, life expectancy did not rise significantly until the early eighteenth century, when it climbed (violent deaths excepted) from 34.7 to 45.8 years for males, and 33.7 to 48.2 years for females.[23]

The most vulnerable ages were the youngest; and, as François Lebrun has shown for the French village of Challain during the last third of the seventeenth century, 18% of the children died in their first month, 35% in their first year, and 53% before they reached the age of 20.[24] Only in a few places in preindustrial Europe did more than half of the children born live to the age of majority. Confronted with the fact that only one of two children born would survive, parents were faced with a situation very different from that of modern families. If they were just to reproduce themselves, their fertility had to be considerably higher than that of the present day. Women could expect to endure considerably more child bearing and raising, for while completed families were not necessarily larger, more children were born simply to meet the needs dictated by a high mortality situation.

The English historical demographer E. A. Wrigley has estimated that, given a life expectancy of 30 years, there must be at least four children born to each family in order that there be at least a 60% chance that one male heir will survive the father. Because societal norms dictated that a son should inherit upon the death or retirement of the father, family strategy required high fertility among both the rural

---

[22] Demos, p. 74.

[23] Laslett, *World We Have Lost,* pp. 103–105; Hollingsworth, pp. 66–70; Chambers, Chapter 4.

[24] Charles Tilly, p. 119.

and urban property-owning population. Fertility patterns might vary at both ends of the social spectrum—among the privileged groups whose death rates were not so appallingly high, and among the landless or the very poor, where considerations of inheritance were irrelevant; but, for what was still the majority of the population in 1700, high mortality dictated high fertility, rising even higher after times of adversity when disease, war, or famine reduced life expectancy below the normal.

Children were to preindustrial society what pensions and disability insurance are to our own. They represented a kind of investment which, while it did not always pay off, was necessary if parents were to have peace of mind about their old age and the perpetuation of their property. A succession of female children or the accidental death of an elder son could destroy the best of family strategies, but the fertile couple who produced four or more children had at least a reasonable chance of fulfilling their hopes for themselves and for their offspring.[25]

What this meant in terms of the age distribution was an abundance of children, with the median age of the population varying from a relatively high 28 years in late seventeenth-century England to figures as low as 21 years, depending on conditions. It has been estimated that, in the English village of Stoke-on-Trent in 1701, 49% of the population were under 20 years of age. In Sweden in 1750 the ratio of those persons aged 15–29 years to every 100 persons aged 30 years and over was 63%. In France in 1776 the ratio was 65%; and as late as 1840 it was approximately 77% in England.[26] This abundance of children and young people is all the more striking when compared to our own times. Today, the percentage of children under 20 in places like Stoke-on-Trent has dropped precipitously and is only 29% of the total population. In England as a whole, age groups up to age 29 compose only 43% of the population, as compared with about 63% in the late seventeenth century.[27]

"We must imagine our ancestors, therefore, in the perpetual presence of their young offspring," Peter Laslett has observed, noting, as have other historians, how little apparent notice adults gave to children, despite their overwhelming numbers. This was due, in part, to the high mortality during the young years and to the fact that parents

---

[25] Wrigley's work cited in Charles Tilly, pp. 119–120.
[26] Laslett, *World We Have Lost,* p. 103; Chambers, pp. 67ff; Herbert Moller, p. 252.
[27] Marsh, pp. 22–26.

could never be sure which of their children would survive to maturity. In such a situation, their attitude was bound to be different from that of the modern parent, not because they were more hard hearted but because, as Rousseau suggested, they could harm rather than help children by paying them the wrong kind of heed. What was the point, he asked, of a training "which sacrifices the present to an uncertain future . . . and begins by making the child miserable, in order to prepare him for some far-off happiness which he may never enjoy?" [28] Parents were advised to prepare the young for the possibility of death, that of their own and of those around them. Conduct books prepared adults for the death of infants, whose passing did not provoke the same kind of grief as older children, conditions dictating that they spare themselves and their offspring extreme disappointment by restraining expectations for the individual boy or girl even into teen age.[29]

Attention naturally focused on the males of the family, for it was through them that wealth and name were to be perpetuated. Customs of inheritance differed from strata to strata, and were not the same in all parts of Europe, however. In England, for example, the nobility, wealthy gentry, and bourgeoisie had come to prefer primogeniture, while the peasantry and artisanate appear to have divided their property more readily, sometimes even giving portions to daughters. In parts of France and western Germany partible inheritance was even more widespread, though there too the eldest son often gained the largest share.[30] Attention given to one child did not necessarily work to the detriment of the other children, for it was generally understood that the well-being of all depended to some degree on the smooth succession in case of the death or retirement of the parents. For example, the loss of family property could result in the forfeiture of the settlement rights of all the surviving children, a blow that could mean a reduction to vagabondage in an age before universal citizenship and the welfare rights attached to it. Thus it was not uncommon for daughters and even younger sons to sacrifice for the good of all by disclaiming inheritance entirely, choosing, in what David Hunt has called "an important gesture of family loyalty," a life of celibacy.[31]

---

[28] Musgrove, *Youth and Social Order*, p. 64.
[29] Hunt, p. 185.
[30] Thirsk, p. 361; Blum.
[31] Hunt, p. 58.

Even where property was partible there were strong pressures in the seventeenth and eighteenth centuries not to distribute the inheritance so thinly as to destroy the property and thereby endanger the entire family.[32] As in the situation of primogeniture, younger children, particularly daughters but also younger sons, were viewed as expendable; produced by the pressure of high mortality on fertility, they were a form of surplus whose utility was greatly diminished once the eldest son inherited the property upon the retirement or death of the father. Family strategy thus dictated a superfluity that, in turn, gave to youth its peculiar character. Well-to-do families could, and often did, provide for surplus sons and daughters, sometimes keeping them at home, supplying them with suitable dowries, or setting them up in other trades or professions without dividing or unduly diminishing family property. The younger sons of the English aristocracy and gentry were customarily established in respectable positions, always available to inherit title or lands if the eldest son should meet an untimely end. The workability of such a system depended, of course, on the acceptance by the younger sons and daughters of a certain measure of downward mobility, a sacrifice sweetened by the fact that their fathers could often afford to set them up well in career and marriage. Yet, throughout the sixteenth and early seventeenth centuries, condemnation to an inferior status by accident of the order of birth often rankled the younger sons. One such, Sergeant Yelverton, bemoaned the plight of those who must uphold the honor of family name on insufficient means: "My estate is nothing correspondent for the maintenance of this dignity, for my father dying left me a younger brother and nothing unto me but my bare annuity, then growing to man's estate and some practise of law, I took a wife by whom I have had many children, the keeping of all being a great impoverishing of my estate and the daily living of us all nothing but my daily industry."[33]

In France and Germany the situation of younger sons was even more precarious, if only because caste lines were stronger there and the children of titled fathers were not permitted to enter many trades and professions. They would seek to maintain their respectability by entering into clerical celibacy or by seeking careers in the army and civil service, but the opportunities fluctuated in a capricious manner,

---

[32] Habakkuk, pp. 24–28.
[33] Quoted in Thirsk, p. 363.

causing much distress among the superfluous sons of the aristocracy.[34] Daughters, too, were in a precarious position, though in countries where Catholicism prevailed the convent was an honorable alternative. We know that the percentage of both males and females who never married was relatively high in preindustrial European society, averaging about 10%. Spinsterhood seems to have been particularly prevalent among the very poor, for whom marriage and remarriage were very difficult. In seventeenth-century English villages the percentage of women aged 25–44 who were either widows or spinsters was almost a third.[35]

The fate of superfluous children was, in fact, much worse among the poor. The Sergeant Yelvertons had to contend with loss of status, but their connections usually protected them against pauperization. The vast majority of the population lived much closer to the minimum levels of subsistence; and even the landed peasantry and urban artisanate were not immune to the pauperization that was the periodic consequence of famine, war, epidemic, and natural disaster. Of the mass of the population, we are reasonably well-informed only about the peasantry and the artisanate; and it is from their historical record that we must attempt to construct a picture of the life-cycle of the preindustrial poor.

IV

We know that peasant sons rarely inherited their father's property until their late twenties, at the time their parent either died or voluntarily retired and settled the farm, in the latter case, on the oldest male in return for assurance of support for the rest of his life. Final settlement would normally include the establishment of dowries for daughters, and annuities or smaller land grants for younger sons. Inheritance of the land or the business allowed the eldest son to marry and immediately begin his own family, thus renewing the cy-

[34] Goodwin, pp. 91f, 104ff.
[35] Stone, "Social Mobility," p. 41.

cle—which, approximately 30 years later, would terminate in his death or retirement—and the passing on of the family property to a new generation. Life expectations of the fathers established the marriage age of the sons at 27 or 28, their wives being 3 or 4 years younger. Brides were often pregnant upon marriage and the first child was expected to arrive soon after the ceremony, followed by others at regular intervals. The wife's career as child-bearer would continue for an average of 10 to 15 years, during which time she would produce an average of 4 to 5 babies, only half of which were likely to survive until the age of 20.[36]

The husband's burden was equally arduous, particularly when, as was the case in most peasant and artisanal holdings, the property was just barely enough to sustain two adults and a small number of children. The size of household was proportional to wealth in preindustrial society, the poor being able to support themselves only with great difficulty. If the property had been inherited by retirement, the surviving old folks were an added burden to the young married couple. In some cases the old man could work for his son, and his wife help with the household chores, but in most cases their deaths were a relief to an already overburdened young family.[37] It was in the first years of marriage, when the children were still too young to contribute to the family economy through their own labor, that things were most difficult. It was common for peasants to hire servants to help work the land or to do household duties during the time their own children were still very young, but this was burdensome and usually did not last beyond the first 10 years of the family life cycle.[38]

The number of live-in servants required by particular families depended on both the size of the holding and the age of the household's own offspring. The more well-to-do peasants were able to hire more servants than their poorer neighbors; and it was the case in most parts of Europe that the wealthier a household, the larger it was in terms of numbers, due to the number of servants who could be

---

[36] The number of children per completed marriage varied considerably according to economic and demographic conditions. Following a plague or famine, the number of children might be larger in order to replace losses. These figures, therefore, represent numbers of children in "normal" times, at the minimum levels of mortality. For a discussion of the complicated question of completed family size, see Chambers, pp. 67–73.

[37] Berkner, pp. 398–401.

[38] Berkner, p. 414.

brought under its roof. Most of these servants were teen-aged boys and girls recruited by the wealthier households from the poorer, a practice which thus served the function of providing relief to those families who found themselves overburdened by surplus children. Paid in terms of room and board, and subordinate to the authority of the head of the household in which they were employed, these youths were effectively provided for, both economically and socially.[39]

For the poor the first years of marriage were the most difficult. Parents eager to have the help of their children and to dispense with paid servants naturally emphasized precocity. As soon as a child was physically ready, he or she was put to work. Little tasks might even be delegated to toddlers, but normally the child began to work at 6 or 7, an age set by custom and physical development. By the tenth anniversary of marriage, the household was becoming more self-sufficient and, unless the holding was large, live-in help was no longer necessary. The household size, therefore, remained relatively stable, the children substituting their labor for that of the departing servants, as indicated in Figure 2.

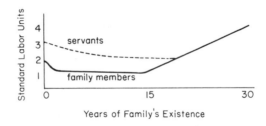

Figure 2 Labor needs of peasant families in preindustrial society [from Berkner, p. 415].

Sometime after the tenth anniversary, the labor of the older children began to become, like that of live-in servants, redundant and a burden. High fertility meant that at some point the family was quite likely to be confronted with more labor than its limited property could absorb. Younger children were, in effect, forcing out the older, who were now in a position to seek their fortunes elsewhere and thus provide relief to their parents and siblings. In late sixteenth-century Ealing, an English village, it appears that boys ordinarily left

---

[39] MacFarlane, pp. 206–209; Tranter, pp. 275ff.

home between the ages of 8 and 15, while girls were moving out between the ages of 9 and 14. Alan MacFarlane has estimated that between puberty (by which he means 14) and marriage, two-thirds of the males and three-fourths of the females were living away from their parents, mainly as servants in other households. Poorer families absorbed fewer servants, and so it was the well-to-do who benefitted from this supply of cheap surplus labor. "The institution of servant-hood might, therefore, be regarded as a disguised means whereby wealth and labour flowed from the poorer to the richer." [40]

This was also the time of life when young men were sent off to schools, apprenticeships, or novitiates in the church. As one might expect, the departure from the family varied somewhat, according to wealth. Lawrence Stone has been able to show that sons of the aristocracy entered Oxford at a little over 15 in the seventeenth century, almost a year and a half earlier than did commoner students. It appears that the latter were needed by their parents for a longer period of time because they were cheaper than hired labor.[41] The similarities among various social strata seem to outweigh differences, however, and it would seem that from 7 or 8 onwards most children were accustomed to a considerable amount of mobility, beginning first with short moves to neighboring households and then, in teen-age, undertaking more elaborate forms of migration, often to towns where apprenticeships and other opportunities were to be found. Wrote Sir John Gibson in 1655 of his own wanderings:[42]

> Crake it had my infancye,
> Yorke did my youth bringe up,
> Cambridge had my jollitie
> When I her brestes did sucke.
> London brought me into thraule
> And wed me to a wife
> Welborne my carefull time had all
> Joyn'd with a troubled life.

Well into the eighteenth century the custom of "claiming kin" was a way families relieved themselves of the burden of surplus children. Friedrich Klöden's parents asked his uncle to take the boy in and

---

[40] MacFarlane, p. 209.
[41] Stone, "Size and Composition," pp. 55–56.
[42] Quoted in MacFarlane, p. 210; on migration, see Chambers, Chapter 2.

train him in the goldsmithing trade. The claim on kin was accepted very grudgingly and young Friedrich became the object of abuse in his relative's household.[43] Where a large town was near, it was common for older children to be sent there, sometimes to prearranged positions, but often on their own to "seek their fortunes." Circulation of young people between London and its surrounding areas seems to have been relatively constant in the seventeenth century, with young boys and girls in their late teens and early twenties going to the city, some returning to their home villages later in life to claim inheritances or to marry.[44] In Austria it was common for servant girls to return to their hometowns to marry and settle down, although there, as in other parts of Europe, many youths were sent off never to return to villages where opportunities for inheritance and marriage were more limited.[45]

V

Peasant society was obviously by no means as free of generational discontinuity as mythology would have us believe. E. A. Wrigley estimates that one-sixth of the English population in the seventeenth century had lived in London at one time or another during their lives.[46] Historical evidence will not permit us to know what part of the youthful migration was cycled back to the home villages, but in a society in which surplus children were a permanent feature, there must have been a sizeable portion who never returned. Fluctuations in population could easily disrupt the delicate balance in any case. In times of population growth, when there were larger numbers of children than usual, even more younger sons and daughters were cut loose to pursue uncertain futures in towns or rural frontier areas. We know that this happened in the period 1550–1630, when the English

---

[43] von Klöden, vol. 1, pp. 215ff.
[44] Stone, "Social Mobility," pp. 30–32; Wrigley, "Simple Model," pp. 47ff.
[45] Berkner, p. 411.
[46] Wrigley, "Simple Model," p. 49.

population doubled and surplus persons poured into waste areas such as fens and highlands, as well as into the expanding towns.[47] Contemporaries believed that they detected growing generational tensions, and there were moves to tighten the authority of the heads of households, workshops, and schools against the "defections and revolts in children of lewd behavior, which have contemptuously prophaned all obedience to parents."[48]

With its limited resources, preindustrial English society could not sustain this population growth. The inevitable result was the disaster of famine and the reduction of fertility by a variety of means, including the delay of marriage, the practice of coitus interruptus, and resort to abortion and infanticide. By the early seventeenth century, fertility was falling among the English aristocracy. The average age of marriage for males born in the cohort 1480–1679 was 24.3 years; the average age for the cohort born 1680–1729 was 28.6.[49] While all the children of the aristocracy were marrying later, and more than before were not marrying at all, it was the youngest sons who bore the greatest burden of self-limitation. Hollingsworth's study of the English peerage shows that by the mid-eighteenth century almost 20% of younger sons remained unmarried throughout their lives, a proportion almost twice that of earlier periods.[50]

It can be shown that the younger, surplus children were also the ones to suffer most, socially and economically, in times of population growth. The reaction of the English aristocracy to the demographic crisis of the early seventeenth century was to enforce stricter settlements on inheritance. There is evidence that fathers were seeing to it that the oldest son got the best education and patronage, leaving the younger with lesser prospects than ever before. The best marriages were also monopolized by the eldest, while many younger sons and daughters were forced to marry beneath themselves.[51] Fortunately for the English aristocracy, the trade and merchant families of London welcomed association with the downwardly mobile nobility; and this, together with expanded opportunities in the military and civil service fields, made their situation considerably better than that of the Con-

---

[47] Stone, "Social Mobility," pp. 20–21, 31.
[48] John Budden, as quoted in Schochet, p. 419; Stone, "Social Mobility," pp. 46ff; also Hill, pp. 151–153, 296.
[49] Hollingsworth, p. 11.
[50] Hollingsworth, pp. 20–22.
[51] Stone, "Social Mobility," pp. 37–38; Stone, "Marriage," pp. 187–88.

tinental nobility, for whom downward mobility was more problematical.

Yet, this retrenchment did not set in before the English upper classes were wracked by generational tensions, which contributed to the turmoil of the English Civil War. Parents had tried to relieve themselves of surplus children by sending sons off to the schools and universities to seek an education. Soon the professions were overcrowded with what contemporaries called an "Egyptian plague of caterpillars," and younger sons began to turn to rebellion. Some were naturally attracted to the new ideas of egalitarianism which were circulating in the seventeenth century, and two, William Walwyn and John Lilburne, were leaders of the Leveller Movement.[52] Others found relief in the New World, where there was, it was said, "worthy employment for many younger brothers and brave gentlemen now ruined for want thereof." [53]

We are best informed about the redundant children of the upper classes, but it appears that conditions were no better, and probably worse, among the lower orders. The population boom of the late sixteenth and early seventeenth centuries brought a flood of settlement and apprenticeship laws in England, all designed to provide for the masterless child and protect society against the threat of these "sturdy beggars." Legislation in 1547 empowered the authorities to indenture a beggar "man child" until the age of 24 and a "woman child" until the age of 20, although the severity of this act caused it to be withdrawn 2 years later. The apprenticeship statutes of 1601 did, however, require that orphaned children apprenticed by the parish be bound until the age of 24. Vagabondage of youth over 14 continued to be punished as a crime; and in certain cases children could be taken from parents who were found to be in perpetual idleness.[54] Parish authorities were further charged with apprenticing begging children between the ages of 5 and 14, so that "they may get their livings when they shall come of age." [55]

Similar tightening of discipline can be found in school and university statutes of the same period. Hobbes was not the only one who believed that parents were relying on schoolmasters and other such

---

[52] Thirsk, pp. 367–371; Hill, pp. 117–118.

[53] From a colonization scheme of 1572, quoted in Thirsk, p. 368.

[54] Pinchbeck and Hewitt, pp. 96–98; on German apprenticeships, see Walker, Chapter 3.

[55] Pinchbeck and Hewitt, pp. 94–95.

disciplinary agents to deal with the problem of superfluous children. John Brinsley wrote in 1627 that boys of 6 were being sent away to school because "if any beginne so early, they are rather sent to the schoole to keepe them from troubling the house at home, and from danger, and shrewd turnes, than for any great hope and desire that their friends have that they should learne any thing in effect." [56] The English boarding (public) schools carried into the eighteenth century a reputation for being dumping places for restless, redundant youth: "To a public school, as a general infirmary for mental disease, all desperate subjects are sent, as a last resource." [57] And since the care of marginal youth was entrusted, in England and on the Continent, almost entirely to bachelors and spinsters, the school therefore served the double function of relieving parents of their surplus children and providing for the employment of older, involuntary celibates.[58]

VI

Given the superfluity of youth and the fact that such large numbers were living away from their families, it is remarkable that even in ordinary times there was not more generational conflict. The obedience of youth was due, in part, to the society's strict enforcement of the Fifth Commandment, which was interpreted to include not only natural parents but all such masters to whom youth was entrusted. Robert Ram defined the "fathers" in 1655 as: "1. Our naturall Parentes, Fathers and Mothers in the flesh. 2. Our Civil Parents, Magistrates, Governours, and all authority. 3. Our spiritual Parents, Pastors, Ministers, and Teachers." [59] He might also have included the economic fathers, guild masters and the like.

---

[56] Brinsley's *Ludas Literarius: or, the Grammar Schoole,* quoted in MacFarlane, p. 207.

[57] Observation made by M. and R. L. Edgeworth in *Practical Education* (1789), quoted in Musgrove, *Youth and Social Order,* p. 48.

[58] Stone, "Literacy and Education," p. 95.

[59] *The Countrymens Catechisme: or, A Helpe for Householders* (1655), quoted in Schochet, p. 431.

Patriarchal government in its many forms was a necessary agent in maintaining the long period of semidependency that constituted "youth" in the preindustrial life cycle. Masters and heads of households had a vested interest in keeping from their charges the full rights of adulthood; for, as long as their life style remained simple and austere, the cost of keeping resident servants and apprentices was relatively cheap. Youths dressed in the manner of adults, but were forbidden luxury clothing. In 1603 three London apprentices were sent to jail for refusing to cut their hair and renounce the sartorial splendor that was causing distress among both their own masters and the local authorities.[60] Masters were also to see to it that youth did not drink, gamble, or seek the company of the opposite sex; and there were curfew laws keeping apprentices and servants off the streets after dark. But perhaps the most effective preventative of the youthful appropriation of adult roles was the fact of living in. There were, as in Germany, laws that forbade youths to marry before they had completed their apprenticeships, but the very fact that young people were dependent on the housholds in which they lived and were rarely paid for their services in money wages prevented them from setting up their own families and thus from putting pressures on already limited resources.

Patriarchalism was certainly important in shaping the character of preindustrial youth, but its effects are hard to separate from another institution much more closely associated with the tradition of youth itself, namely fraternity. As a major organizing principle of the seventeenth and eighteenth centuries, the concept of brotherhood—and, to a lesser extent, sisterhood—gave form and meaning to most of the institutions, apart from the household, with which youth came into contact. Horizontal bonding of young single persons was a feature not only of the schools and universities, but also of many of the professions, the army, the bureaucracy, and the clergy as well. The clergy was the only one in which celibacy was an essential aspect of the brotherhood; but, as a requirement of apprenticeship and as a kind of extended rite of passage, it was a feature of all trades and professions. In the crafts, journeymen's associations upheld the ideal of continence and the delay of marriage, relying on an elaborate imagery and ritual of "brotherhood" to solidify the social and moral bonds within their group. Entry into the French *compagnonnages*

---

[60] Pinchbeck and Hewitt, p. 233; for similar sumptuary legislation in Germany, see Dorwart, pp. 45–50.

and the German *Gesellenverbände* involved elaborate initiation in which the candidate was formally divested of his original identity as member of a particular family; subjected to symbolic baptism in the presence of a "godfather" who was chosen from among his new brothers; and given a nickname which was to be kept secret from all outsiders.[61] The objectives of both student and artisan ceremonies were moral as well as professional, impressing on the initiate his obligations to the ethical code of the craft and the "honor" of its membership. Injunctions against violation of the rules were couched in Biblical language, and the image of the family—the masters as fathers, the journeymen as good sons or, as they were sometimes called in France, "good cousins"—was frequently invoked. Expressing this interlocking system of fraternal and paternal authority, the journeymen printers of sixteenth-century Lyon proclaimed: "Masters and Journeymen are and ought to be one body together, like a family and a fraternity." [62]

Fraternal institutions provided one of the strongest controls over the young, particularly for those youths who were migrant from their families and localities. The journeymen's tradition of wandering apprenticeship, known as the *Wanderjahr* in Germany, "tramping" in England, and associated with the *tour de France*, was a highly institutionalized arrangement by which members of the trades were cared for and protected while on the road. Wandering across the face of Europe, moving from one house of call to another in search of employment or, where that was not available, assistance, was the way young skilled workers traditionally sustained themselves before returning to their hometowns, attaining their masterships, and marrying. The houses of call, which French artisans liked to call "Mothers," were in fact a substitute family. They could also serve as places of organization and agitation against abusive masters, from which strikes and boycotts could be carried forth.[63] Yet, perhaps a primary function of the *Wanderjahr* was to take young men out of the marriage market during those years when such a step would have had disastrous results for the entire community, and thus prolong the state of semidependence until a place for them opened up in the normal course of the generational cycle.

---

[61] On the initiation ceremonies of journeymen's societies, see Stadelmann and Fischer, pp. 67–76; Coornaert, pp. 152–171.

[62] Natalie Davis, "Trade Union," p. 53.

[63] Coornaert, pp. 225–230.

The celibate tradition of schools and universities served much the same purpose for another class of young people. There too a combination of paternal and fraternal government served to institutionalize and regularize the prolonged period of youth. Masters imposed the same moral and social restrictions on their pupils, whether they were 12 or 25. Oxford University rules which cloistered young men as if they were children, subjecting all offenders to the birch without regard to age, reflected the pervasive patriarchalism of the seventeenth and eighteenth centuries.[64] At the same time, however, a great deal of freedom was allowed the students to organize themselves and create fraternal forms of self-government. Older youths took charge of the younger, and up to the early nineteenth century many of England's most prestigious boarding schools were ruled, in large measure, by their students. Pupils had their own rites of initiation for newcomers, which reinforced the solidarity of the group against the masters.[65] In Germany, the parallels between student and craft practices were even more evident. There the novice student, called the *adolescens*, was subjected to a prolonged hazing, lasting up to a year. Not until he passed severe social and moral tests was he admitted to the company of his peers as an "honorable fellow" (*ehrlicher Bursch*).[66]

There too tension existed between the pupils and their masters; but, on the whole, the most enlightened educators of the day, including Philip Melanchthon, looked favorably upon the tradition of student self-discipline, despite its excesses.[67] The fraternal spirit complemented the goals of Latin education in any case. These were, as Walter Ong has suggested, as much social as they were intellectual; for education in a difficult and increasingly alien language was not functional in an economic sense but did serve as a kind of prolonged rite of passage for boys entering elite status, reinforcing the boundaries between them and the common people. Noting the parallels between the sex-segregated schools of the Early Modern period and the cohorts of novices in primitive society who are cloistered from women during their initiation period, Ong notes that "peoples of simple culture have, almost universally, a systematic ceremonial induction of adolescent youths into full participation in tribal, as op-

---

[64] Pantin, pp. 5–8.
[65] Mack, pp. 31–34, 38–42.
[66] Waas, pp. 15–18.
[67] Waas, p. 19; Ariès, pp. 241–252.

posed to family and clan, life." [68] In this case, however, it was the prolongation as well as the separation functions of the rite of passage that were important. Latin education served to isolate boys from the world, particularly from the world of women, for whom classical languages were still a mystery in the sixteenth and seventeenth centuries. Humanists like Sir Thomas Elyot were quite explicit about the necessity of this separation: "After that a childe is come to seven years of age, I holde it expedient that he be taken from the company of women, savynge that he may have, one yere, or two at the most, an auncient and sad matrone attending on hym in his chamber." [69] The vernacular, like the women who spoke it, was viewed as a danger; Latin, as an instrument of segregation, came to be looked upon as toughening the moral fibre. As the tongue of an exclusive all-male society, it served the same purposes as the secret signs and lingo of the crafts in prolonging youth.

Universities also had their fraternal organizations, ranging from the elaborate German regional brotherhoods (Landsmannschaften) to the more informal groups which helped organize student life in the Oxford colleges. To a greater or lesser degree, they all provided social welfare and moral support, even, as in the case of some German fraternities, offering funeral benefits to their members. The convivial customs of student fraternities found their parallel in other preprofessional institutions, such as the English Inns of Court, the Parlement of Paris, or wherever educated bachelors gathered. The fraternities of young clerks and lawyers were most visible at festival and holiday times, when corporate groups participated in civil pageantry, playing pranks, mocking the foibles of their elders, and generally turning the patriarchal social order upside down for a brief moment of fraternal revel. The tradition of youthful mockery was borrowed from the Medieval Feast of Fools, a Christmas custom in which novices and choir boys inverted the religious order and honored a "boy bishop" elected from their ranks, parodying and mocking their regular superiors. By the sixteenth century, once the Feast had been expelled from the French church, its functions were absorbed by secular fool societies (société joyeuse), the most famous of which was the Parisian Enfants-sans-souci, composed, as the name implies, of the young bachelors of the city. Closely associated with it was the Kingdom of Basoche, made up of clerks of the Parlement of Paris. Similar customs

[68] Ong, pp. 115–116.
[69] Ong, p. 122.

were observed in the Oxford and Cambridge colleges and at the London Inns of Court; and carnival societies were also common in Germany, where bachelor members of the professions elected their Prince of Fools and paraded his insults on selected occasions.[70]

On the surface, these fraternities would seem to threaten patriarchy, but their toleration by adults hints at their real functions, which were profoundly moral and conservative. The elders undoubtedly relished the release that the festival revels represented, but they also appreciated the need for conviviality and control for young persons away from home. The academic calendar prevented Cambridge students from returning home on holidays, and it was for this reason that the masters there opposed the abolition of the Christmas version of the Feast of Fools, when this was proposed in the mid-seventeenth century. As one of the dons put it, in the conviviality of those few days "they more discover the disposition of Scholars then than in the twelve months before." [71] Only when the urban fool societies began to dabble in political and religious controversy did they come in for official disfavor; and even then many managed to linger on into the eighteenth century.[72] At Cambridge the Christmas revel lasted until 1881, by which time most students no longer stayed in college over the holidays, due to the accessibility of improved transportation.[73]

VII

Craft, student, and professional fraternities met the needs of youths who were on their own in the cities or traveling in search of scholarship or training. They were, however, minority institutions in a society in which more than 85% of the population lived on the land. The patriarchal household met the requirements of the majority of youth, and the dutiful father of the house saw to it that those en-

---

[70] Welsford, pp. 204–212.
[71] Quoted in Welsford, p. 218.
[72] Welsford, pp. 194–195.
[73] Porter, pp. 283–285.

trusted to his care observed the rituals of family life—sitting down to the common meal, observing the round of prayers and church-going, retiring and rising at hours prescribed by the seasons and the economy. But however carefully he might try to oversee his charges, there were still times when they could escape the paternal eye. In preindustrial society, slack seasons were common enough and in summer, when the chores were done, warm evenings provided opportunity for unregulated free time. In addition, there were those occasions when young people were moving between households, times that were regulated to some degree by the seasonal "hiring" fairs which had a special meaning in the calendar of the young.

In England, the spring and fall dates marking the beginning and end of the growing season, when masters bargained with their servants and laborers, were popularly associated with customs and festivals of the young. May Day, which coincided with one of the most important hiring fairs—called "Pack Rag Day"—had been traditionally associated with dancing, games, and general revelry.[74] Its significance derived not only from the fact that great numbers of youths came together in the market towns, but also from the fact that it was one of those brief but intense moments of release from the discipline of labor and of dependence on the patriarchal household. In Lincolnshire, another major revel occurred in midsummer when, as Philip Stubbs described it in the late sixteenth century,[75]

> all the wildheads of the parish, conventing together, choose them a grand captain (of all mischief) whom they ennoble with the title of "my Lord of Misrule," and him they crown with great solemnity, and adopt for the king. This King anointed chooseth forth twenty, forty, threescore or a hundred lusty guts, like to himself, to wait upon his lordly majesty and to guard his noble person. . . . Then march these heathen company towards the church and churchyard, their pipers piping, their drummers thundering, their stumps dancing, their bells jingling, their handkerchiefs swinging about their heads like madmen, their hobbyhorses and other monsters skirmishing amongst the rout. . . . They have also certain papers, wherein is painted some babblery or other of imagery work, and these they call "my Lord of Misrule's badges." These they give to everyone that will give money for them to maintain them in their heathenry, devilry, whoredom, drunkenness, pride or what not. And who will not be buxom to them and give them money for these their devilish cognizances, they are mocked and flouted at not a little.

---

[74] Hobsbawm and Rudé, pp. 38–39.
[75] Stubbs's *The Anatomie of Abuses* (1583), as quoted in Barber, pp. 27–28.

Stubbs's account is not without its biases, for he was one of the sternest critics of youth and an enemy of frivolity in any form. While May dancing and midsummer revels may have produced excesses, the highly ritualized social theater of the Lords of Misrule and similar youthful cohorts had another, strongly moral, side. Such mummery was in fact an expression of a highly organized and disciplined youth culture that existed at the village level across Europe. These youth groups took various names—Abbeys of Misrule in France, *Brüderschaften* in Germany and parts of Switzerland—but they showed a remarkable similarity in form and purpose. Theirs was the fraternity of rural youth in the sixteenth and seventeenth centuries, performing functions of social control and moral support similar to the student and corporate brotherhoods of the towns.

We know little of the historical origins of village youth groups, though it seems they must have been an integral part of rural life for centuries. They were strongest in Early Modern Europe in those areas where communities were not yet deeply divided between rich and poor. There they involved all the youth of the village from the age of about 14 until marriage. While the main groups were primarily male, female cohorts sometimes formed satellite bodies. Whether membership was in any way obligatory cannot be determined, but in those areas where village unity was still pronounced it seems likely that almost all unmarried youth were involved.[76] In Germany, entry usually coincided with confirmation, and there appear to have been certain initiation procedures, complete with hazing, for the novices. A strict hierarchy of age prevailed in most cases, the bachelors in their mid-twenties exercising leadership until marriage forced them to drop out of the group. Permanent bachelors were tolerated until 30 or so, and then ceased to exercise influence over the younger members. Thus, barring a dearth of marriage partners or some disruption of the normal village flow of inheritance opportunities, the youth groups were constantly changing in composition.[77]

As far as can be determined, the solidarity of the group found no support in separate economic functions or living arrangements, as is the case of age cohorts in some African societies. Neither sex lived separated from the usual household units, except where herding or similar pastoral occupations drew youths away from the villages for

---

[76] Wikman, pp. 40ff; Hornstein, pp. 119ff; and Natalie Davis, "Reasons of Misrule," pp. 51–57.

[77] Wikman, pp. 363–370.

brief periods of the year. This applied mainly to pasture regions, where even the girls might sleep apart in summer; yet, even there, most of the youth's working day was spent in the company of adults, leaving only the idle hours—evenings, holidays, slack seasons—for peer group activities.

While the group's economic functions were nil, their civic and moral duties were recognized as being highly significant. In some parts of Early Modern Europe, youth groups still served as local militia, drilling together and participating as a group in the civil ceremonies of their communities.[78] But even where central authorities had taken over military functions, youth was often mobilized by the church, which gave their groups prominence in religious processions marking the important days of the Christian year. The identification of youth with Christian symbols of regeneration derived from earlier pagan association of the young with the powers of fertility, a notion still popular among the peasantry. Midsummer dancing and courting that marked pre-Christian summer revels became an established part of St. John's Day during the Medieval period; and the church's sanction of games and other youthful activities on Shrove and Easter attest to further links between pagan traditions and the Christian notions of regeneration.[79]

The importance of their functions was reflected in the high degree of organization attained by youth groups in the Siebengebirge region of western Germany and the Graubünden area of Switzerland.[80] There, in the sixteenth and seventeenth centuries, they had their own written law, with a primitive court system complete with fines and other punishments. These self-regulating bodies appear to have evolved along with militia and other civic functions, but their major concern appears to have been moral and sexual conduct rather than purely civil matters. Although it is difficult to generalize about a phenomenon that took such different forms and was known by various names according to geographical region, it would seem that chief among the Early Modern youth groups' responsibility was the regulation of communal sexuality, particularly the access to marriage.

We know that German *Brüderschaften* exercised tight control over the eligible females in their villages, limiting access not only of their

---

[78] Hornstein, p. 120.

[79] Spamer, pp. 215–221; Porter, pp. 97–146; Natalie Davis, "Reasons of Misrule," pp. 41–49.

[80] Hornstein, p. 120.

own members but also of intruders from the outside and of older men who might pose a threat to the pool of brides. K. Robert Wikman's fascinating study of premarital customs in northern Europe confirms the impressions of generations of folklorists that these village bands played a most important role in regulating courting patterns, even to the point of influencing the choice of mates. Socializing, which most often took the form of nighttime visiting, was managed largely by the group itself, whose norms permitted the visiting of girls in their bedrooms but stopped short of legitimizing sexual intercourse for any but the betrothed. The rigorous rules of "bundling" were designed to prolong chastity to the point of betrothal and to regulate access to the marriage market. Younger boys who showed themselves too precocious in courtship were dealt with severely by the older lads; and girls who were known to be promiscuous were also coerced, their doorways decorated with the obscene symbol of the gorse bush.[81]

The behavior of male outsiders and widowers was carefully scrutinized. Girls are known to have been equally jealous of older women, widows and spinsters, who posed competition for the attentions of their young swains.[82] Village youths could be brutal toward those who they felt endangered their own chances of marriage, but violence was usually the last resort in a society where ritual symbols of antagonism were still readily available. Youth had at its disposal an ancient stock of frightening effigies, rough music (profane songs), and mocking pantomime with which to deal with its enemies.[83] Ready with tin pans and horns under the lecher's window, and quick to join the charivari of the second wedding of an old man and a young bride, the Brüderschaften and the Abbeys of Misrule were self-interested enforcers of the moral and social equilibrium of village life.

In a typical rural charivari, a recently remarried widower might find himself awakened by the clamor of the crowd, an effigy of his dead wife thrust up to his window and a likeness of himself, placed backward on an ass, drawn through the streets for his neighbors to see.[84] Paying of a "contribution" to the Lord of Misrule might quiet his

---

[81] Wikman, pp. 367–372; Spamer, pp. 170–175, 202–204; Myrdal, pp. 42–45.
[82] Natalie Davis, "Reasons of Misrule," pp. 53–54; Wikman, pp. 363–365, 371–372.
[83] Hole, *English Folklore*, pp. 16, 24; Porter, pp. 111–112; Natalie Davis, "Reasons of Misrule," pp. 53–54; Edward P. Thompson, "Rough Music," pp. 285–312.
[84] Descriptions in Edward P. Thompson, "Rough Music," pp. 287–288.

youthful tormentors, but by that time the voices of village conscience had made their point. Second marriages invariably drew the greatest wrath and, by contrast, endogamous marriages of young people of roughly the same age were the occasion of the youth groups' rejoicing. In that case, the functions of charivari were reversed and the couple were accompanied by a noisy crowd to their wedding bed, the ritual send-off of its former members by the peer group. The marriage feast, and the Abbey's participation in it, symbolized the central purpose of the youth group, which was to provide a prolonged rite of passage from roughly the onset of puberty to the point of marriage.[85]

Of course, it was over the selection of mates that the preindustrial forms of fraternity were most likely to clash with paternal interests. Parents were naturally concerned with marriage as a means of improving the family's holdings and status in the community, and it was not uncommon for well-to-do peasants to withhold their daughters from peer group activity in order to protect this vital interest. In times of severe population growth and pauperization, such as the late sixteenth and early seventeenth centuries, the power of the youth groups must have undergone severe challenge. We know that peer group structures were weaker in areas of social and economic heterogeneity, particularly in England where the division of the rural population into the landed and the landless was perhaps the most advanced. While the customs of Misrule survived in various parts of Britain, the corporate forms of the Abbeys themselves did not.[86] Yet, there is no reason to believe that economic modernization resulting in the disruption of communal unity necessarily meant decline for the youth groups. It may be that, in the seventeenth and eighteenth centuries, these groups became even more important as what Robert Wikman has called a "kind of corrective to paternal despotism."[87] The survivals of the charivari certainly served a function much like that of the "rituals of rebellion" in some African societies, expressing the collective morality and commitment to tradition by calling attention to lapses of both the young and old alike.[88]

---

[85] On the participation of youth groups in marriage ceremonies, see Spamer, pp. 176–186; Hole, *English Folklore*, pp. 21–23.

[86] Edward P. Thompson, "Rough Music," pp. 295–296.

[87] Wikman, p. 359.

[88] See Gluckman, pp. 39ff.

VIII

Transplanted traditions of fraternity flourished in town as well as countryside, and as late as the early nineteenth century, the signs of Misrule could still be read in Lancashire weaving communities. Sam Bamford remembered that "a gorse bush indicated a woman notoriously immodest; and a holly bush, one loved in secret; a tup's horn intimated that a man or woman was faithless to marriage; a branch of sapling, truth in love; and a sprig of birch, a pretty girl." [89] Yet, the demographic situation of the towns tended to be different, with the pool of eligible men and women less restricted and the concerns of youth less centered on the problems of inheritance and control of access to marriage. Many of the young migrants to the preindustrial city had given up hope of a landed inheritance and thus had no vested interest in maintaining or regulating the traditional marriage market. They tended instead to be more concerned with bread prices and wage levels, with the result that the old rural forms of charivari were turned to new ends in sixteenth- and seventeenth-century cities.

Both Natalie Davis and Edward Thompson have noted a pronounced shift, in urban settings, from charivaris against second marriages to protests against nagging wives and, in the case of early nineteenth-century England, wife beaters.[90] Whatever changes in the status of the female may have been involved, this change indicates a decline of the traditional concern with the pool of eligible mates. Decreasing anxiety about the marriage market was paralleled, however, by rising discontent with other aspects of life, and with increasing frequency the instruments of Misrule were directed against economic and even political targets. The Abbeys of Misrule in the larger sixteenth- and seventeenth-century French towns tended to form along occupational, neighborhood, and class lines, adapting tradi-

---

[89] Quoted in Edward P. Thompson, *Making of English Working Class*, p. 406.
[90] Natalie Davis, "Reasons of Misrule," pp. 65–66; Edward P. Thompson, "Rough Music," pp. 296–302.

tional rituals to new forms of protest. In sixteenth-century Lyon, for example, the guise of a traditional *société joyeuse* served as cover for a clandestine organization of journeymen printers. The Company of the Griffarins, as they called themselves, was locked in economic struggle with the masters of the trade, a conflict that took on the character of class rather than generation. The Griffarins welcomed journeymen of all ages, including married men not usually admitted to an Abbey of Misrule or a *société joyeuse*. These were men without hope of inheritance, who had taken the step of abandoning the celibate state while still journeymen; it was not suprising that for them the charivari had lost its original meaning.[91]

Rituals of rebellion, which youth had once monopolized, were losing their age specificity. In Languedoc, the instruments of Misrule were taken up by whole peasant villages in their protests against both the exploitation by larger landowners and the taxation and conscription by the state. According to Emmanuel Le Roy Ladurie, the youth groups of sixteenth-century Côtes du Rhone were "cells for insurrection." [92] In England, a familiar figure among the Lords of Misrule, called "Mother Folly"—a man dressed in women's clothing, with face masked or blackened—played a prominent part in rural uprisings from the seventeenth through the early nineteenth century.[93] And in their desperate defense of the just price, eighteenth-century English crowds often transformed rough music, traditionally expressive of moral indignation against lechers, into instruments of class conflict. The miller's legendary prowess with young women who came to his mill became a convenient metaphor for a different kind of exploitation, economic rather than sexual.[94]

> *Then the miller he laid her against the mill hopper*
> *Merry a soul so wantonly*
> *He pulled up her cloaths, and he put in the stopper*
> *For says she I'll have my corn ground small and free*

Sexual and economic abuses have always been closely associated in the popular mind; and it may be that exploitation of luckless girls by old men, employers, and heads of households, was increasing by

---

[91] Natalie Davis, "Trade Union," pp. 51–55.
[92] Natalie Davis, "Reasons of Misrule," p. 69.
[93] Edward P. Thompson, "Rough Music," pp. 305–308.
[94] Edward P. Thompson, "Moral Economy," p. 103.

the early eighteenth century due to the desperation of the poor and the breakdown of the old moral pressures, including the youth group.[95] In any case, obscene gestures and profane songs that still carried a trace of their original purpose were finding their way into political, economic, and even religious controversy. Much to the displeasure of the church and secular authorities, French Abbeys, such as the Dijon *Mère Folle,* the Cornards of Lyon, and the *Enfants-sans-souci* of Guyenne, were active in various types of sedition during the sixteenth and seventeenth centuries. Increasingly, these Abbeys and others like them came under official censure, resulting ultimately in their dismemberment.[96]

By the time Louis XIII banned the *Mère Folle* in 1630, many of the other *sociétés joyeuses* had lost their association with youth as such, and had become age heterogeneous. Most included married as well as bachelor members, making obsolete their original function of prolonging the celibate condition. Among the literate population, the cartoon and the written satire were replacing the street theatre of the old Abbeys of Misrule as carriers of social and political criticism.[97] Only by retreating behind corporate walls could the ancient traditions of youth maintain their authenticity; and it was in the Oxford and Cambridge colleges, as well as at the Inns of Court, that the customs of youth remained most pure. We can detect some of the forms of Misrule in the merrymaking of the London "rakes" of the eighteenth century, ill-bred young gentlemen whose wild pranks and violent behavior demonstrated none of the moral or social purpose of the Abbeys of old, however. The rakes and their counterparts on the Continent tended to be cynical individualists who scoffed at the concepts of temperance and chastity. Their collective behavior took on a bizarre, anarchical flavor, with gangs of young gentlemen, of which the "Mohocks" were the most notorious, roaming the London streets, attacking bystanders, accosting helpless women, and generally calling into disrepute the traditions of Misrule.[98] No longer tied to calendar occasion, and random rather than ritualistic in character, the revels of this new kind of youth group marked the beginning of a new phase in the social history of youth.

----

[95] Causes of increasing illegitimacy rates are discussed by Edward Shorter, pp. 329–345.

[96] Natalie Davis, "Reasons of Misrule," pp. 66–69.

[97] See Welsford, pp. 207–218.

[98] T. S. Graves; Jones, pp. 29–30, 140ff, 155–156, 174, 200, 210.

IX

In the villages of Europe, however, youth groups preserved their functions well into the nineteenth century. Henry Mayhew, touring Germany in the 1860s, came upon functioning male and female cohorts whose "bundling" practices he, as a good Victorian, misinterpreted as licentiousness.[99] Athletic contests that pitted bachelors against married men continued in English villages well into the nineteenth century, as did many of the traditional revels associated with hiring and holidays.[100] We cannot be sure whether they were regulated by organized peer groups, but we know that courting habits in areas like Cambridgeshire remained highly ritualized until very late in the nineteenth century. There, pregnant unwed girls were still being serenaded with rough music at the time of the First World War.[101]

In the cities first and in the countryside later, the unique conditions which had required of youth a long period of self-denial were disappearing. The decline of traditional corporate and communal forms of youth coincided with the emergence of capitalism in agriculture and commerce, with the growth of towns, and with the increase of centralized state control. Even before the coming of massive industrialization and urbanization, there were signs that the old forms would have to either adjust to new conditions or disappear. With the decline of the peasant economy, the connection between inheritance and marriage was dissolving, opening up new possibilities for the young. But of equal importance with the economic changes was the demographic transformation that was beginning in the middle of the eighteenth century. This was to change the developmental cycle of the family and, with it, the parameters of childhood, youth, and adulthood.

---

[99] Mayhew, *German Life*, pp. 25, 426.
[100] Mingay, p. 250; also Manning, pp. 312, 317, 319; Hole, *English Sports*, p. 56; Brailsford, pp. 207ff.
[101] Porter, pp. 8–9.

A bourgeois couple shy from a parade of Paris street urchins during the Revolution of 1848 in this selection from Honoré-Victorin Daumier's "Alarms and Alarmists" series, done in 1848. Reproduction of Plate 40, "The Dangerous Children," published in Howard P. Vincent, *Daumier and His World* (Evanston, Ill.: Northwestern University Press, 1968).

2

Troubled Youth: The Consequences of Modernization, 1770–1870

Generational tensions often characterize societies in the first stages of economic and political modernization, and Europe was no exception.[1] Charles Fourier was exaggerating only to a degree when he described the social and economic conditions as causing "fathers to desire the death of their children and children to desire the death of their fathers."[2] The theme of "sons against fathers" was a familiar one in both the life and literature of the early nineteenth century, leading James Fazy to publish in 1828 his *On Gerontocracy*, a work in which he voiced the frustrations of a post-Napoleonic generation whose hopes and career ambitions had been raised by the democratic revolution only to be thwarted by the Restoration. The figures of the young student and ragged street urchin in Delacroix's famous painting, "Liberty Leading the People," stuck in the minds of contemporaries, for whom anything associated with youth now had radical connotations; thus the names of avant-garde artistic and intellectual movements such as the *Jeunes France* and the "Young Germans," as well as the titles of revolutionary nationalist movements like Mazzini's "Young Europe."[3]

The traditional association of youth with renewal and regeneration served any number of purposes. "Place the youth at the head of the

---

[1] Eisenstadt, *Modernization*, pp. 26–31; also Eisenstadt, *Generation to Generation*.
[2] Fourier, p. 282.
[3] de Sauvigny, pp. 238–240.

insurgent masses; do you not know what strength is latent in those young bands, what magic influences the voices of the young have on the crowd," wrote Mazzini.[4] But the magic, once released, was not to be monopolized by the left—once the tables were turned and the revolutionaries were installed in power, it was inevitable that the traditions of youth should be appropriated also by the conservatives. This happened in France soon after the Terror, when the *jeunesse dorée* paraded their contempt for revolutionary discipline in the cause of counterrevolution.[5] Later, in England, after that country's first electoral reform, a new generation of conservatives, led by Benjamin Disraeli, formed the Young England Movement; its tactics including many of the old devices of Misrule, Karl Marx was led to describe it as "half lamentation, half lampoon." [6]

Beneath these manifestations of unrest lay the profound demographic, economic, and social changes that were transforming agrarian Europe into the world's first industrialized and urbanized society. Modernization affected different groups in different ways, and in the period 1770–1870 the traditions of youth were redrawn along class lines, with the laboring classes developing their own distinctive youth culture organized around the urban neighborhood gang, and the upper and middle classes creating forms exclusively their own, including the modern student movement and bohemianism. This process was sometimes simply a matter of replacing the older traditions of youth, but more often it involved adapting their characteristics to new conditions. Tradition did not always stand in the way of change, but interacted with it in ways that made custom itself an important agent of transformation. The layer upon layer of youth cultures deposited during this and later periods were a product of a dialectical process that must be explored with respect to continuity as well as to change.

---

[4] Mazzini quoted in Herbert Moller, p. 241.
[5] Lefebvre, pp. 49–55, 80ff.
[6] Marx and Engels.

I

John Stuart Mill called this the "age of transition," when "mankind have outgrown old institutions and old doctrines and have not yet acquired new ones."[7] "Transition" applies not only to economic and political structures, but to the family and the individual life cycle, both of which underwent fundamental transformation in the period 1770–1870. A major factor was the steep rise in population that began in the middle of the eighteenth century. The population of Europe rose from approximately 125 million in 1750 to 208 million a century later, increasing to almost 300 million in 1900. During the late eighteenth and for a greater part of the nineteenth century, each successive generation was larger than its predecessor, and younger age groups increased even beyond their high preindustrial proportions, the ratio of the age group 15–29 to the age group 30 and over reaching almost 65% in the late eighteenth century, and over 70% in England by the 1840s.[8]

Although the causes of the eighteenth-century population explosion still remain to be explained by historical demographers, it is clear that this growth took place initially under the same conditions of high mortality and high fertility that had been characteristic of preindustrial society. Child mortality did not begin to fall significantly until the late nineteenth century. Sharp fluctuations in death rates, caused by famine, epidemic, and uncertain food supply, tended to disappear by the middle of that century, but conditions in the new industrial cities were not such as to lower the death rate among children and in many places this actually increased. So it was in Glasgow, for instance, where the death rate of children under 10 rose from 1 in 75 in 1821 to 1 in 48, 20 years later.[9] In Prussia, a country where industrialization and urbanization occurred mainly in the second half of the century, the infant mortality rate for 1000 live-born males rose

---

[7] Mill, p. 3.
[8] Herbert Moller, p. 250.
[9] Morley, p. 7.

from 213 in the early 1860s to 222 at the turn of the century, only then dropping to the current levels of about 20 per thousand as the impact of modern medicine and sanitation began to have its effect.[10]

Of course, mortality rates varied enormously by region and class. As a rule, the more densely populated a district, the higher the death risk.[11] Wealth also played a prominent part, the English aristocracy setting the pace of improvement in its own country, with its life expectancy rising from 42.4 years for the cohort born 1690–1729 to 54.9 years for the cohort born 1830–1879.[12] Life chances were proportional to position in society, as indicated by the fact that in London in 1830 life expectancy for the gentry and the professional middle classes was estimated at 44 years; for the tradesmen and clerks, 25 years; and for the laborers and their families, 22 years.[13] After the aristocracy, the middle classes showed the greatest improvement in infant mortality. But for the vast majority of the laboring classes, who made up 85% of the population, the loss of children remained a fundamental fact of life until the beginning of the twentieth century.[14] *Why Weepest Thou?*, a book for mourners published in 1888, expressed the experience of this age of transition.[15]

> *And yet again*
> *That elder Shepherd came: my heart grew faint—*
> *He claimed another lamb; with sadder plaint,*
> *Another!—she who, gentle as a saint,*
> *   Ne'er gave me pain . . .*

Reduction in fertility rates followed the same social and chronological sequence as mortality, apparently beginning first with the upper classes, followed by the middle and lower-middle classes, and reaching the laboring poor only toward the very end of the nineteenth century. Class differences in fertility and mortality resulted in a striking disparity in family size among various classes. In the decade 1890–1899, families of the English professional middle class averaged 2.80 persons, about half that of manual laborers, whose families were

---

[10] Wrigley, *Population and History*, pp. 164–171.
[11] Anna Weber, pp. 343, 361.
[12] Hollingsworth, pp. 66–70.
[13] Morley, p. 7.
[14] Banks, *Prosperity and Parenthood*, pp. 194–195.
[15] Morley, p. 15.

still preindustrial in size, averaging 5.11 members.[16] The average for the total population at the time was 4.34, evidence that prior to 1900, family limitation was practiced by only a small minority of the English. In France, family limitation appears to have set in on a widespread basis as early as the late eighteenth century, but this was an exception to the European pattern of the continuance of high fertility among the mass of the people until the end of the nineteenth century.

We have seen that in preindustrial Europe it was precisely this condition of high fertility and high mortality, combined with a particular pattern of inheritance and marriage, that required the removal of children from their families for that part of their life cycle defined and institutionalized as "youth." The onset of industrialization and urbanization did not immediately alter the demographic conditions underlying this traditional strategy of family survival but did change inheritance and marriage patterns in such a way as to seriously disrupt the old developmental patterns. This was most apparent among the lower strata of society, particularly among peasant and artisan groups being deprived of land and craft by the new economic order and thus being left with neither wealth nor trade for their children to inherit. Charles Fourier claimed to have overheard four artisans, "a little above the poorest class," discussing their prospects:[17]

> "I'm asking that girl in marriage because she'll have money; the family is comfortably set. You can be sure I don't want to be a sucker again. Take a wife who hasn't a penny, then the children come; it's the devil to take care of them, it's hell."
> "Then you had a lot of them?" said one of them.
> "I had six—feed all that and the wife!!!"
> "What? Six? Oh! good heavens! a worker who hardly earns a thing, to feed six children!"
> "Yes, six; but they all died, fortunately for me. And the mother's dead too."

As Fourier and others pointed out, such distress was not limited to the poor or the landless. The father who refused to give up the land to his son was commonly referred to as the *père qui vit trop* (father who lives too long) by French peasants; and the nineteenth century saw a renewed attack on the law of primogeniture in England as well

---

[16] Wrigley, *Population and History*, pp. 186–187.
[17] Fourier, p. 282.

as on the Continent.[18] Faced with the disruption of old patterns of both paternity and fraternity, youth of all classes began the painful reassessment of traditional habits and values. The result of this process was an abundance of new styles of behavior, each representing the attempt of a different segment of the young population to come to grips with the challenge of the new industrial age.

II

Rapid growth of population would have been sufficient to cause severe strains on traditional age relations, but the fact that this was also accompanied by the breakdown of the traditional linkage between inheritance and marriage meant that the status of youth was fundamentally altered, giving birth to new patterns of personal and group behavior only vaguely foreshadowed in earlier periods of expansion. In England, the process began with the agricultural revolution of the eighteenth century, which involved the massive enclosure of land and the final reduction of the peasantry to the status of landless wage laborers. The early phases of the capitalization of agriculture favored the young by increasing their earning power. Increased production of foodstuffs for a market economy meant more intensive use of wage labor and a decline of old patriarchal arrangements, including payment in board and room. Demand for child and female labor rose until the end of the Napoleonic Wars, encouraging the rural population of England to increase at a steady rate despite the near subsistence levels on which the new rural proletariat were forced to exist for most of the period.[19]

Rural society was dividing into three relatively well-defined ranks —larger landowners, tenant farmers, and landless laborers—who viewed one another with increasing suspicion. The tradition of having laborers and servants "living in" had become socially and economically unacceptable to the landowning elites and many of the farmers, who no longer wanted their sons and daughters sitting down

---

[18] Thirsk, p. 376; on similar controversy in France, see de Sauvigny, pp. 384ff.

[19] On these changes, see Slicher van Bath, pp. 195–208; Hobsbawm and Rudé, Chapters 1–2; Wolfram Fischer, pp. 415–435.

at the same table with common folk. Where servants were kept, they were "below the stairs," no longer a part of the family as had been the case in the old patriarchal household. Market-oriented landowners were finding that board and room were an unprofitable way of paying for labor in any case. William Cobbett, who complained of these new habits as an "infernal stock-jobbing system," described the decline of one such traditional boarding arrangement:[20]

> Everything about this farmhouse was formerly the scene of plain manners and plentiful living. . . . But all appeared to be in a state of decay and near of disuse. There appeared to have been hardly any family in that house, where formerly there were, in all probability, from ten to fifteen men, boys, and maids. . . . Why do not farmers now feed and lodge their workpeople, as they did formerly? Because they cannot keep them upon so little as they give them in wages. This is the real cause of the change.

The same class that in the sixteenth and seventeenth centuries had so jealously guarded the patriarchal system was now willing to give young laborers their independence, even encouraging them to set up their own households, because it was now economically advantageous to create an abundance of wage labor.

The rural poor had traditionally relieved themselves by placing their children in the homes of their betters, but now they had either to keep them at home or to push them further afield into the new industrial cities. The latter alternative did not really become operative in England until the 1830s and 1840s; and it appears that co-residence of parents and children was increasing in the late eighteenth and early nineteenth centuries. In any case, this was what the rural welfare system encouraged, for it gave grants in addition to wages to families with children. Witnesses reported that "men who receive but a small pittance know that they have only to marry and that pittance will be augmented in proportion to the number of their children. . . . But there was one thing better than to marry and have a family, and that was to marry a mother of bastards. . . . As one young woman of twenty-four with four bastard children put it: 'If she had one more, she should be very comfortable.' "[21]

Although their object of procreation was no longer to secure a male heir, the rural poor still regarded large numbers of children as the

[20] Quoted in Redford, p. 77.
[21] Redford, p. 83.

best guarantee of a comfortable old age.[22] Subsisting on the newly
discovered foodstuff, the potato, rural laborers continued to produce
large families. In Ireland, a tradition of partible inheritance had
tended to subdivide the land into tiny plots, but parents continued
to follow a strategy of high fertility.[23] "It is general practice with them
to divide their land into portions, which are given to their children as
they get married. The last married frequently gets his father's cabin
along with his portion of the ground, and there his parents like to
stop, from a feeling of attachment to the place where they have spent
their lives." [24] In the end, the Irish strategy produced disastrous rural
overpopulation and famine, causing thousands of young men and
women to begin emigrating in the 1840s, and ultimately forcing upward the age of marriage for those who remained behind. A land of
unusually young families in the early nineteenth century, Ireland rapidly returned to a situation of strict primogeniture after the disastrous
1847 Famine, thereby also returning to a system in which younger
sons resigned themselves to long bachelorhoods.[25]

Rural overpopulation threatened in England also, at least until 1830.
Families following a strategy of high fertility in what was still a high
mortality situation continued to produce a surplus of older youth,
who were pushed out of the home as the number of offspring became too great. No longer subject to the discipline of "living in," and
having access to wages, these youths were now able to set up their
own households. Welfare arrangements also encouraged young marriage, thus contributing further to the population boom. Many seem
to have settled near their kin, showing no eagerness to migrate in the
traditional manner. The parish system of welfare, which granted benefits only to those who could prove their right of settlement, had a
good deal to do with this; and during the period 1751–1831, migration from England's agricultural counties actually fell.[26] The resulting
situation of competition at low wages and unemployment was felt
most strongly toward the end of the 1820s, producing a crisis which
broke forth in 1830 in the massive uprising of the rural poor known
as the "Swing Rebellion."

Not surprisingly, it was young unmarried men who were among the

---

[22] Mingay, p. 241.
[23] Michael Anderson, *Family Structure*, pp. 81–83.
[24] Quoted in Michael Anderson, *Family Structure*, p. 82.
[25] Musgrove, *Youth and Social Order*, pp. 78–79.
[26] Hobsbawm and Rudé, pp. 42–43; Hammond and Hammond, p. 204; Redford,
Chapters 4–5.

most active machine-breakers and rick-burners of that year. According to the historians of the movement, these were the ones who "suffered most from pauperization, since they received least from the parish and were most likely to be forced into the most degrading and useless kinds of parish labour, e.g. on the road-gangs which provided only too justified centres of disaffection." [27] But social custom had as much to do with the form that rebellion took as did the structure of the work force. Here we find the traditions of youth adapted to serve the purposes of economic protest. Rituals of Misrule proved effective in organizing entire communities against exploitation; masking was a feature of the early phases of machine-breaking; and processions, reminiscent of Whitsun or Plough Monday youth festivals, became regular means of rallying a crowd, intimidating the masters, making "collections" from the rich in the name of the poor. The leaders of the protest, who, like the mythical fellow "Swing" from whom the movement derived its name, liked to fancy themselves "captains," playing that role in a fashion that reminds one of the Lords of Misrule of Stubbs's day. Eyewitnesses reported the rioters as "being in general very fine looking young men, and particularly well dressed as if they put on their best clo' for the occasion." [28] Similar recourse to the traditions of youth was evident in other rural disturbances of the era, particularly in the so-called "Rebecca Riots" of 1839 in Wales, where the avenging "Rebeccas"— men dressed in women's clothing, with faces blacked in the tradition of mummers—attacked toll houses and destroyed crops in the name of economic and social justice.[29]

III

Similar interactions of tradition and change were evident in other parts of Europe where the demand for labor induced increasing numbers of youth to remain in their villages rather than migrate in the

---

[27] Hobsbawm and Rudé, p. 62.
[28] Hobsbawm and Rudé, p. 211.
[29] Williams, Chapters 7–8; Edward P. Thompson, "Rough Music," pp. 305–309; Edward P. Thompson, *Making of English Working Class*, pp. 418–429.

traditional manner. In the cantons of the Zurich highlands, the peasantry had begun to supplement its farm income by home industry, receiving cotton from urban jobbers, weaving it, and then selling it back again. The new source of income allowed these communities and others like them all over Europe to sustain a much larger population than had been previously possible.[30] Domestic industry was particularly attractive to those who had no prospect of landed inheritance, and its immediate effect was to break the traditional tie between inheritance and marriage. Income from weaving allowed young couples to evade parental control and establish households at an earlier age. According to the reports of the local clergy, most of whom viewed such developments with considerable alarm, precocious courting was rampant in the cantons by the middle of the eighteenth century. Youth of both sexes and of all ages mixed freely during the idle hours, enjoying the forms of sociability once reserved only for older youth.

Introduction to the lore, if not the actual experience of sexual intercourse, was apparently becoming accessible to youths at an earlier age than previously. It was reported that "the young boy starts as soon as he is confirmed, and almost as if that were an initiation ceremony, begins to prowl after one or more girls." [31] And because the competition in the marriage market was becoming more intense, due to the fact that both girls and boys who earlier would have had to emigrate for the lack of work or inheritance were now remaining at home, even the fair sex was becoming more aggressive. "Knowing they cannot get a man in any other way, [girls] open their chambers to these night boys and abandon themselves in the certain or uncertain hope, that, in the case of pregnancy, they will not be left to their shame." [32]

The traditions of bundling were serving an increasingly larger peer group. Nights spent in socializing proliferated; young people, who now had pocket money from their own labors, indulged themselves in drink and dress in ways that horrified their elders. To the previously limited circle of peasant sons and daughters were added children of the poor and the landless, who with a tiny plot of land and a loom were now able to subsist in their home parish.[33] "Early mar-

---

[30] Braun, especially Chapter 2; for a general survey of domestic industrialization, see Charles Tilly and Richard Tilly.

[31] Quoted in Braun, p. 68.

[32] Braun, p. 68.

[33] Braun, pp. 69–71.

riages between people, who have two spinning wheels but no bed, happen fairly often," [34] it was remarked at the time. Bitter attacks on "beggar weddings" by the clergy and the richer peasantry were in vain, however, for youth had not only strength of numbers but the traditions of Misrule with which to resist their elders. Meddlesome old people were visited with old fashioned tin panning, their fences wrecked and gardens pulled up.[35] Bans on Sunday dancing and ordinances against night visiting went largely unheeded, not only for the resistance of the young themselves but for the acquiescence of many parents, who were forced to accept—as a consequence of their own poverty and the desire to push older children out of the home to make room for younger—the liberties of their offspring, including early marriage.

Disappearance of inheritance meant that the bargaining power of the fathers was greatly reduced and the advantages of the eldest children diminished. The older generation's frustrations were reflected in their complaints about youthful extravagance, an almost universal lament in the eighteenth century. Every evidence of precocious consumption, even the buying and reading of novels, was viewed as dangerous self-gratification.[36] Yet, the employment opportunities offered by domestic industry appear also to have kept children at home longer and strengthened the bonds between parents and children who were coresident. Even when sons and daughters set up their own independent households, they often continued to pay an allowance to their parents as a kind of insurance premium against old age. As one domestic worker described it:[37]

> My wife and I are getting old. We cannot work so much any more. We also have three children, two of whom pay us each week an allowance of 30 Batzen. Only one daughter still helps us with our work. We work only as much as we can and feel is necessary, and make out with what the other two children give us. It is very hard to find workers and day laborers, to keep a boy and girl, because board and wages are so high. Thank God, we can make out well with what the children give us.

As Rudolf Braun has described it, children were becoming "boarders" in their own families, and kin ties, once based on the tyranny of inheritance, were being replaced by a more pragmatic arrangement

---

[34] Braun, p. 66.
[35] Braun, p. 121.
[36] Braun, pp. 120–127, 148–154.
[37] Braun, p. 85.

that allowed the young person considerable freedom to marry and establish his or her own household, though continuing to contribute to the support of the aging parents. Clearly, economic change had tipped the balance somewhat more in the favor of youth as against the parents, but where it also created local employment opportunities and eliminated the need both for "living in" and migration, it was allowing family members to remain together for longer than ever before.[38] In the Zurich highlands, "youth" was no longer a period spent away from home, and its two boundaries, childhood and adulthood, were not so clearly marked as before. Early teenage, now spent in coresidence with the parents, was beginning to blend with the former, while early access to courting and the acquisition of the sumptuary symbols of maturity were blurring distinctions at the adult end as well.

Domestic industry was but a half-way house on the road to industrialization. The weavers of the Swiss cantons survived into the early nineteenth century, when their livelihood was destroyed by competition with factory-manufactured goods. There is probably no more pitiful example of this kind of doomed occupation than the English hand-loom weavers, whose prosperity had also been enhanced in the early stages of industrialization only to have the craft ultimately destroyed by the introduction of mechanized weaving beginning in the 1820s. Up to that point, the yarns produced by factory-spinning provided the weavers and their children with abundant employment, encouraging a family economy in which parents were able to keep their children at home for longer periods of time, passing on to them a valuable inheritance of skill and culture. For the weavers' children the work place was both school and recreation. "My work was at loom side, and when not winding my father taught me reading, writing, and arithmetic," remembered one weaver's son. Another reminisced that before the coming of factories "there was no bell to ring them up at four or five o'clock. . . . There was freedom to start and to stay away as they cared. . . . In the evenings, while still at work, at anniversary times of the Sunday schools, the young men and women would most heartily join in the hymn singing, while the musical rhythm of the shuttles would keep time. . . ."[39]

The collapse of domestic weaving and similar home trades meant the breakup of the family, and by the mid-nineteenth century the

---

[38] Braun, pp. 80–89.
[39] Quoted in Edward P. Thompson, Making of English Working Class, p. 291.

weavers had one of the lowest rates of generational continuity among the Lancashire working classes.[40] Having nowhere else to turn, older weavers stuck to their dying craft. They discouraged their children from following the trade, however, and sent them instead to the factories where the prospects of a decent wage were now much greater. The separation of the generations was not without much pain and suffering, as in one nineteenth century lament:[41]

> If you go into a loom-shop, where there's three or four pairs of
>   looms,
> They all are standing empty, encumbrances of the rooms;
> And if you ask the reason why, the old mother will tell you plain,
> My daughters have forsaken them, and gone to weave by steam.

Acceptance of factory employment was not easy for the older skilled artisan. Not only was its discipline unlike that of the home, but it meant disruption of the family economy and a loss of status besides. There was bound to be a good deal of generational conflict between parents preoccupied with such traditional values as honor and children seeking a future in the new industrial world. Such tensions were most likely to revolve around the institution of apprenticeship, the prime regulatory device of the traditional crafts. In England, apprenticeship was already at issue in the second half of the eighteenth century, when the functions of this youth-prolonging institution began to be undermined by conflict between indentured lads and their masters. Much of the fault lay with the latter who, like the rural landlords, were finding the old boarding arrangements less and less profitable, both economically and socially. Many London masters were taking on boys only for their cheap labor, teaching them nothing, and then encouraging them to break their contract so that they might claim the forfeited premiums. Most adversely affected were those youths least able to defend themselves, orphans and pauper children who were apprenticed by parish authorities, under the Elizabethan statute of 1601, from the age 10 or 12 to 24. As early as 1700 we hear a complaint that was to be echoed time and again until this long indenture was abolished in 1844:[42]

---

[40] Michael Anderson, *Family Structure*, pp. 121–122.
[41] Quoted in Edward P. Thompson, *Making of English Working Class*, p. 308.
[42] George, p. 277.

> Apprentices put out by the parish are frequently placed with poor,
> ill-natur'd or unskillful masters, who either force them from them by
> a bad maintenance and severity, before their times are out, or when
> they are out send them from them but bunglers in their trade, or
> masters of such a one as will turn to no account.

Unwanted apprentices were hired out as cheap manual labor, shipped to the colonies, turned over to naval press gangs, sometimes even murdered.[43] By the end of the eighteenth century, living in the master's house was increasingly rare, which led to the large numbers of runaways recorded during the period. "Though many do miscarry through their own fault," noted one contemporary, "yet that very many do miscarry either through the carelessness and negligence or the harshness and unreasonableness (or which too often happens) through the ill designs and practices of their masters. This is so common and notorious that there is no part of the nation which hath not marked examples of such unhappy young men, who might have been very useful in their generation, but by these means are driven into ill-courses, or become either altogether useless to the public and a burden to their relations."[44] Francis Place remembered that besides himself only one of the other young men with whom he was apprenticed on Fleet Street, London, ever gained a mastership in his trade.[45]

Unburdening themselves of the expense of feeding, boarding, and otherwise looking after their apprentices, many English masters were violating the patriarchal order. Even as early as 1775 it was reported that there were "but a small number of masters in these days who can or will keep their apprentices within door in the evening when their shops are shut."[46] The practice of paying wages in lieu of living in encouraged the violation of the indenture's ancient strictures: "Taverns and alehouses he shall not haunt, at cards, dice, tables or any other unlawful game he shall not play, matrimony he shall not contract, nor from the service of his said master day or night absent himself."[47] Brawling, drunkenness, and resort to prostitutes appear to have been widespread not only in England but in other European cities. Remembered Francis Place: "I went frequently among these

---

[43] George, pp. 230ff.
[44] Quoted in George, p. 278.
[45] George, p. 230.
[46] Quoted in George, p. 277.
[47] Quoted in George, p. 280.

girls—that is—I went with other lads . . . and at that time spent many evenings at the dirty public houses frequented by them. . . . We were all sons of master tradesmen, or persons of some consideration, yet among us this bad conduct was suffered to exist unchecked, uncontrolled." [48]

In England, general obligatory apprenticeship (with the exception of parish apprenticeship of orphans and pauper children) was abolished in 1814. The revolution in France abolished guild regulation there, but in other continental countries, notably Germany, the custom was much slower to disappear. Everywhere, however, the traditions that had once been a functioning part of the artisanal life-cycle were becoming sources of tension, particularly when industrial competition was causing a decline among the crafts. Masters continued to take on apprentices, not for the purpose of training but as a source of cheap labor. When the German journeyman, Johann Dewald, went out on his *Wanderjahr* in the 1830s he found the old well of hospitality dry. Stopping in Lahr, he noted the master there to be "a skinflint, a miser, who counts every spoonful the journeymen put in their mouths and cannot complain enough about how dear food is, so that one almost would vomit it up if one were not afraid the mistress would make another meal out of it. She is his image and not a whit better. Besides, to him the best of the experienced journeymen is no more than a young apprentice." [49]

Finding no work with masters in neighboring Bohemia, Dewald worked for a short time in a factory there. But he felt his status as journeyman demeaned and did not like the pace of the work: "all day long one has to do the same thing and so loses all sense for the whole. Of course it has to be so in a factory, but I can't adjust to it and always feel as if I only half ply my trade." [50] Many like Dewald, bereft of a future in their craft and unwilling for reasons of status and habit to enter factory work, found themselves extending their *Wanderjahr* beyond the usual limits, sometimes becoming permanent nomads. During the 1830s, 15,000 to 20,000 journeymen carpenters, tailors, and other German craftsmen were resident in Paris; and another 10,000 Germans found work in London.[51] The tradition of the

---

[48] Quoted in George, p. 282. Similar trends in German apprenticeship are described in Stadelmann and Fischer, pp. 76–114.
[49] Quoted in Eugene N. Anderson *et al.*, p. 108.
[50] Eugene N. Anderson *et al.*, p. 116.
[51] Schieder, pp. 93–110.

Gesellenverbände served them well in this respect, for it allowed them to sustain themselves away from home and family.

Thus the renaissance of the traditions of the *Wanderjahr*, tramping, and the *tour de France* in the immediate post-1815 period. Beneath their romantic trappings these institutions revealed the dire needs of a class of young men who were increasingly cut adrift from their chosen occupations. The authorities, fearful of the political results of vagabondage, made travelling difficult, but the journeymen persevered, summoning tradition in defense of their tramping rights. In France, the *compagnonnages* were undergoing a revival under the leadership of Agricol Perdiguier, who argued the moral and social benefits to the young and gained the support of some industrialists who found that journeymen belonging to these associations were better behaved and more reliable than other working men.[52] In England, too, the "tramping system" found new uses, particularly in times of strikes or depressions when trades would send off some of their members so as to relieve themselves.[53] In both England and France, families were left behind for months at a time, as the artisan passed from one house of call to another. "Those who were not married used to tease those who are about the wives they had left in solitary. How often homesickness drives the oldest to return home before their time!" remembered one French artisan.[54]

The journeymen's lodges, or "Mothers" as the French called them, continued to serve as substitute families, fraternities of "brothers" who recognized one another with secret signs and handshakes. Partly to escape repression by authorities, partly to fill a social and emotional void, the rituals of fraternity bloomed in the early nineteenth century. The colorful ceremonies of the *compagnonnage* attracted the attention and admiration of intellectuals like Victor Hugo, and for a time the reforms of Agricol Perdiguier found support within the Romantic Movement.[55] But the underpinning of the artisanal revival was essentially social and economic rather than cultural, and as the trades upon which these youth-prolonging institutions were based were absorbed into the industrial system the traditions of the *Wanderjahr* were bound to fall into disuse.

---

[52] de Sauvigny, pp. 251–254.

[53] Hobsbawn, "Tramping Artisan," pp. 34–45; for France, see de Sauvigny, pp. 206–207.

[54] Quoted in Chevalier, p. 427.

[55] Coornaert, pp. 71–72.

Before they disappeared entirely, however, the institutions of the journeymen served an unexpected purpose. Once the regulators of the flow of candidates to mastership, they became part of a broader movement demanding the abolition of all corporate privilege, a movement with strong political overtones. By the 1840s German journeymen were asking the abolition of the corporate structure of which they had been a part. Their *Gesellenverbände* had broadened the basis of membership, offering hospitality to fellow workers regardless of craft and admitting married men.[56] Furthermore, the traditions of the *Gesellen*, with their oaths of secrecy and networks of contacts over wide territories, proved well-suited to conspiratorial activity. Journeymen living in Switzerland and France were in close contact with offshoots of Mazzini's Young Germany movement, and a tradition of conspiratorial activity was established then that even as late as the 1870s still served the outlawed German Social Democratic Party.[57]

But it was earlier, in the Revolution of 1848, that the extent of the radicalization of young artisans was fully revealed. Journeymen in Saxony took advantage of the newly won freedom of association to demand the abolition of the rules of celibacy that prevented any married journeyman from becoming a master. Fellow craftsmen in other parts of Germany were attacking settlement restrictions and demanding easier access to trades closed to them by guild restrictions. "Things had changed since the eighteenth century days when journeymen had been the most ardent defenders of the guildsman's honor," writes Mack Walker. "They were leaving the guild corporation for the outsider class, and calling for reentry on those terms." [58] In 1848 there were, according to the young printer journeyman Stephan Born, "two age levels, not two classes" in conflict in Germany. But Born, who had been influenced by the writings of socialists, including Karl Marx, was himself a part of a new generation who tended to identify not with the masters of their trades but with a broader working class.[59] The real situation was as Gottfried Kinkel described it: "Half the artisans belong to the bourgeoisie and visit the casinos . . . ; the other half sends its children to the poor house

---

[56] Schieder, pp. 39–44, 82–92.
[57] For the personal experiences of one young printer's journeyman, see Born, pp. 27–33, 42–46; also Stadelmann and Fischer, pp. 216–223; Schieder, pp. 14–44.
[58] Walker, p. 365.
[59] Born, p. 29.

and lives a mean and miserable life on its daily earnings. Among the artisans themselves an aristocracy has arisen—namely, the aristocracy of the better coat." [60] And for Born, and many young artisans like him, the aristocracy of the better coat was now the enemy.

It was precisely at the point of their dissolution that the traditions of the journeymen were most politically explosive. Violent protest during the early nineteenth century was characteristic of groups attempting to protect their traditional status against the forces of modernization about to overwhelm them. The crowds of 1830 and 1848, like those of 1789, were composed, for the most part, of respectable, settled artisans, shopkeepers, and journeymen who were fighting defensively, though with the modern weapons of democracy, against an increasingly alien world. Those just beginning or attempting to begin their careers were often most deeply involved. The rebels were neither very young nor very old, as was shown by the Paris Revolution of 1830 in which 54% of those killed were between 20 and 35. [61] In Berlin, where journeymen were particularly conspicuous among the dead of the March Revolution of 1848, the role of youth was but another act in a series of protests and revolts that had begun with the so-called "tailors' rebellion" of 1830. [62] Conservatives tended to associate the actions of the young with the heedless gamin of Delacroix's "Liberty Leading the People"; and one German wit included in his "Recipe for a Rich Riot" a dash of the Berlin street urchins— but it was not these street nomads who gave their lives on the barricades. [63] On the contrary, the journeymen insurgents of 1830 and 1848 were neither rootless nor without tradition. "These journeymen were highly mobile," Richard Tilly has noted, "but we must remember that for journeymen artisans such as tailors, high geographical mobility did not necessarily imply, thanks to the institution of the *Wanderschaft,* uprootedness in a social sense." [64] Once a source of stability, this and other related institutions of working youth were now vehicles for rebellion. An old consciousness of brotherhood carried within it the seeds of a new. All over Europe, ancient notions of fraternity were being broadened along class lines to encompass all working men, regardless of trade, marital status, or age. [65]

---

[60] Kinkel quoted in Noyes, p. 26.
[61] Figures from Pinkney, p. 257.
[62] Richard Tilly, p. 31.
[63] Pinkney, p. 256.
[64] Richard Tilly, p. 32.
[65] Hobsbawm, "Ritual," p. 162; Noyes, Chapter 8; Coornaert, pp. 280–282.

IV

The spread of capitalism worked to transform the economic institutions of working youth. Shifts in population, associated with the
same process of industrialization, contributed to a similar transformation of their social life. The massive urbanization that began in the
third and fourth decades of the nineteenth century radically altered
the migratory traditions of youth and contributed to the replacement
of institutions associated with it by forms better suited to the modern
city. Newcomers to the city were heavily concentrated in the age
brackets we associate with youth. Charles Booth found that of those
migrants from English villages to London in the 1880s, some 80%
were 15 to 25 years of age; and these figures seem representative of
European internal migration as a whole.[66] The age distribution was
not new, but its one-way character was. Young people were not circulating back to the villages as before, but were becoming permanent
residents of the cities in much greater numbers. The rural areas of
Europe were beginning to be depopulated in the second half of the
century.

We can see this in Paris beginning in the 1830s, when masons and
carpenters, who had once left their wives behind while they made
a seasonal visit to the city, began to settle there permanently. Traditional migration cycles slackened and the hiring and lodging places
of the itinerant crafts began to lose their appeal. The Indian summer
of the *compagnonnage* was coming to an end as industrialization and
urbanization eliminated the economic and emotional needs that
it had once served. Romantics like George Sand viewed their
disappearance regretfully:[67]

> In Paris the *compagnonnage* is tending increasingly to become
> lost and dispersed over the great field of work and varied interests.
> No association could hope to monopolize work in Paris. In any event,
> the skeptical spirit of a more advanced civilization has put an end to

---

[66] Anna Weber, pp. 280–281; Redford, especially Chapter 1.
[67] Quoted in Chevalier, p. 430.

the gothic customs of the *compagnonnage;* too soon, perhaps, for a fraternal association covering all the workers was not yet ready to replace the association.

In England, tramping was being kept alive by the necessity to provide relief in hard times. Older workers were the first to abandon it when they found that they could use undergrounds and street cars to find work within the larger urban regions in which they lived, without the necessity of leaving home. Late in the nineteenth century young apprentices still travelled, but their institutions eventually fell into disuse due to economic modernization.[68]

Industrialization and urbanization were, in fact, tying young workers closer to their families and neighborhoods as the century progressed. Middle-class observers described family life in the factory towns of England as characterized by "parental cruelty, and carelessness, filial disobedience, neglect of conjugal rights, absence of maternal love, destruction of brotherly and sisterly affection," [69] but these accounts do not square with the economic and demographic facts of the period. Conditions of extreme poverty, combined with high levels of fertility, were bound to create generational tensions, yet kin ties remained surprisingly close. In the first phases of industrialization, the predominant forms of domestic spinning and weaving encouraged families to stay together, children working with parents. The invention of water-powered spinning in the 1790s brought that part of the process within factory walls and introduced a period when child labor was highly sought after. In the first decades of the nineteenth century, 80% of the workers in English cotton mills were children, but as heavier machinery was introduced skilled adult male spinners took command. They tended to hire their own children as scavengers at the age of 8 or 9, promoting them to the job of piecing cotton as they matured, and finally teaching them to spin at the ages of 17 or 18.[70] In this way the master spinner was able to preserve a great deal of paternal authority, preserving his family intact until the 1820s. Witnesses described this form of family economy diminishing rather than encouraging youthful immorality.[71]

> It is fathers or friends who work in factories, and they have all a
> common interest in checking immorality among the younger assist-
> ants, both boys and girls. . . . Now, even if none of their own chil-

---

[68] Hobsbawm, "Tramping Artisan," pp. 46–47.
[69] Peter Gaskell, quoted in Perkin, *Origins,* p. 150.
[70] Smelser, p. 189.
[71] Quoted in Smelser, p. 190.

dren were working with them, yet they have all a common interest as fathers in discountenancing indecencies. . . .

In the mining industry, too, early industrialization seems to have reinforced patriarchism. It was reported there that "the collier boy is, to all intents and purposes, the property of his father (as to wages) until he attains the age of 17 years, or marries." [72] Only when the factories increased in size and the complexity of the production process displaced the master spinner did paternal authority in textiles wane. [73] Even then, however, kin continued to be of prime importance in finding and holding employment in most industrial communities. This was true not only for sons and daughters of the operatives themselves, but for migrants from the rural areas who came to the industrial towns to "claim kin" and thus to find work. Because many employers continued to find it convenient to recruit from families of their most loyal workers, the factory remained a source of extended family unity. [74]

Young people were moving from the overpopulated countryside to the factory towns in search of high wages and marriage opportunities. [75] This movement brought relief to the rural areas and allowed a stabilization of family life there. [76] Sometimes, however, a young man or woman would act as advance party for those at home, encouraging them to come along once contacts and opportunities had been established. Such was the strategy of the Henry Bannerman family of Perthshire, Scotland, who sent their eldest son to seek his fortune in industrial Manchester. "He took a small warehouse in Marsden Square, and prospered so well as to induce his father to throw up the farm and bring the whole family south. . . . The new firm was styled Henry Bannerman and Sons, four out of the five sons having joined." [77] It is significant that the firm took the father's name; apparently the patriarchal principle could survive even this kind of relocation.

The Bannermans were fortunate. Most migrants to the cities never came to own their own businesses and most ended up in factory employment. Because children were hired so readily, parents often

---

[72] Quoted in Musgrove, *Youth and Social Order*, pp. 68–69.
[73] Smelser, pp. 199–201.
[74] Michael Anderson, *Family Structure*, pp. 115–119.
[75] Anna Weber, pp. 318–329; Banks, "Population Change," pp. 281–285; Wrigley, *Population and History*, Chapter 5.
[76] On this point, see Wolfram Fischer, pp. 423–435.
[77] Quoted in Redford, p. 136.

found themselves dependent on them. "The father remained unemployed or under-employed and became dependent in his declining years on the earnings of his children, in a manner which remained common until recently in manufacturing districts," writes Arthur Redford.[78] One witness reported that "generally people who have been distressed in their families and their affairs broken up . . . are apt to go as little colonies to colonize these mills. . . ."[79] Often a ladder of migration was established between a particular village and the neighborhood of some industrial town. Because in many factory and mining occupations control of jobs still lay with the older males, foremen and leaders of work gangs, kin could be summoned from the countryside with reasonable assurance that jobs would be waiting for them. Kin would lodge the newcomers in their own houses while they broke into the industrial system. Places for female domestics were often obtained in the same manner, with relatives who worked in a particular house putting in a good word for them. In some cases, whole families might be brought to the city, but it was more common for rural people to "lend" their younger members first, with the more firmly rooted elders following later, if at all.[80]

In effect, factory industrialization had successfully adapted traditional rural habits of migration to its own uses. But in the process, the traditional family strategy was radically transformed, particularly for those who became resident in the cities. No longer were they forced to send their children away at a certain age; now there was every advantage in keeping them at home during that part of the life cycle, namely youth, that had once been associated with the *Wanderjahre*. In English cotton towns, working class families were now actually receiving rather than sending children, as Michael Anderson has shown in his study of Lancashire household structure (Table 1).

Noticeable is the rise of lodgers and the decline of servants living in, but even more striking is the number of resident kin. Anderson has shown that 28.3% of the kin resident in Preston households were "parentless children," some of them orphans but many of them youths taken in as immigrants seeking work in the town.[81] Not only had industrialization encouraged families to keep their own young children longer for the wages they could bring in, but now there was

---

[78] Redford, p. 186.
[79] Quoted in Edward P. Thompson, *Making of English Working Class*, p. 307.
[80] Michael Anderson, *Family Structure*, pp. 101–106; for similar findings, see Lees, pp. 359–385.
[81] Michael Anderson, *Family Structure*, pp. 112–123, 148–159.

TABLE 1

Household Composition of Residents Other Than Parents[a]

	Kin	Lodgers	Servants and apprentices
Preindustrial households, 1564 to 1821	10%	<1%	29%
Preston, 1851	23%	23%	10%

[a] Figures from Michael Anderson, "Household Structure," p. 220.

more coresidence of young married couples and their elderly parents. Factory employment was making three-generation households not only socially but economically desirable, because the elderly person could look after the grandchildren and thus allow the mother to be out at work.[82] In turn, children were able to offer a new kind of social security to their parents.

Parents and children were remaining together longer, a fact clearly reflected in the differences in residence patterns between boys and girls in Preston and those in the surrounding countryside, as shown in Table 2.

TABLE 2

Children Residing with Their Families in 1851[a]

		Preston	Villages in surrounding Lancashire
Boys	10–14	92%	77%
	15–19	79%	56%
	20–24	65%	53%
Girls	10–14	86%	86%
	15–19	67%	62%
	20–24	62%	46%

[a] Figures from Michael Anderson, *Family Structure*, p. 85.

Of course, the wages that young persons earned in factory employment could work in the opposite manner by encouraging greater

---

[82] Michael Anderson, *Family Structure*, pp. 55–67, 143–146.

independence on their part. It was reported at the time that "children frequently leave their parents at a very early age in the manufacturing districts. Girls of sixteen, and lads of the same age, find that they can enjoy greater liberty, and if not greater comforts, that at least they can have their own way more completely in a separate home, and these partings cause little surprise or disturbance." [83] Cheap lodging houses beckoned to those who yearned for personal freedom, and there is evidence that in large cities young people, being on their own, formed a separate sub-culture apart from kin. "Children frequently pay for their own lodgings, board, and clothing. They usually make their own contracts, and are in the proper sense of the word free agents." [84]

However, Anderson has calculated that, given the wage scales of the factory towns, few could afford to live out until the late teens or early twenties. Indeed, there were strong economic incentives for males to remain at home until 16 or 17, females even longer.[85] Until then, they contributed to the family purse, holding back a share for their personal enjoyment and savings. Living more cheaply at home than they could in a lodging house allowed youth to build a nest egg for future marriage, while at the same time fulfilling obligations to parents and siblings. "The children that frequent factories make almost the purse of the family, and by making the purse of the family they share in the ruling of it and are in a great state of insubordination to their parents," wrote one anxious observer of this arrangement.[86] Yet few children deserted their families and, by our contemporary standards, kin loyalty remained remarkably strong. In comparison to the rural situation, where the father's control of inheritance guaranteed submission, relations between parents and children were indeed more equal; but poverty and the uncertainties of daily life, including health, accident, and unemployment, were still so pressing that most parents and children were still bound together by necessity.

For working-class families, poverty was a cyclical phenomenon closely associated with the number and age of the children. When offspring were very young and not yet employable, there was more than a 50% chance of the family being below the poverty line. The situation was best when at least half the children were employed, but

---

[83] Quoted in Michael Anderson, *Family Structure*, p. 124.
[84] Quoted in Musgrove, *Youth and Social Order*, p. 68.
[85] Michael Anderson, *Family Structure*, pp. 126–132.
[86] Michael Anderson, *Family Structure*, p. 131.

worsened again when all the offspring were married and parents were left alone.[87] This explains the observation of one eyewitness who observed that "nothing can be more warm and keen than the affection of parents throughout the cotton districts for children, *so long as they continue children.* . . ."[88] It would seem that the older youth were dispensable, though not in precisely the same way as they had been in preindustrial society. Wages of younger siblings could benefit the teenagers of the family by bringing the family purse to its highest level, thus allowing them to set up separate lodgings or even marry. Anderson argues that younger children also enjoyed certain advantages, however, precisely because they came along when the family earnings were greatest and they sometimes had the advantages of schooling that were denied to the first-born.[89]

In any case, the life cycle of working-class children appears to have been drastically changed by the mid-nineteenth century. The old distinction between dependent childhood and semidependent youth on the one hand, and youth and the independence of adulthood on the other, had become blurred by the fact that young people were staying at home longer and leaving only a short time before setting up their own independent households. But we cannot yet talk about a phase of life like that which we know as "adolescence" replacing the traditional semidependent status of youth. For while the teen-aged lived at home, their family situation—large numbers of siblings and crowded living space—was still such that a large part of their social life continued to be organized around traditional peer groups. In short, despite the new residency patterns, demographic and economic factors perpetuated the utility of youth groups that were very similar to those found in preindustrial society.

V

At this point we have less than adequate information on peer-group structures in nineteenth-century cities. However, it would ap-

---

[87] On poverty cycle, see Michael Anderson, *Family Structure*, p. 31.

[88] Quoted in Michael Anderson, *Family Structure*, p. 76.

[89] Michael Anderson, *Family Structure*, pp. 75–76.

pear that many of the rural traditions of youth were adapted by youthful migrants to meet their needs in an urban setting. There is strong evidence, for example, of peer groups exercising strong moral control over their members. Henry Mayhew, whose studies of mid-nineteenth century London life were concerned with the very lowest elements of that society, found that even among the supposedly promiscuous ranks of juvenile street peddlers a certain code of honor prevailed. Boys were known to discipline their girls for infidelity, sometimes with a brutality that Mayhew found quite reprehensible.[90] Gangs of youth, ages 14–20, appear to have had the same sense of territoriality as village youth groups, with the same fierce hostility for outsiders, particularly rivals for the affections of local girls.[91] Gangs took on the names of their neighborhoods or baptised themselves with more colorful designations. In Manchester, gang life was generally known as "scuttling," an expression of "a kind of wish to assert the supremacy of their own neighborhood against that of some neighboring one." [92] A hierarchy of age was evident, with the younger members, aged 14–17, concerned mainly with sex-segregated pursuits such as sport and gambling, leaving to their older "brothers" the control of and access to serious courtship. Girls appear to have formed satellites to the male groups, often acting as a cause of peer group solidarity against outsiders but having no strong structure of their own. Once courtship began, at about 17 for boys and somewhat earlier for girls, the peer group again provided a kind of setting for its activities. Having no place other than the streets and public houses to carry on their acquaintance rituals, young lovers developed the seasonal custom of "promenading" in large groups. On summer nights, the streets of both large and small English towns would be crowded with young people until ten o'clock or so, at which time they returned to their homes to prepare for another long day of labor.[93]

Of course, peer loyalty could serve more dubious purposes, and the criminal bands of young pickpockets, footpads, and other artful dodgers who populated the cities of fiction and fact in the nineteenth

---

[90] Mayhew, *London Labour*, p. 470.

[91] Montague, p. 244.

[92] Russell, *Manchester Boys*, p. 43.

[93] Montague, pp. 234–254; Urwick, "Conclusion," pp. 300–308; Russell, *Manchester Boys*, p. 115; Rowntree, *Poverty and Progress*, p. 470. On German urban youth in the eighteenth century, see Helmut Möller, pp. 55ff. Harrison, pp. 238ff. Similar customs still exist in parts of Wales; see Frankenberg, pp. 62–63.

century displayed similar tightly-knit structures. However hard honest parents tried to steer their children from these gangs, sometimes bringing them into court when beyond control, there was always the danger of delinquency. As one English magistrate explained:[94]

> It is really a difficult thing to keep children constantly in the house; they must be allowed by poor parents to go about, even for air and exercise. . . . [The magistrates] are placed in this painful situation, that we cannot counsel a parent to prosecute a child to conviction, and yet, by not prosecuting, we know that they must go on till they become hardened in crime.

Studies of prostitution in the same period indicate that peer-group pressure was a powerful force in leading girls astray, though it would seem in the case of both male and female delinquents that it was orphans and runaway children, not those living with or near their parents, who were most frequently recruited to life-long careers in crime.[95] We must be quite careful here to separate casual delinquency from persistent criminality, both of which await further intensive study.

The little we know about gang behavior is colored, unfortunately, by the perspective of middle-class observers, who tended to interpret comradery as deviance and found in contacts between the sexes little except licentiousness. In English cities, groups of young people perpetuated the traditions of village life within their local neighborhoods. Its streets were their village green, and a marriage feast, fair, or visiting circus their special occasion for fun and ceremony.[96] Nineteenth-century schoolmasters found it virtually impossible to maintain attendance on days that children viewed as rightfully theirs; and even as late as 1914 Oxford school logs recorded low attendance for days before and after traditional holidays.[97]

The street gang was in some sense the school of the poor, bringing together young people from early teens to mid-twenties in a com-

---

[94] Quoted in Tobias, p. 165.

[95] Tobias, pp. 161–163; Bongert, pp. 49–90. On prostitution, see Henriques, pp. 97–125; Bloch, pp. 315–335.

[96] Bray, "Boy and Family," pp. 8–32; Montague, pp. 239ff.

[97] Porter, p. 19. My own survey of several Oxford elementary school logs turned up similar low attendance on traditional dates, like May Day and Guy Fawkes Day, and at times when a civil or commercial attraction was in progress. On the effect of annual fairs, see Alexander, p. 26.

prehensive learning situation. It was through the peer group that the young person gained a sense of place and a measure of individual worth. "Understand it [the street] and you hold the key to many of the riddles of social morality," wrote E. J. Urwick, "and let this too serve to explain how it is that the majority of boys and girls for whom the home does so little and for whom the school has so little chance of doing much, nevertheless grow up into decent and respectable citizens instead of lawless and licentious ne'er-do-wells." Social relations between the sexes were precocious by middle-class standards, beginning as early as 14, but most flirtations were innocent enough, closer to childish love games and horseplay than adult intimacy. "Granting the greater coarseness of words, the more flagrant faults of habit and behavior, we question whether a comparison of sins and self-indulgence would work out at all to the disadvantage of the town labouring class as a whole," concluded Urwick.[98] His collaborator, Lily Montague, found that serious courtship began in the late teens, but that a prolonged period of acquaintanceship intervened before actual betrothal. Even though working-class youth married early, long betrothals were honored, with girls testing the "steadiness" of their boyfriends before marriage.[99] Courtship was known among the respectable English working class as "walking," a term that underlined its public, ritualistic character. As in the village youth groups, friends seem to have acted as a kind of social and moral jury, leading Urwick to observe: "The glaring publicity of the street is all on the side of town youth's virtue." [100]

Yet, the traditions of city youth were not necessarily identical to those of the village, being no longer inclusive of such a broad range of social ranks as before. The growth of residential segregation by class had the effect of giving each urban neighborhood a specific social character, perhaps encouraging greater cohesion than had been the case when various classes inhabited the same area. In the sixteenth-century cities studied by Natalie Davis, social divisions caused the decline of age-homogeneous groups, but the nineteenth-century city may very well have produced the opposite effect precisely because the removal of adults to their place of work meant that parents had to reply on semiautonomous peer groups as extensions of their moral authority. So the typical fair weather street scene:[101]

---

[98] Urwick, "Conclusion," pp. 298, 310.
[99] Montague, p. 243; Hewitt, pp. 38–40, 81–84.
[100] Urwick, "Conclusion," p. 310.
[101] Quoted in Michael Anderson, *Family Structure*, p. 104.

> The doors of the houses stand hospitably open, and younger children
> cluster over the thresholds and swarm out upon the pavement. . . .
> The people all appear to be on the best of terms with each other, and
> laugh and gossip from window to window, and door to door. The
> women, in particular, are fond of sitting in groups upon their thresh-
> olds, sewing and knitting; the children sprawl about beside them, and
> there is the amount of sweethearting going forward which is naturally
> to be looked for under such circumstances.

What strikes us here is the equilibrium between paternity and fraternity. Parents concerned with the day-to-day struggle for survival
in a hostile economic environment were more than willing to turn
over tasks of education and supervision to the peer groups. In turn,
the urban youth groups were ready to support the interests of the
parents when occasion demanded. The ritual of Misrule remained an
instrument of popular protest in French cities throughout the early
nineteenth century, becoming appropriately the title of Daumier's
satirical newspaper, the *Charivari*, in the 1830s.[102] Despite intergenerational tensions, young and old were united in defense of their
class interests. In Oxford, the traditional Guy Fawkes Night activities
of November, 1867, became a vehicle for economic protest, when
bands of men and boys roamed the streets, shouting for lower bread
prices, and ultimately gathering under the windows of Balliol College
to support a strike of masons there. After two nights of tumult, town
and university authorities readied troops, but found it more expedient
to turn students loose against the crowd. Members of the University's
cadet corps, armed with clubs, surged into the streets on the third
night. That evening the ritual battle between town and gown took
on the aspect of class warfare, as the traditions of one segment of
English youth were pitted against those of another in a melee of un-
accustomed violence.[103]

As the century wore on, youthful pranks were more likely to be
directed against another object of general working-class distrust, the
schools. Here again we see the solidarity of old and young; and in
many parts of England, parents encouraged rebellion against school
authorities when compulsory education interfered with what they
believed to be their right to their children's work.[104] Poverty and in-

---

[102] Natalie Davis, "Reasons of Misrule," p. 75.

[103] "Reports of Riot"; also "Gown and Town Rows," pp. 380–381; Plowman, pp.
215–220.

[104] For one such case in Oxford, see ms. source D, St. Frideswide's, September 26
and October 2, 1889. For London, see Booth, pp. 206–230; and Rubinstein, pp. 61,
85–86.

security bound young and old together, and anything that turned
the children from the home or cut their contributions to the common
purse was viewed with the dismay George Sims attributed to a London costermonger in the 1870s:[105]

> It's the School Board what gives 'em these notions, a-stuffin'
>   boys' heads full of pride,
> And makes 'em look down on their fathers—these School
>   Boards I ne'er could abide.
> When I was his age I was working', a-wheelin' the barrer for
>   dad,
> And a-fetchin' the stuff from the markets, when horses was
>   not to be had.

We have seen how the corporate traditions of the laboring poor
gave birth to new forms appropriate to an urbanized and industrialized society organized on a class basis. The neighborhood gang, the
various rituals of social protest, and the economic and political redefinition of "brotherhood" were all products of a period of struc-
tural demographic and economic change. Not surprisingly, similar
transformations were affecting the upper orders of society as well.
There, too, the traditions of youth were fundamentally altered, producing new youth-prolonging structures to serve this other strata of
troubled youth.

VI

If transition is a proper characterization of the status of youth
among the poor, it is also a fitting description of the changing life-
cycle of the sons and daughters of the well-to-do. Until the 1860s and
1870s, when family limitation became widespread among the well-
to-do, large numbers of children were for them also a form of social
security, though in the sense of preserving family name and property
rather than as contributors to current income. Large families were

---

[105] Quoted in Rubinstein, p. 60.

still necessary to guarantee a male heir, for while child mortality was lower among these elites, it was not yet so in the 1830s that parents could expect more than three-fourths of their children to reach the age of 20. This was the mortality rate recorded among the English clergy at that time, and while it is difficult to verify it for other middle-class groups, it probably represented the average.[106] In any case, the fact of child mortality was an oppressive presence until very late in the century, reflected in children's tales designed to prepare boys and girls for death, in paintings such as Archer's "The Empty Cradle," and in other morbid decorations of mid-Victorian interiors.[107]

All this reflected a certain fatalism that the rich shared with the poor. Rousseau and other pedagogues had reminded them that large investment in a young child's training was a relatively poor risk. This was not callous advice, for Rousseau was one of the leading proponents of a new, more sentimental, attitude toward the child, which caught the imagination of the educated classes at the end of the eighteenth century.[108] But for much of the nineteenth century this concern could never be without its ambivalence so long as the awful facts of death loomed as large as they did for most families. The time of the modern family, characterized by Philippe Ariès as focusing its attention on "helping the children to rise in the world, individually, and without any collective ambition . . . ," had not yet fully arrived on the stage of social history even by 1870.[109] In any case, the sentimentality about young children did not extend to youth, for in this age of transition the treatment of them reflected a family strategy that, while modified by new economic and social conditions, was still in many respects traditional, regarding younger sons and daughters as expendable to what Ariès would call the "collective ambition."

It must be remembered that relatively high mortality encouraged high fertility until the 1860s and 1870s; and because the mortality rate among children of the higher classes was beginning to decline in the middle of the nineteenth century, persistent high fertility was resulting in even more superfluous children than had been the case earlier.[110] The problem of what to do with younger sons and daughters was due as much to the changing social pretensions of the middle

---

[106] Banks, *Prosperity and Parenthood,* p. 195.

[107] Archer's painting and other maudlin objects of Victorian sensibility are included in Morley, illustration nos. 1,3,4,6.

[108] Musgrove, *Youth and Social Order,* pp. 63–64; Ariès, pp. 365–407.

[109] Ariès, p. 404.

[110] Banks, *Prosperity and Parenthood,* especially Chapter 10.

classes as to population growth, however. As a group, they were the first to give up the practice of sending children out to live in the households of others. The aristocracy, with its networks of patronage, could be sure of placing its children properly, but the *nouveau riche*, whose social status was still shaky, worried about any loss of status that might result from their children's being associated with the class of people who were hired servants.[111] Girls were the first to abandon the traditions of service, and because the Victorian middle classes frowned on public education for women, there was no alternative for them but to remain at home until marriage or, if spinsterhood was their fate, to move into the home of a brother or some other relative.[112] With respect to their sons, the middle classes were divided between the entrepreneurial elements, who up to the mid-nineteenth century normally brought them into their businesses after some kind of apprenticeship, and the professional families, for whom formal education was the key to career. This latter group preferred to educate their young children within their own households during the late eighteenth and early nineteenth centuries, again partly for fear of associating them with the lower orders in the neighborhood schools. In withdrawing their sons from the local grammar schools, the English middle classes were following the lead of the landed elites, who had already abandoned these institutions in the eighteenth century.[113] Until the boarding (public) schools became popular in the 1830s and 1840s, many children of the well-to-do appear to have remained at home until their middle teen years, when the surviving males either went on to university study or, more often, began apprenticeships in business or the professions. As late as 1861, some 40,000 English boys, 15–20 years of age, were living at home without visible occupation or outside schooling. Apparently, most of these were sons of the propertied classes.[114]

Traditional forms of maintenance, such as tramping, were simply socially unacceptable to the expanding middle classes. Taking sons directly into the family business was the cheapest mode of accommodation, but this was hardly a help to the professional elements. They shared with the aristocracy an abhorrence of trade and were determined to have their offspring follow them in their own, or similarly

---

[111] Ariès, pp. 396–99.

[112] Crozier, pp. 32–35.

[113] Hans, pp. 28–29 and Chapter 9; Crozier, pp. 18–23; Musgrove, *Youth and the Social Order*, pp. 37–46. On German developments, see Stephen, pp. 64–72.

[114] Publication/report, *Parl. Papers* V, p. 135.

prestigious, professions. "Clergymen beget clergymen and barristers; barristers beget barristers and clergymen and the scions of the professional classes have generally to get a draught of the Lethe of penury before they desert their conventional status, and take to selling anything but their wits. . . . The professions absorb aspirants from all classes, but return few or none to their source," noted the *Saturday Review* in 1857.[115]

Even in the eighteenth century, training for the professions was becoming a long, drawn-out affair. Mid-nineteenth-century English doctors and lawyers were typically older as a group than businessmen or entrepreneurs, a condition that reflected their extended preparation.[116] By mid-century, the cost of domestic education or grammar schooling to the age of 17 or 18, plus 5 to 7 years of articled apprenticeship beyond that, was often over £2,000.[117] In England, only the civil service was really open to sons of modest means, for even the army required purchase of commission. The situation on the Continent was much the same, with the exception that in countries like Prussia the civil service at its higher levels also required university training in law, making it as expensive as the other professions.[118] And added to the formal costs of education were the social overheads of eligible young bachelors, who had to keep up appearances in order to be professionally and socially acceptable.

Little wonder that the English Schools Inquiry Commission of 1868 found the professional classes desperate about the cost of education. "Having received a cultivated education themselves, they are anxious that their sons should not fall below them. . . . They have nothing to look to but education to keep their sons on a high social level."[119] Their special anguish was well-depicted in J. C. Hudson's *Parent's Handbook* of the early 1840s:[120]

> The pride and satisfaction with which a father regards his first, and as yet only son, in the days of cockades, white frocks, and naked knees, are exchanged for anxiety and apprehension, when, some eighteen years afterwards, he sees himself surrounded by a half a dozen full-

---

[115] Quoted in Reader, p. 120.
[116] See age structure of Preston professions in Michael Anderson, *Family Structure,* p. 27.
[117] Figures from Banks, *Prosperity and Parenthood,* pp. 173–196.
[118] Gillis, *Prussian Bureaucracy,* pp. 49–53.
[119] Publication/report, *Parl. Papers* I, p. 18.
[120] Quoted in Banks, *Prosperity and Parenthood,* p. 195.

grown and fast-growing candidates for frock coats, Wellington boots, walking-canes, watch guards, and cigars.

From the middle of the eighteenth century on the Continent and from the 1820s in England, there is evidence of parents desperately seeking relief from this burden and resorting to any means to start sons precociously on careers regardless of the consequences for the individual. Parents were bargaining for the cheapest apprentice premiums, indifferent to the quality of training. Unscrupulous doctors, lawyers, and other professionals would take on a boy merely for his labor, teach him nothing, and then blame his examination failures on his idleness.[121] Where parents turned to secondary education, they were hardly less discriminating. In England, grasping schoolmasters took advantage of parental gullibility to establish schools like Dotheboys Hall in Dickens' *Nicholas Nickleby*, horrid dumping grounds for unwanted lads. Prussian teachers reported that parents pushed their children with unreasoning haste through school and on to university. Boys were arriving at the university at such tender ages in the late eighteenth and early nineteenth centuries that the Prussian state was forced to contemplate prescribed examinations in order to halt abuses which included the bribery of teachers.[122] Authorities were afraid of the consequences, however, for as one official put it: "One is dealing here not only with common people and understanding parents, but with influential and rich people, who would raise an uproar against such a law as an arbitrary intervention by the state." [123] By 1818 a school-leaving exam was introduced, but not before standards of promotion had been made mockery of in many districts: "The order and discipline among the students is thereby almost totally destroyed, so that between students and teachers conflict instead of peaceful, trustful relationships appropriate to such things now prevails." [124]

The condition of English public schools of the same period were comparable, if not worse. They, too, had become dumping grounds, both for sons of the gentry and for the offspring of the upper-middle classes, most of whom had no prospects of going on to the university and were in public school simply to gain a bit of social polish before seeking their fortunes in the army, the colonies, or, in last resort,

---

[121] Reader, p. 119.
[122] Schwartz, vol. 1, pp. 67–71.
[123] Schwartz, vol. 1, p. 107.
[124] Quoted in Schwartz, vol. 2, p. 94.

business.[125] English boarding schools, prior to the Arnoldian reforms of the 1830s, were "great seminaries, where hundreds of bad and good boys are promiscuously mingled, where the time of boys is so entirely at their own disposal, that of four and twenty hours but two or three àt the utmost are spent under the master's eyes; and of the remainder, when we deduct what is employed in the important business of purveying, in quarreling and in play, we find little left for the purpose of voluntary improvement." [126] Without a defined future or a reason to study, the schoolboy of the early nineteenth century viewed teachers as captors rather than mentors. Discipline, either abysmally lax or brutally harsh, inevitably triggered rebellion; and the early nineteenth century was punctuated with violent schoolboy revolts, the last of which was at Marlborough College in 1851.

Much of the blame can be placed on grasping schoolmasters, to whom the academic success of their boys mattered only as "advertisement to their schools." [127] But the 1868 Schools Inquiry Commission placed responsibility elsewhere: "Too often parents seem hardly to care for education at all. Too often they think no education worth having that cannot be speedily turned into money." [128] Reverend Charles Evans, headmaster of a Birmingham grammar school, noted the tendency of parents to "throw the responsibility of the entire education of their children upon the school, ignoring their own responsibility." [129] Other teachers complained that parents withdrew boys before their education was complete, thinking little of their long-term future and only of immediate advantage. Masters were nearly unanimous that parents had no respect for the goals of the local grammar schools and that, while day schools were reported to work in Scotland, where parents carefully planned and supervised their children's education, "in England, at any rate at present, parents do not seem able to make day schools as efficient places of teaching as good boarding schools." [130]

The Commission took heart from the growing popularity of the reformed boarding (public) schools, but their attraction also appears to have been partly a function of parental desire for relief. "They feel themselves child-ridden," observed Reverend Edward Lowe, "the

---

[125] Musgrove, *Youth and Social Order*, pp. 48–49.
[126] Quoted in Hans, p. 182.
[127] Publication/report, *Parl. Papers* I, p. 17.
[128] Publication/report, *Parl. Papers*, I, p. 15.
[129] Publication/report, *Parl. Papers* I, p. 543.
[130] Publication/report, *Parl. Papers* I, p. 44.

accommodation of small houses, the domestic arrangement of small houses, the class of servants in small houses, and all that sort of thing, suggest the advantage it is to the parents to board their children at school and not to have their big boys always at home." [131] Still, such schools were increasingly expensive, and as late as the 1860s the professional middle classes had found no way of relieving themselves of the burdens of their high fertility. Furthermore, the conditions of those whose "circumstances compel them to live in small houses with large families" was getting worse, for the fall in child mortality that was recorded among that class between 1830 and 1870 meant that even more offspring were surviving to be educated. [132] As T. H. Marshall was later to put their plight: "It may be possible to bring ten children into the world, if you have only to rear five, and while one is 'on the way,' the last is in the grave, not in the nursery. But if the doctor preserves seven or eight of ten, and other things remain equal, the burden may become intolerable." [133]

Demographic crisis was compounded by the peculiarities of early nineteenth-century economic growth, which did not provide adequate employment opportunities for the educated. Among the aristocracy, the problem of younger sons returned in the eighteenth century, particularly on the Continent, where impoverished noblemen became a burden on both state and society. In Prussia, where military and civil service had previously provided acceptable employment for that group, these occupations were no longer sufficient to meet the demand of both the nobility and the expanding middle classes, who were now challenging the old elites' monopoly on preferred positions. At the end of the eighteenth century there was the first of a series of crises of underemployment among the educated, producing an unprecedented level of generational awareness among Prussian youth. Talented young men, the likes of Friedrich Schleiermacher and Friedrich Wilhelm Schelling, could find no other occupation than that of tutoring the children of the wealthy. Henri Brunschwig has written of a whole generation whose frustrations adversely affected their health, turned them against society, and, if we are to believe contemporary accounts, led to an unprecedented rash of suicides. [134] For those without prospect of employment or marriage, youth itself be-

---

[131] Publication/report, *Parl. Papers* V, p. 50.
[132] Banks, *Prosperity and Parenthood*, p. 194.
[133] Quoted in Musgrove, *Youth and Social Order*, p. 65.
[134] Brunschwig, pp. 177–179, 266–269.

came a nightmarish state of existence, reflected in the literature of the *Sturm und Drang* movement, whose heroes were inevitably cast in the role of young outlaws. This was the generation that wept at reading Goethe's *Sorrows of Young Werther* and identified with Schiller's *The Robbers*. Theirs was not a political movement in the usual sense of that term, though in their adoption of the "Werther costume," comfortable coat and shirt open at the neck, they were making a statement of rebellion against the highly formalized society of the eighteenth century. "It hardly occurred to anybody in my youth to envy the privileged class or grudge them their privileges," Goethe wrote in 1790, "but knights, robbers, an honest Third Estate, and an infamous nobility—such have been the ingredients of our novels and plays during the past ten years." [135]

This first generation of young romantics aroused the antagonism of their elders, who accused them of every excess. The sedition of the young was purely spiritual, however. They came together in the 1770s in small, informal groups like the Göttingen *Hainbund* to discuss ideas and nourish the thought of moral self-preservation. The essence of this and other self-styled *"Bruderbünde"* of the period was "to spread religious virtue, sensibility, and pure innocent spirituality." The *Hainbund* made of male friendship a kind of secular religion, making of youth itself the repository of all that was socially and culturally holy.[136] This tradition went back to the founding of *Der Jüngling* in 1747, one of the journals of the "moral weekly" category that were so popular among the German educated class during the period. This paper set itself against the dominant social mannerisms of the day, imports of French fashions and tastes that came in for increasing criticism at the end of the eighteenth century.[137] The association of effeminacy with cosmopolitanism, and masculinity with native German fraternal custom, had its roots in the same rebellion against all that was privileged and therefore French. The ladies of the exclusive salons were viewed with the same contempt as the courtesans, thus reinforcing the cult of maleness that was a part of the movement from the beginning. Spiritual rather than physical however, the homoerotic element in early romanticism's fraternalism was perhaps to have been expected among a body of young men who, through no fault of their own, had been excluded

---

[135] Quoted in Holborn, p. 328; Hornstein, pp. 170ff.
[136] Muchow, *Jugend und Zeitgeist*, pp. 29–56.
[137] Hornstein, pp. 149–164.

from all privilege, including the company of women of their own class.[138]

Demographic and economic conditions were less severe on English youth of a similar background. England's younger sons were better provided for by the expanding economic opportunities at home and abroad. Furthermore, the aristocracy's traditional powers of patronage and purchase appear to have remained adequate for its needs until the 1870s, when considerations of merit began to undercut its traditional monopolies.[139] There was talk of the need for Protestant convents for unmarried daughters in the eighteenth century, but nothing like the crisis of the seventeenth century arose among the gentry and middle classes until the third decade of the nineteenth century, when overcrowding began to appear in the English professions. By the 1850s primogeniture was again being criticized and elaborate schemes devised to provide respectable employment for surplus youth. The most ambitious project was that of Thomas Hughes, the self-appointed protector of the interests of the English upper classes, who collected £150,000 to found a colony for younger sons in backwoods Tennessee. Appropriately called "Rugby," Hughes's settlement was to combine the attractions of tennis and fishing with the genteel but profitable employments of farming and horse-breeding. It lured several young pioneers in 1879, but, as the historian of the experiment explained: "They were Englishmen of culture and refinement and at one period their supply of Worcester sauce became exhausted and their agonies were terrible to witness. But even this disaster was followed by a greater. This was the failure of *London Punch* to arrive on time. . . . Then again the country was unfavorable for the playing of lawn tennis." [140] Two years after it began, Tennessee's Rugby collapsed.

Many a young gentleman had been forced to emigrate under much less attractive circumstances. The Napoleonic wars had provided outlet for young energies through military service, but, with the demobilization and the economic depression that followed 1815, troubles already apparent in the eighteenth century were intensified. On the Continent many turned to higher education as a way of attaining or maintaining status, but there, too, the professions were not expanding at a rate sufficient to absorb the numbers of qualified graduates.

---

[138] Muchow, *Jugend und Zeitgeist*, pp. 90–92.
[139] F. L. M. Thompson, pp. 70–75.
[140] Quoted in Thirsk, p. 377.

Already, in the 1830s, German parents were being told that "the number of young people who have completed their studies is already more than sufficient to occupy all the positions." Enrollments declined for a time and then shot upwards again in the 1840s, the cause of W. H. Riehl's pessimistic observation: "Germany produces greater intellectual product than it can use and support."[141] In France, the situation was much the same, there being "want of straight and regular paths in which steady industry or persevering ambition may insure success in life."[142]

In both Germany and France, industrial development was still proceeding too slowly to absorb more than small numbers of educated youth. And even had it been faster, the traditional disdain of the educated for commerce would have prevented most of these young men from taking advantage. Until the middle of the nineteenth century, higher education remained everywhere classically rather than technologically oriented, preparing the young almost exclusively for the clergy, law, medicine, and civil service. As the crisis of overcrowding worsened, access to salaried position, marriage, and, in effect, to adulthood itself was progressively delayed. Among candidates for the Prussian higher bureaucracy, the age of tenured appointment was increasingly postponed. In the 1830s a Prussian administrative trainee of the *Assessor* rank waited an average of 6.6 years for his first salaried post; by the 1850s the waiting period was over 10 years.[143] As the educational process became more rationalized and bureaucratized, schooling itself was extended. Students were arriving later at the university (median age of 17 years at Oxford in the 1590s; median age of 19.7 in 1900) and staying longer. Lawrence Stone estimates that the whole English educational process was extended 5 or 6 years between the seventeenth and nineteenth centuries, a trend apparent on the Continent as well.[144] Precocity, so much desired by the parents, had become socially and professionally unattainable for the sons.

For many, family resources were too small to ride out a prolonged period of training. Some, like Stephan Born, were forced to abandon their schooling when family funds failed and seek employment in the

---

[141] O'Boyle, p. 477; Gillis, *Prussian Bureaucracy*, p. 66.
[142] O'Boyle, p. 489.
[143] Gillis, *Prussian Bureaucracy*, p. 43.
[144] Stone, "Size and Composition," pp. 51–54. For German university statistics, see Zorn, pp. 321–339.

trades.[145] Others turned to less socially acceptable intellectual occupations, such as journalism, where they gave vent to their social frustrations and generational grievances. These young men were fated by background or ambition to "follow one of the liberal professions, the law or medicine . . . or to gain a precarious livelihood by the public press, or to solicit (long, perhaps, and vainly) employment in public office. Agriculture and commerce are repudiated as beneath young men who are attempting at one go to overleap many steps in the social scale." [146] They were, as W. H. Riehl described them, Europe's "intellectual proletariat," inclined to be politically radical or, if not so oriented, involved in the various elite youth-prolonging counter cultures and organizations that had proliferated since the eighteenth century, many of them sprouting from a single root, namely that of freemasonry.

VII

Circles of serious young men, bound together by shared intellectual and moral concerns, were already common in mid-eighteenth-century Germany. As a schoolboy, Goethe had vainly sought to join such a group which called itself the *Philandria*. Though not much older than he, its members turned him down because his reputation for wild behavior was an affront to their image of themselves as a "league of virtue." [147] Although the future genius was never initiated into that priggish company, he was later to be associated with freemasonry, which in its goals, organization, and constituency was strikingly similar to that schoolboys' organization. Indeed, it was not by accident that the *Philandria* later evolved into a masonic lodge, for the history of masonry and that of elite youth-prolonging organizations were tightly interwoven for much of the eighteenth and nineteenth centuries.

The origins of freemasonry provide us with clues as to why this movement exerted such an extraordinary attraction on upper and

---

[145] Born, pp. 6–9.
[146] Quoted in O'Boyle, p. 489.
[147] Friedenthal, pp. 30–31.

middle class youth, beginning in the eighteenth century. As the name implies, it borrowed heavily from certain craft traditions, notably that of the itinerant masons, whose system of lodges was attracting considerable attention among the educated class as early as the late seventeenth century. The masons' world was an intensely moral one. Its journeymen were protected against social mishap and personal failing by a series of strict rules to which novices committed themselves in elaborate, ofttimes exotic, initiation ceremonies. Ritual not only protected the secrets of the trade, but encouraged a peer group solidarity that was reflected in the generous mutual aid that distinguished this and other itinerant crafts during the Early Modern period.

Beginning sometime in the seventeenth century, individuals of middle- and even upper-class origin began to join mason lodges. By the early eighteenth century some of the "operative" lodges had been transformed into "speculative" lodges, whose functions were purely social and cultural rather than economic. In 1717 the first Grand Lodge of this new freemasonry was founded in England, the beginning of a movement that quickly spread to the Continent.[148] The new speculative masons appear to have been attracted originally to the craft traditions by both their exotic character and the social-moral fellowship that they represented. Occult practices associated with craft rites were to become increasingly popular as the century progressed, but, initially at least, these seem to have been secondary to the warm, convivial atmosphere of the lodges themselves. "Refreshment, smoking and conversation, in circumstances of ease rather than elegance, and undisturbed by the society of women, in which many a man can take a rational pleasure"—these were the primary attractions of this new form of fellowship.[149]

Masonry represented a rejection of the exorbitant social and economic demands of court and salon. Although socially it was a middle- and upper-class movement, fashion, connection, and patronage counted less among its circles. The tradition of mutual aid was also refreshing to those contemptuous of or exhausted by social climbing, one of the reasons it attracted so many young intellectuals, among them a large number of *déclassé* persons. The lodges provided a supportive structure for the duration of that long social moratorium that was the fate of this group. As a single-sex organization with a

---

[148] On the origins of freemasonry in England, see Knoop and Jones; also J. M. Roberts, pp. 17–25.
[149] Knoop and Jones, p. 315.

strong moral code it served as protection against disastrous liaison and premature marriage. Membership attracted not only those itinerant pleasure-seekers like Casanova, who found that the lodges comprised a convenient international network for their exploits, but more sober bachelors, looking for decent, respectable companionship.[150] Customs that for centuries had served the tramping artisan were now adapted to meet the needs of another, even more mobile, social class.

Like the craft from which it took its name, freemasonry divided its membership into a number of grades, roughly corresponding to age. Lodges were active in recruiting young men to their apprentice and journeymen's ranks; and in Germany they were particularly successful in penetrating the traditional student fraternities, the *Landsmann-schaften*, thereby altering their character from that of regional associations to broadly-based national organizations by establishing within them a series of interlocking cells called *Orden*. Ultimately the *Orden* detached themselves from the parent lodges and became strictly student organizations, but they continued to operate as a moral counterweight within the student community. Under masonic influence, the initiations of the traditional fraternities took on a more elevating character by the late eighteenth century, shedding many of the brutal, senseless features that had been accumulating during the previous two centuries.[151] At the same time, the small, semisecret *Orden* served as a vehicle for the more occult forms of freemasonry that, after 1770, were becoming increasingly popular among old and young alike. Adam Weishaupt, the leader of the exotic Illuminati fringe of German freemasonry, found the secret student societies to be a useful instrument, and all over the Continent and in England young men were soon dabbling in cabalistic rituals, experimenting in alchemy or the mysteries of Mesmerism.[152] And because the Illuminati and other mystical branches of masonry were also devotees of radical libertarianism and egalitarianism, fraternity in this case also became a kind of "underground," spreading ideas subversive to the established order.[153] Little wonder that the influence of freemasonry on the young was the cause of increasing concern in the years just be-

---

[150] J. M. Roberts, p. 56.

[151] Schulze and Ssymank, pp. 161ff; Muchow, *Jugend und Zeitgeist*, pp. 47–52.

[152] On France, see Viatte, pp. 33–37, 104–139; Brunschwig, pp. 217–269; Epstein, pp. 94–97.

[153] Darnton, pp. 81–115.

fore 1789 and that, with the advent of the French Revolution, authorities in other parts of Europe moved to ban the brotherhoods.

The appeal of the occult went deeper than its political tendency, however. Henri Brunschwig has shown how widespread was the attraction of both mysticism and magic on the educated young at the end of the eighteenth century. For them, it was a kind of secular religion, a stabilizing element in a whirling world of change, in which traditional religion and conventional social ritual had lost meaning.[154] Poor health and frayed nerves had driven the young Goethe to search for the philosopher's stone. Under the direction of his Pietist friend, Fräulein von Klettenberg, he passionately explored the occult, from the mysteries of the zodiac to the magic incorporated in the writings of Pietist writers, including Swedenborg. Together these seekers explored alchemy, associating personal spiritual regeneration with the transmutation of metals.[155] Troubles of the heart as well as the body were believed to be exorcised by absorption in the occult and it was no accident that the Rosicrucians, one of the most exotic offspring of eighteenth-century freemasonry, devoted themselves to experimentation with drugs in search of what they regarded as the secret of perpetual youth.[156]

The occult, Mircea Eliade informs us, often contains in its practices rites of initiation and passage.[157] In the case of the freemasonry of the late eighteenth century, these appear to have had youth-prolonging functions. Parallel to the craft brotherhoods from which it drew its inspiration, masonry was "like a family and a fraternity," serving to ease the lonely passage from childhood to adulthood by creating a new, almost monastic code for this elite of troubled bachelors. Thus, one fictitious son explains to his father his enthusiasm for the movement:[158]

> Our secret meetings stir our hearts. We experience sacred hours devoted to the brotherly love of mankind as we assemble in a quiet place far removed from the bustle of the world. Such a place is rightly called a "temple" since all profane relationships lose their significance there. A prince becomes a simple brother, the most humble of his subjects can communicate with him on the basis of perfect equality. Every man

---

[154] Brunschwig, pp. 217–220.
[155] Friedenthal, pp. 66–68.
[156] Epstein, p. 109.
[157] Eliade, pp. 123–124, 132–133.
[158] Quoted in Epstein, p. 97.

is a brother to every other regardless of distinctions of rank and religion. Every meeting of the lodge strengthens me tenfold in my resolve to walk the thorny path of life as an upright and free man. My heart expands and embraces all the world—in short, I become a cosmopolitan in feeling.

The imagery of freemasonry was both fraternal and patriarchal. Its organization was hierarchical and at the same time fundamentally egalitarian. And from it would spring a whole set of organizations— student movements, revolutionary conspiracies, utopian experiments —which would have a continuing attraction for educated youth well into the nineteenth century.

VIII

Before moving on to later youth cultures, we should not neglect another set of eighteenth-century movements that were also to deposit their own traditions. These were the anti-institutional evangelical groups, such as German Pietism, and English Quakerism and Methodism. Pietism established the model of small devotional groups, patterned consciously on the simple piety of the early Christians. The rejection of social convention, and the concept of brotherhood and sisterhood, coupled with a strong emphasis on worldly success, had great appeal to the young, not only in Germany but also in England and America.[159] Quakerism, for example, was most successful in converting younger sons and daughters in their late twenties and early thirties, precisely the groups that could no longer find fellowship within their own family circle.[160] The religious institution of conversion carried with it the social salvation of "second birth" into a community of believers, and it was through the evangelical revivals of the eighteenth and nineteenth centuries that countless youth found support and a sense of direction that their background and situation could not provide.

Pietist communities, such as Herrnhut in Germany and Bethlehem

---

[159] Holborn, p. 140.
[160] Vann, pp. 641–642. For America, see Greven, pp. 119–134.

in Pennsylvania, went still further in institutionalizing religion's youth-prolonging character. There, the community was organized around age-graded, sex-segregated "choirs," which functioned to instill simultaneously both the skills needed in this world and the piety required by the next. Children were separated at an early age from their parents and brought up in separate lodgings, where they were encouraged to reject all sibling jealousies and to view all persons as their brothers and sisters. Religious fellowship blended with a kind of social utopianism which sought to minimize social and generational conflict through the abolition of private property and, thus, inheritance. In place of old traditions of celibate youth were substituted a series of age groups, with elaborate rituals marking each stage of a passage from childhood to adulthood that was controlled largely by the peers themselves.[161]

Little wonder that Pietism had such a powerful appeal for troubled youth. Goethe was attracted for a time to the Herrnhut community near his native city, reporting himself "almost" converted.[162] There was hardly a figure in the "Sturm und Drang" generation of young German intellectuals who was not touched at one time or another in his youth by the spiritual or moral goals of the movement. Rejecting infant baptism and concentrating its energies on conversion after puberty, Pietism reinforced the special significance of youth as a period of moral and spiritual regeneration. Pietists were among the first to concern themselves as well with social welfare of youth, taking the lead in founding both schools and orphanages in eighteenth-century Germany.[163] Two of the most important figures of the later German student reform movement, Friedrich Schleiermacher and Jakob Friedrich Fries, were both educated in Pietist institutions.

English Quakerism and Methodism also produced leaders in the field of educational and moral reform. In their early stages, they, too, emphasized the intimate fellowship of believers, sharing social as well as spiritual concerns. Although there exists no systematic study of the early membership of Methodism, it would seem that many who were attracted to it were young, single individuals for whom that non-institutionalized faith held a social appeal. Pietism had had a direct effect on the form of Methodism, through the Moravian Brethren with whom Methodism's founder, John Wesley, had close contact in the

---

[161] Gollin, pp. 68–83.
[162] Friedenthal, p. 65.
[163] Holborn, p. 135.

1720s.[164] As a young man still seeking a calling in life, Wesley had found strength and direction among the pious Brethren, a fellowship whose model he followed in establishing his own evangelical movement. In America, about which we are somewhat better informed, Methodism appears to have had a particularly strong appeal for socially and geographically mobile youth. As late as the mid-nineteenth century, New England colleges were still experiencing waves of revivalism and, in many, conversion to the fellowship of believers attained the status of a major institution in student life.[165] Conversion, which had become associated with late teenage by that time, served to mark a "new beginning," the first departure from family, sustained and legitimized by Christian fellowship.

Evangelical religion was a vehicle for emancipation, and, as such, was bound to be the center of generational controversy. George Whitefield was accused, during his 1740 American revival, of creating "division of families, neighborhoods and towns; the contrariety of husbands and wives; the undutifulness of children and servants." [166] There is no doubt that the emotive imagery of Methodism, which Edward Thompson has described as "by turns maternal, Oedipal, sexual and sado-masochistic," was reflective of complex intergenerational tensions that were the product of a rapidly changing economic and social system. Turning to a Heavenly Father and entering into the Brotherhood of Christ was undoubtedly a way of reconciling the break with family, a socially acceptable way of setting off on a long and difficult passage to adulthood. Not only among middle-class youth but working men, too, conversion was both a spiritual and social turning point.[167] Methodist experience of "New Birth" brought forth many famous "boy preachers" from the ranks of the laboring poor, taught them the rudiments of leadership along with the skills of literacy, and ultimately helped them toward active involvement with the early labor movement. "Conversion of some kind is, of course, a commonplace in labour movements," writes Eric Hobsbawm. "British ones, however, are particularly archaic in so far as the conversion was normally a traditionally religious one, or a political one which took religious form." [168]

---

[164] Walsh, pp. 140, 148.

[165] Hall, vol. 2, pp. 281–282, 287.

[166] Gaustad, p. 32.

[167] Edward P. Thompson provides a brilliant discussion of the complex forces involved in working-class conversions, in *Making of English Working Class*, pp. 365–374.

[168] Hobsbawm, "Ritual," p. 141.

IX

Eighteenth-century traditions of fraternity, particularly the masonic and academic, were to take on an increasingly political meaning after the French Revolution, mainly because the authorities, in their efforts to root out all opposition, made the secrecy of the brotherhoods all that much more attractive to conspirators. As for the French Revolution itself, its contribution to the new traditions of youth was complicated by the fact that old forms of youth could serve both it and its enemies. There can be little doubt that, for many young men, 1789 constituted a personal turning point, improving their prospects by opening careers to talent and abolishing feudal inequalities of inheritance.[169] Paris on the eve of the Revolution, remarked Mallet du Pan, was "full of young men who take a little facility to be talent, of clerks, accountants, lawyers, soldiers who make themselves into authors, die of hunger, even beg, and turn out pamphlets." [170] From this *proletariat de bacheliers* were recruited the likes of Marat and Brissot, young men of uncertain or failed careers, who would find their vocation in revolution. And, of course, they would be joined by another youth, Napoleon Bonaparte, whose meteoric rise would continue to inspire the imagination of ambitious youth well into the nineteenth century.

Not surprisingly, the Revolution also developed its own conception of the phase of life between childhood and adulthood. As the demands of foreign and civil war became ever more pressing on the Republic, this became frankly spartan in its orientation. Youth had its place in the civil ceremonial of the Revolution, emphasizing the military and civic duties of the age group rather than its special rights or privileges. The major revolutionary festivals of 1793–1794 were devoted as much to the wisdom of age as to the virility of youth; and the theme of generational harmony was given prominence along with the special regenerational role of youth in revolutionary ceremony. The annual *Fête de la Jeunesse* saw boys of 16 ritually inducted

---

[169] Darnton, pp. 112–113.
[170] Darnton, p. 94.

to the duty of bearing arms; and at 21 a second rite of passage transformed them into adult citizens, men shouldering the burden of national defense, women the responsibility of bearing the children of the Republic.[171] Gone were the rituals of Misrule, with their inverted social roles, for now republican virtue required that young and old exchange gifts and blessings.

Such rituals of reciprocity were meant to reflect a new society, in which fathers and sons were united in a broader feeling of fraternity. However, social divisions and generational tensions remained, and when the spell of the Jacobin terror was broken in 1794, many of the traditional rites of youth burst forth with astonishing vigor. The infamous *jeunesse dorée*, the gilded youth of the middle and upper classes, flaunted the memory of civic puritanism with foppish dress, obscene speech, and decadent manners. Their contempt for the Jacobin Revolution took the ancient form of the charivari, the revel, and the masked dance. Staging balls in honor of those who had fallen in the Terror, these youths mocked the fathers of the revolution with obscene *danse macabre*, staged on the site of cemeteries destroyed by the Jacobins. Their debauch knew no limits, their women no modesty; and for the concept of universal fraternity they had nothing but derision.[172]

Traditions of youth served both ends of the political spectrum, both in support of revolutionary France and in opposition to it. Nowhere was this more apparent than in the strange career of Filippo Buonarroti, the *déclassé* son of an Italian nobleman, who had found his own "second birth" in identification with the Revolution and who, until his death in 1837, was to serve as "father" for a series of conspiratorial organizations that had strong appeal to uprooted young men of similar background. Like so many of the others who were involved in the formation of political brotherhoods in the early nineteenth century, Buonarroti was the product of eighteenth-century freemasonry, with its love of ritual, mystery, and hierarchical organization. His most important secret society, the *Sublimes Maîtres Parfaits*, founded in 1809 in opposition to Napoleonic dictatorship, reflected masonry's preoccupation with rites of passage. For "Papa" Buonarroti the young novices of his organization were young knights receiving their initiation into the secrets of revolution.[173] That few ever got the

---

[171] Ozouf, pp. 573–574.
[172] Lefebvre, pp. 47–55; Mathiez, pp. 81ff.
[173] Eisenstein, pp. 74ff.

chance to put their plotting into action, and none, including Buonarroti himself, ever saw any of their plans succeed, apparently mattered less than the fact of belonging. This, in any case, was the effect that Buonarroti had on his most devoted follower, Alexander Andryane, who, at the age of 24 and still without a purpose in life, was inducted into the *Sublimes Maîtres Parfaits* in elaborate masonic fashion.

Some of the conspiratorial brotherhoods borrowed their ritual directly from freemasonry; others owed theirs to the original source, the trades themselves. It seems likely that the anti-Napoleonic Italian conspiratorial movement, known as the "Carbonari," traced its forms back to the journeymen's confraternity of charcoal burners, the *Charbonnerie*, which operated in the forests of Franche-Comte and the Jura before 1789. Sometime during the Revolution, some of this organization's lodges had begun to initiate non-operative members, including soldiers, sharing with them the conviviality of the *"bons cousins,"* as the journeymen charcoal burners liked to call themselves. Among the initiates was Pierre Joseph Briot, a left-wing revolutionary, who ultimately brought the traditions of the *Charbonnerie* to Italy and there set up the first of the Carbonari conspiratorial brotherhoods in 1808.[174]

The fraternal tradition of the trades and freemasonry proved well-adapted to secret conspiracies. Their hierarchical organization afforded a useful model; their oaths and rituals were suitable cover against the authorities. Furthermore, the leading conspirators could borrow from the familial imagery of both to reinforce their position and power. Buonarroti was not the only leader to style himself as the "father" of his movement. Friedrich Ludwig Jahn, Germany's first politically-inclined youth leader, also called himself *Vater*, combining with this paternalism the fraternal traditions that he had encountered earlier in his career as a student and a freemason.[175] Jahn's gymnastic societies, founded in 1810, served the cause of patriotic resistance to Napoleon; and his faith in the regenerative power of youth found echoes in other major intellectual figures, including Johann Fichte, himself a former freemason, and Friedrich Schleiermacher and Jakob Fries, both of whom had been influenced by Pietism.

The streams of religious and intellectual thought that had shaped eighteenth-century German youth groups thus gave form to the ideology and organization of their more political nineteenth-century

---

[174] J. M. Roberts, pp. 283–286.
[175] Schulze and Ssymank, pp. 69, 216–224; Wentzcke, pp. 72–85.

counterparts, beginning with the gymnasts and culminating with the student reform movement, the *Burschenschaften*, which was founded in 1815 at the University of Jena in the name of "Honor, Liberty, and Fatherland." Although the impulse for its founding was patriotic, much of the appeal of the *Burschenschaften* was the same as the youth-sustaining organizations that had gone before. "Let your community of youthful fellowship, your federation of youth, be a model for the national state," the students were told by Fries.[176] His inspiring words were spoken at the Wartburg Festival of 1817, an event that linked the anniversary of Luther's rebellion against the Pope with youth's patriotic crusade against another foreign enemy, France. "Reveal to us the pure life of the *Burschen*," students were urged; and they set about purging student life of its custom of precocious wenching and drinking, regulating the fierce dueling tradition, and generally improving the tone of university towns. Student reformers wore beards as a sign of their manhood, but their initiation rites included oaths of chastity and temperance not unlike monastic vows. Indeed, we find the same distrust of female companionship that was evidenced in the earlier Pietist and Masonic movements, and which can be traced back to the celibate condition of students in the late Medieval universities. Jahn's gymnasts, and groups within the *Burschenschaften* like the Giessen University "Unconditionals," carried this youth-prolonging tradition to an extreme by associating patriotic and moral virtue with a totally Spartan existence. *Vater* Jahn, dressed in his rough peasant costume, was a symbol of the contempt for French fashion which, in the mind of the students, was associated with effeminacy and weakness. The "Unconditionals" carried this sado-masochism so far that they regarded self-annihilation—assassination of the enemies of the German people, followed by ritual suicide—as the greatest possible act of virtue. This was the mentality that inclined Karl Sand, in 1819, to murder the conservative poet Koetzebue and then attempt to stab himself, an act of extremism that brought down official repression on even the mild reformist majority of the *Burschenschaften*.[177]

---

[176] Wentzcke, pp. 94–95, 211ff.
[177] Wentzcke, pp. 160–165; Feuer, pp. 63–64.

X

Perhaps it was inevitable that older moral traditions of youth would take on the violent features of an age of revolution and military adventure. But the Spartan mentality that can be detected in some aspects of the French Revolution and again in the German resistance to Napoleon was relatively rare among the other elements of early nineteenth-century youth movements. Mazzini's "Young Europe" organization had little about it, even in its nationalism, that can be called fanatical or militaristic. On the whole, it followed the humanitarian trend evident in the eighteenth century, abhorring violence as a means, and attaching to youth a profoundly moral purpose and meaning.

Nothing could contrast more with the mentality of the "Unconditionals" than the self-styled "Children of Saint Simon," one of the many utopian movements in which youth played such an important role. Its gentle "Father," Barthelemy Prosper Enfantin, and his disciples were unmarried men and women in their twenties and early thirties, many of whom were graduates of the Ecole Polytechnique. They had given up their careers in what amounted to a prolongation of youth, in the name of social harmony and universal love. Despite their reputation for libertinism, the movement's commune outside Paris was monastic in its asceticism. From 1830 to 1832, the "Father" and his "Children" lived in a balance of paternal and fraternal harmony, initiating novices in elaborately-staged ceremonies, hearing public confessions, and generally encouraging the spirit of selfless cooperation that they held in opposition to the competitiveness and division of the emerging capitalist industrial order.[178]

Frank Manuel has written that "the Saint-Simonians help us to comprehend that total loss of identity, that oceanic feeling (to follow Freud), which men of the nineteenth and twentieth century experienced when they successfully lost self-awareness in the ardent periods of nationalist, socialist, and communist movements."[179] He might

---

[178] Manuel, pp. 149–194; Talmon, Chapter 1; Charlton.
[179] Manuel, p. 192.

have added, to follow Erikson, that in the case of the Saint Simonians and the other Romantic utopias that attracted educated youth, the postponement of adult identity was necessary to self-preservation. Ultimately the Children of Saint Simon would disperse from their commune and move on to successful careers in engineering and business. Critics took this to be proof of the failure of communalism, but in fact it was the strong emotional and moral support that they found in utopia that allowed these young people to move on beyond its cloistered walls. Unlike the natural fathers who had let down their sons and daughters, communal leaders like *Père* Enfantin and Father Noyes of the Oneida Community in New York State were apparently succeeding in making adults of their children.[180]

All utopians of the early nineteenth century were vigorous in their condemnation of the existing family economy, but none more so than Charles Fourier, himself a rebel against his own petite bourgeois upbringing. Fourier was aware of the conditions that lay behind the intergenerational tensions of his age and he spoke with conviction about the need for change:[181]

> To speak frankly, the family bond in the *civilizee regime* [his term for contemporary society] causes fathers to desire the death of their children and children to desire the death of their fathers. It is much worse in the case of distant relatives. Could there be anything more infamous? A few rich families are the exception that confirms the rule, which applies mainly to the poor who make up seven-eighths of the population. The rule, however, applies as well to many families of the middle and wealthy classes, where brothers love one another like Cain and Abel.

Fourier's solution, similar to that of the Pietists, was to remove children from their parents at an early age, thus eliminating the psychological as well as economic causes of conflict. Age-grouped, but not puritanically sex-segregated as were the Herrnhut communities, boys and girls would proceed through a series of educational phases, each of which would be keyed to their natural instincts and interests. In plans that seem to have been inspired by the traditions of his native Besançon, Fourier envisioned a series of self-regulating youth groups, called "Juvenile Legions" and "Juvenile Bands," which would

---

[180] On the paternalism of leaders of various student movements, see Feuer, p. 22; on John Humphrey Noyes, "Father" of the utopian Oneida community, see Carden, Chapters 1–2.

[181] Fourier, p. 280.

serve as instruments of education and social control. They would operate autonomously, relying on the natural bonding instincts of the young to bring out the goodness and energy of that stage of life. "Young souls, hearts, that are fresh, exhibit in the exercise of social virtues, such as friendship, philanthropy and devotion to the collective good, a degree of ardor and disinterestedness which is rarely found in adults." [182]

Fourier's hopes for the peer group, like his faith in social harmony in general, were doomed to disappointment. The communal institutions that were his models were fast disappearing, and even the flurry of utopian experimentation that was occurring in the late 1830s and early 1840s in both Europe and America could not sustain them. In Paris itself, the strong hopes surrounding youth were giving way to despair. The failure of the French Revolution of 1830 seemed to sap the energies of the revolutionaries, and youth turned in new directions, many toward more anarchical, amoral life-styles associated with bohemianism. Wrote Alfred de Musset: "The richest became libertines; those of moderate fortune followed some profession and resigned themselves to the sword or to the robe. The poorest gave themselves up with cold enthusiasm to great thoughts, plunged into the frightful sea of aimless effort." [183]

Bohemianism was the product of Paris' extraordinary ability to attract to it the youth of the provinces. There, as students, they were largely on their own, living as aliens within working-class neighborhoods, unsupervised by their teachers, unwanted by the authorities.[184] They were cut off from their families by poor transportation and the lack of long vacations. The old custom of boarding at the home of a family friend was going out of style, and to add to the difficulty of the young was the fact that the professions were becoming overcrowded.[185] By the 1830s the city was full of young men who had nothing better to do than to spend their days at the cafe, forever thumbing through newspapers, talking politics and scandal. Balzac described them as "some rich, others poor, all equally idle . . . who, with no outlet for their energies, threw themselves not only into journalism and conspiracies, literature and art, but into the most extravagant excesses and dissipations." [186]

---

[182] Fourier, p. 326.
[183] From de Musset, p. 344.
[184] de Sauvigny, pp. 238ff; Mazoyer.
[185] de Sauvigny, pp. 243–245; Ariès, pp. 398–399.
[186] Quoted in Graña, p. 23.

A pattern had become so well-established that it was common to refer to *les jeunes gens de Paris* as a definable group, with its own roles and subculture. "The youth of Paris" had acquired a special meaning, as Frances Trollope discovered when she visited the city in 1835: "*La jeune France* is another of those cabalistic forms of speech by which everyone seems expected to understand something great, volcanic, and sublime." [187] Later, Henri de Mürger would popularize the term "Bohemian," borrowed from the French word for "gypsy" and carrying with it the connotation of vagabondage that was part of the self-image of this cohort. Emerging in the late 1820s and spreading rapidly in the wake of the disappointments of the Revolution of 1830, bohemianism quickly established itself in the tolerant Latin Quarter, where almost overnight it became a mecca for tourists like Mrs. Trollope, who described denizens with "long and matted locks that hang in heavy, ominous dirtiness. . . . The throat is bare, at least from linen, but a plentiful and very disgusting profusion of hair supplies its place. . . . Some roll their eyes and knit their dark glances on the ground in fearful meditation; while others there be who, while gloomily leaning against a statue or a tree, throw such terrific meaning into their looks." [188]

We find among the bohemian youth of the 1830s the same fascination with bizarre styles, outlandish behavior, and strange language that characterizes their counterparts today. Contempt for work, preoccupation with the present to the exclusion of all thought of past and future, resistance to order and discipline—all the signs of prolonged social moratorium—were common then as now. Eastern religions, with their mind-extinguishing mysticism, enjoyed great popularity. The occult, the alchemistic, and the satanical, anything that could obliterate the demands of adulthood, all were the rage.[189] We find students experimenting with rites of initiation suggested to them by the novels of Scott and Cooper, acting—as Theophil Donday pictured them—as "artists to the core, pipes puffing, sardonic of eye, their heads adorned with the Liberty Cap; the bearded Young France, ready for the orgy. . . ." [190]

For many, Paris was an orgy, the loss of virtue and purpose. Yet,

---

[187] Trollope, p. 31.

[188] Trollope, p. 124.

[189] These themes are discussed in Schenk, pp. 6, 125–151; Hobsbawm, *Age of Revolution*, pp. 306–323; Parry, pp. 13ff.

[190] Quoted in Graña, p. 77.

the occult carried with it something of the eighteenth-century moral tradition; and in the experimentation with ritual we can find another link to the youth-prolonging traditions of the past. In 1846, students at the Sorbonne formed a Suicide Club, pledging to defy bourgeois morality through that ultimate act of rebellion, self-destruction.[191] Parisians were relieved to learn that only one death actually resulted, but even in this madness there remains a glimmer of earlier traditions of youth. The traditional carnival revel was still part of the Parisian calendar and bohemia's sense of the bizarre and grotesque blended well with its ceremonies of Misrule. The counterculture of the young artists and intellectuals was an extension of the tradition of the *société joyeuse* and it had a certain appeal even to the stuffy bourgeoisie. The same middle class bought paintings like "Young Venetian after an Orgy" because, as one historian has noted, these had an appeal which, "like the masked balls, were socially approved channels for the forbidden." [192] For the youths themselves, bohemia was a kind of prolonged carnival, an avoidance of roles in the real (adult) world to which most knew they must ultimately turn. Alexander Dumas remembered of his youth that "I had put on, along with the others, a mask." [193] Youth made life an art and, in turn, writers like Victor Hugo made art of youth. Robert Schumann ended his *Carneval* with the rebellion of the young against the philistinism of the old; and no Romantic play was without its young rebel.[194]

In their desire to be different, the bohemians created their own conformity. Stendhal, who was born in 1783, remembered that in his youth "I was full of heroes of Roman history: I looked upon myself as a future Camillus or Cincinnatus . . ." [195] French youth in the 1830s were also searching for models, but their heroes were more likely to be poetical spirits, like Lord Byron. "Young people found a use for inactive strength in the affectation of despair," commented Alfred de Musset. "Scoffing at glory, religion, love, at everybody, is a great consolation for those who do not know what to do. . . . And it is easy to believe oneself wretched when one is only empty and bored." [196] Detached from, yet still drawing on, old traditions, the

---

[191] Graña, pp. 79–80.
[192] Pelles, pp. 97, 144.
[193] Quoted in Pelles, p. 114.
[194] Schenk, p. 27.
[195] Quoted in Pelles, p. 114.
[196] Pelles, p. 85.

counterculture of the 1830s was one more of the new forms of youth that were a product of this age of transition.

XI

Paris was exceptional among European cities, and the new youth culture which it produced found no immediate counterparts, even in industrialized England. In the more backward parts of Europe, tradition lingered much longer, interacting with political and economic movements until the middle of the century. In 1848 the journeymen's movement and student radicalism came together in Germany in what seemed the long-awaited revenge of the sons against the fathers. But the grand alliance of youth that Mazzini and others had been talking about since the 1830s did not materialize.[197] While it was the fondest wish of the middle-class students to replace the formal "Sie" with the comradely "Du," thus breaking down structured social roles, the young workers demanded instead that the adult dignity attached to formal address be extended to all members of the society.[198] Furthermore, workers and students could not agree on the meaning of "fraternity." For the former, the concept was coming to mean not the brotherhood of all mankind, but the solidarity of their own class against the capitalist bourgeoisie. For the students, too, the meaning of fraternalism was narrowing. Soon after 1848 the egalitarianism of the progressive student movement gave way to the snobbish comradeship of the highly conservative dueling organizations, the *Corps*. Social and political changes that had previously disturbed the generational balance and ushered in new traditions of youth on each level of society were now reinforcing rather than ameliorating class divisions.

For the working youth, ancient traditions of fraternity had become the instruments of forging a precocious identity with adult comrades. Recourse to the traditions of youth served precisely the opposite

---

[197] On the background of Young Germany's contact with the journeymen in the 1830s and 1840s, see Schieder, pp. 30ff.

[198] Noyes, pp. 127–128.

function for the middle classes, however. Among their ranks, too precipitous an entry into the status of adulthood meant forfeiture of future opportunity. Individual success required long training and delayed gratification, and the new middle-class youth cultures, even those considered "deviant" by society, complemented this condition. Thus, while youth cultures of different classes might draw on a similar historical heritage, by midcentury they were moving in very different directions.

Boy cadets at Charterhouse School in the 1870s. Second from left is Robert Baden–Powell, later to become famous as a general and the founder of the Boy Scouts movement. Reproduced by permission of the Johnston Historical Museum, Boy Scouts of America, North Brunswick, New Jersey.

3

Boys Will Be Boys: Discovery
of Adolescence, 1870–1900

The failed revolutions of 1848 marked a turning point in the political history of youth, effectively terminating Europe's first period of student unrest and ending the independent role of the young within the working-class movements as well. Not until 1900 would youth again take to the public stage, and then in very different forms and in support of new causes. The traditions of radicalism and bohemianism survived to renew themselves in the socialist youth movements and the artistic avant-garde of the turn of the century, but at that point they were joined, and even overshadowed, by a new set of youth movements that tended to be focused on the narrower spectrum of youth we now call "adolescence." Not only were the new organizations younger in constituency, but their sense of fraternity was both more nationalistic and socially conservative. By 1900 the symbol of youth as a regenerative force was shifting from left to right, revealing the changed status of the young in European society.

In England we can detect this process beginning in the 1850s, starting with the upper and middle classes and then gradually trickling down to the lower orders. During the Crimean War one of the traditional festivals of Misrule, Guy Fawkes Night, became the occasion for outbursts of patriotic venom. The effigy of Czar Nicholas replaced that of Guy on the November bonfires, and although such substitutions were not new—Napoleon, too, had been burned at the beginning of the century—the accompanying enthusiasm for juvenile marching and drilling in the name of Queen and Country was unprecedented.[1] The threat of war with France at the end of the same decade produced a movement to form rifle corps within the elite boarding schools; and at Oxford the Volunteers, a university militia which had lapsed after the Napoleonic Wars, sprang up again after Edmond Warre wrote a stirring letter to the London *Times* in April 1859:[2]

> I suppose that when next term begins there will be some thousands of us strapping young fellows up there, whose average height, weight, and activity might, I have no doubt, equal, if not excel, that of any regiment in H.M.'s service. In three years they will be scattered all over the Empire. What useful results might not ensue from their being instructed as well in the *ars militaris* as in the *ars logica*. . . . Why should not the Royal Oxford University Volunteers be embodied and drilled in Port Meadow? . . . . Two hours' drill two or three times a week would set us up bravely, and a blue flannel tunic and white trousers would not ruin anybody.

International crisis passed and Warre's Volunteers graduated without a test of their fighting spirit. Eight years later, however, the university cadets were to be sent into battle, in this case against a town crowd agitating for redress of economic grievances. In putting down the rioters, Oxford's young gentlemen proved that defense of class was inseparable in their minds from defense of country.[3] By the end of the century, many traditional rituals of Misrule had become similar instruments of conservative nationalism, culminating in the wild outburst of Mafeking Night of May 18, 1900, and in the attacks on pro-Boer peace meetings by students, clerks, and other young professionals in the days that followed.[4]

The utility of turning folk custom to patriotic purpose became in-

---

[1] In Oxford, Nicholas replaced Guy in 1854. Two years later, those householders who did not illuminate their windows in celebration of victory had their panes smashed. Plowman, pp. 48, 88. Other examples of conservative uses of traditional youth rituals are provided by Edward P. Thompson, "Rough Music," pp. 308–309.

[2] Quoted in Newsome, p. 224; Plowman, pp. 30–32.

[3] Plowman described the attack of the students upon the bread rioters as follows:

> I shall never forget their swift and joyous onrush. In a spirit of keenest enjoyment, with an estatic shout, they fell upon the mob in front of them with irresistible determination, and mowed them down as though they had been grass. In fancy, I can hear now the rapping of staves on the heads of the discomfited disturbers, intermingled with the cries of the wounded [p. 220].

[4] On the Mafeking Night and that which followed, see Price, pp. 132–176.

creasingly obvious to elites in the late nineteenth century; and when the antiquarian, Percy Manning, went looking in the 1890s for authentic traditions of youth, he found to his disgust that the May singing and dancing in the Oxfordshire villages was more often an officially-sponsored exercise for school children than an authentic example of folk custom. Gone were the spontaneous revels; absent, too, were the social satires associated with the traditional mummings. What was left were pious ditties and artificial diversions, shorn of all social meaning. "I was in hopes that I had found a good thing," Manning wrote after a visit to May Morning at Yarnton Manor, "but the children followed it up with some milk-and-water rubbish that they had been taught in school." [5]

In England, traditional dancing, mumming, and hunt festivals had been in decline since the 1850s. Manning found that by 1900 not only were the occasions once presided over by young men and women being abandoned to children of a much younger age, but that the class composition of the participants was also changing. This was true of the First of May in Oxford itself, where the crowning of a king and queen, once entered into by youth of all social ranks, had become the rite of the very lowest of youths, the poor chimney sweeps, who managed to keep the tradition only with difficulty in the face of harassment by city officials. The profane version of the hymns sung on May Morning from the top of the Magdalen College tower had long since been expurgated, making the whole occasion more the quaint tourist attraction it is today than the boisterous revel it had been earlier in the nineteenth century.[6] Festivals like the Whit Hunt in Oxfordshire's Wychwood Forest were also a thing of the past, perpetuated at the turn of the century by gypsies and other "undesirables," but no longer respectable as far as the mass of the rural population was concerned.[7] Morris dancing and the mumming associated with it had fallen into such decline that it took the attentions of urban folklorists to revive them. From photographs taken in the 1860s, Percy Manning had been able to identify two former dancers, whom he encouraged to teach songs and steps to younger men. But even Manning's desire for authenticity was not strong enough to dis-

---

[5] Ms. source B, Manning Collection, Scrapbooks and notes, MS Top Oxon d 199, pp. 192–193.

[6] Ms. source B, Manning Collection, Scrapbooks and notes, MS Top Oxon d 199, p. 119; Manning, pp. 307–309.

[7] Ms. source B, Manning Collection, Scrapbooks and notes, MS Top Oxon d 199, pp. 166, 186–88, 258; Manning, pp. 309–315.

place his Victorian sense of decorum and when his dancers made their first appearance in Oxford in 1899, not only were their lyrics clean of the good-humored profanity, but the antics of the traditional Lord of Misrule were missing.[8]

The tendency for youth to lose its autonomy and become an instrument of adult interests was resisted most strongly among the laboring poor. Yet, by 1900, traditions of Misrule were dying in the better sorts of working-class neighborhoods, revealing changes there that paralleled what was happening to middle- and upper-class youth. Behind both the decline of the journeymen's movements and the disappearance of student radicalism lay deeper transformations that not only eased the demographic and economic strains that had been a cause of troubled youth earlier in the century, but altered the life-cycle itself in such a way as to bring forth new forms of fraternity in the place of old. Youth's loss of political and social independence reflected the fact that a significant segment of that life-phase, the adolescent years 14–18, was becoming increasingly dependent. While older youth retained much of its earlier autonomy, becoming even more identified with the status of adulthood, this younger age-group was losing access to the economy and society of adults as it became increasingly subject to parental and other institutional controls. The moral autonomy attributed to youth by earlier generations was giving way to new kinds of conformity associated with a more mindless kind of physical vitality. In turn, this was reflected in the public image of the young, changing from Delacroix's rebels on the barricades, youth at war with society, to the late-nineteenth-century recruiting posters, glorifying youth at war for their society.

I

The discovery of adolescence belonged essentially to the middle classes, the first group, apart from the aristocracy, to experience a drop in child mortality and the consequences this entailed. The no-

---

[8] Manning's role is documented in the Bodleian Library, MS Top Oxon d 200. Also see Beerbohm.

bility was able to absorb larger numbers of surviving children, because of both its greater wealth and the firm tradition of primogeniture that allocated subordinate roles to younger sons. The middle classes, particularly their professional elements, having no comparable resources and not wishing to penalize the last born, turned to family limitation as the only way to relieve their burden. Although the actuality of the two-child family was still some way off, the English middle classes, and other groups claimant to that social status, were beginning to adapt it as an ideal in the 1860s and 1870s as a means of bringing into line with their incomes the growing expense of raising and educating children. Among this group, the situation of the early nineteenth century, with its superfluity of sons and daughters, was thereby gradually ameliorated; and instead of each successive generation being larger than the next, each was now smaller among those groups practicing family limitation.[9]

Family strategy had changed from one of high to one of low fertility, altering parental attitudes toward the children in the process. Increasingly, each individual child was treated (according to sex) without prejudice to his or her place in the birth order. "Give the boys a good education and a start in life," wrote J. E. Panton in 1889, "and provide the girls with £150 a year, either when they marry or at your own death, and you have done your duty by your children. The girls cannot starve on that income, and neither would they be prey of any fortune hunter; but no one has a right to bring children into the world in the ranks of the upper middle class and do less."[10] The consuming concern that had previously been reserved for the very young child appears to have been extended to older youth as well, not simply out of sentimentality but with the realization that the investment in long, expensive education should be carefully planned and conscientiously protected, rather than left to chance as had so often been the case in the first half of the century.

One aspect of this new care and concern for older children was the longer period of dependence that youth was now subjected to. Girls of the middle classes were kept at home until marriage, tightly supervised by their parents until they passed safely into the bosom of another family. An interest in female education was growing in the second half of the nineteenth century, partly as a result of surplus young women for whom marriage did not beckon; but this was

---

[9] Banks, *Prosperity and Parenthood*, Chapters 10–12.
[10] Quoted in Banks, *Prosperity and Parenthood*, p. 163.

still suspect among a group who believed that "love of home, of children, and of domestic duties are the only passions they [women] feel." [11] Boys had greater autonomy, but their careers were also being carefully supervised by the parents, who, recognizing the decline in traditional kinds of apprenticeship, were taking a much greater interest in secondary education. Even businessmen, for whom classical education had previously held little attraction, were increasingly concerned to gain for their sons the benefits of schooling to 16 or 17, even when they expected the lads to join theirs or some other business.[12] James Templeton, master of the Mission House School in Exeter, told the English Schools Commission of 1868: "Instead of what I heard in my younger days, a parent saying, 'I have done very well in the world. I was only six or twelve months at school,' the acknowledgment of such a man will now be. 'I had no such advantages or opportunities in my early life; I should like my son to be something of an educated man, and to have far greater advantages than I have had.' " [13] A similar trend was noticeable on the Continent, where the decline of apprenticeship was also the product of parental desires to see their children have not only the intellectual but the social benefits of elite schooling.[14]

The *Edinburgh Review* wrote in 1876 of an upper middle class which was "conscious that its retention of the advantages which it enjoys is still dependent on the mental activity by which they were gained; and keenly alive to the aesthetic and intellectual pleasures, the upper middle class seems the least likely of all to neglect its own educational concerns." [15] The Schools Commission found them likely to keep their children in school the longest, to 18 or 19, and then to send them on to the university. But even the less well-to-do of the middle classes showed a similar concern, motivated by a desire to attain a similar privileged status. An ironmonger, Edmund Edmundson, testified in 1868 that because the traditions of apprenticeship had recently decayed, tradesmen's traditional prejudice against Latin education was diminishing. "The fact is, if a boy is not well educated he cannot keep his position in society. Society twenty years ago, as

---

[11] Acton, p. 213.

[12] Crozier, pp. 33–42; Zorn, pp. 329–334; Ringer, Chapters 1–2.

[13] Publication/report: Parl. Papers IV, pp. 744–745.

[14] Musgrove, *Youth and Social Order*, pp. 46ff; Musgrove, "Decline of Educative Family," pp. 377–404. For Germany, see Roessler, Chapter 5.

[15] Quoted in Banks, *Prosperity and Parenthood*, p. 191.

I recollect it, was a totally different thing to what it is now." [16] The bias of the self-made man, never so strong to begin with on the Continent, was giving way all over Europe as the middle classes became increasingly dependent on the schools to guarantee a future for their progeny.

Smaller numbers of children encouraged longer coresidency, particularly on the Continent, where secondary education was organized around the day school. The growth of secondary education in the second half of the nineteenth century had made secondary schools locally available even in moderately-sized towns, making the need for boarding out while going to school much less prevalent than it had been earlier. Improved transportation facilitated the movement of pupils within urban areas where neighborhoods were not served by their own schools, and thus, by 1900, most French and German secondary students were living with their parents, leaving home only when they went on to the university or entered careers. Even in England, where the boarding tradition was continued and expanded during the second half of the century, longer vacations and better transportation were making contact between parents and their children much more frequent.

Whether a child was sent away to school or not, parents were assuming a much greater role in the supervision of the entire training process of each of their sons and daughters. German fathers were notorious for the strictness with which they oversaw their sons' training. They cloistered both boys and girls within the narrow confines of the home, allowing them only limited contact with the world outside, and then only for the purposes of formal training and education. The age of the patriarchal household, with its multiple economic and civil functions, was past by 1870, many of the prerogatives of the father having been usurped by factory, state, and school. Yet, the authority of the fathers persisted in what often seemed an outdated, tyrannical manner. Hans Heinrich Muchow has perceived a cultural lag operating in the fathers' slowness to adjust to the transition from the large multifunctional household to the small nuclear family unit: "Out of habit, he held onto the role, however, and thus pressed down on the nuclear family as a superfather [*Übervater*], especially on the growing children, who from the nursery onwards were subject to every impulse of their paternal master." [17] Little wonder that the sons

---

[16] Publication/report: *Parl. Papers* V, p. 487.
[17] Muchow, *Sexualreife und Sozialstruktur*, p. 54.

of the German middle class looked back on the earlier semidependent traditions of youth, especially the *Wanderjahr*, with a certain nostalgia. Trapped during their teen years between the tyranny of the home and the demands of the rigorous German academic school, the *Gymnasium*, they had lost contact with the sustaining force of the old peer-group structure and the autonomy which that represented.

In England, parental concern was no less intense or comprehensive, but, there, an alternative to fatherly tyranny offered itself. On the Continent, boarding schools and military academies remained the monopoly of the aristocracy, while in England this tradition was broadened to include a growing part of the middle class. The reform and expansion of the boarding (public) schools was a key instrument of the compromise between middle-class aspirations and aristocratic values that took place in the mid-Victorian period. The attractions to the social climbers were obvious: "In the great schools, which possess famous traditions, and in which the pupils come for the most part from the houses of gentlemen, there is a tone of manners and a sentiment of honour which goes far to neutralize the disadvantages of too early withdrawal from the shelter of home." [18] For parents who were worried about sending their children away at an age that demanded care and protection, there was the assurance that "the master in this case stands in the parent's place, and to do his work properly ought to be clothed with all the parent's authority." [19] Whether a boy remained at home for his schooling or was sent away to a boarding institution was obviously less important to the European middle classes than were the social controls associated with that education. The universal result was a state of dependence longer than that experienced by the previous generation: in effect, the creation of a new stage of life corresponding to what we now call "adolescence."

At its lower limit, adolescence was divided from childhood by the lines newly-drawn between primary and secondary education. Whereas, in the early nineteenth century—when, for reasons of tradition and expediency, parents encouraged the precocity of their children—boys of the ages 8 to 19 had been thrown together in English public schools, in 1868 it was reported that "it has now become a very common practice not to send boys to such a school as

---

[18] Publication/report: *Parl. Papers* I, p. 45.
[19] Publication/report: *Parl. Papers* I, p. 43.

Harrow or Rugby till 13 or 14, and to have them prepared at a preparatory school with boys of their own age."[20] Stricter age-grading and a deemphasis on precocity were also reflected at the other limit of adolescence by the growing uniformity of the age of matriculation to the university. The age distribution of entrants to Oxford University (Table 3) demonstrates the striking trend toward a new set of

TABLE 3

Age Distribution of Matriculants to Oxford University (in percentages)[a]

Age	Year					
	1810	1835	1860	1885	1910	1960
13						
14	1					
15	1	1				
16	7	2		1		
17	25	24	10	5	2	2
18	34	48	48	34	18	30
19	16	15	30	40	45	31
20+	16	10	12	20	35	37

[a] From Stone, "Size and Composition," Table XI.

norms, establishing a clear boundary between adolescent years of secondary schooling (14–18) and the status of "young adulthood," lasting from university entrance until marriage at 30.[21]

The period 1830–1890 was the most age-homogeneous in Oxford's history. Thereafter, graduate admissions increased the number of entrants who were over 20, but this does not detract from the point that the day of both the precocious and the laggard was clearly past. Neither parents nor schoolmasters were interested any longer in pushing boys in the manner common earlier. Precocity itself was in disrepute, associated with street urchins rather than respectable schoolboys. "How I dread mannikizing a boy," stated Warden Sewell of Radley College. "It is to be just as bad as opening an egg and

---

[20] Publication/report: _Parl. Papers_ I, p. 89.
[21] On age grading, see Airès, Chapter 4.

finding an advanced chicken inside it. What say to a baby with whiskers, or mustachios? No, keep boys boys—children children—young men young men." [22]

Sewell was writing in the late 1850s, when this new tripartite division was giving "boyhood" a concrete meaning it had not had previously. The emergence of boyhood (and later girlhood) was reflected in the changing children's literature of the time, which was undergoing its own peculiar age-grading. Prior to the middle of the century, magazines such as *Youth's Monthly Visitor* had aimed their moral homilies at an undefined audience that covered both sexes and ranged from mere children to young adults. The appearance in 1855 of *Boy's Own Magazine*—followed, after it had demonstrated its commercial succcess, by *Boy's Own Paper, Boy's Penny Magazine, Boys of England,* and a host of other competitors—signaled a momentus change in public attitudes, at least among the middle classes who were the initial subscribers. Not only were the new papers sex-segregated, but they reinforced the stereotypes favored by the Victorian bourgeoisie, "the image of the public school boy for males, Women in the Home for females." [23] By the end of the century, children's literature was further subdivided, there being magazines for babies, children, adolescents, and young adults, each reflecting a well-defined norm of what behavior ought to be at each stage of the life cycle.[24]

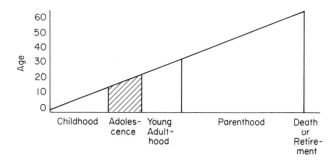

Figure 3   Life cycle of middle class, 1900.

"They [parents] desire very often, above everything else, that their boys should be like other boys, and not marked off as peculiar," re-

---

[22] Quoted in Musgrove, *Youth and Social Order,* p. 55.
[23] Darton, p. 293; Turner, *Boys Will Be Boys,* pp. 66–72; Avery, pp. 139–148.
[24] Darton, p. 314.

ported the Schools Inquiry Commission.[25] An important part of being like everyone else was conformity to the conventions of the middle-class life cycle, which by 1900 had already enshrined adolescence as a part of the natural order of respectable society. (See Figure 3.)

II

Low mortality and low fertility made adolescence possible, but the real crucible of the age-group's social and psychological qualities was the elite secondary school. In England, the invention of adolescence was the unintended product of the reform of the public schools, whose beginnings are usually associated with the era of Thomas Arnold's tenure as headmaster at Rugby, 1827–1839. Arnold and the other reformers of his generation were the products of that earlier era of troubled youth, whose own training had been precocious and who themselves had known nothing like the adolescent stage of life that was to ensue from their reforms. As university students in the 1820s, they had felt the spiritual and social ferment of the times. Most had been touched by Evangelicalism and had at one time or another felt themselves "saved" by its fellowship. The social forms from which they drew strength were those typical of the age of transition—small, intimate circles of friends, such as that which Thomas Arnold shared with John Keble and J. T. Coleridge at Oxford. Coleridge wrote of "the members rather under the usual age, and with more than the ordinary proportion of ability and scholarship. . . . One result of all these circumstances was, that we lived on the most familiar terms with each other: we might be, indeed, we were, somewhat boyish in manner, and in the liberties we took with each other; but our interest in literature, ancient and modern, and in all the stirring matters of that stirring time, was not boyish; we debated the classic and romantic question; we discussed poetry and history, logic and philosophy; or we fought over the Peninsular battles and the Continental campaigns with the energy of disputants

---

[25] Publication/report: *Parl. Papers* I, p. 17.

personally concerned in them. Our habits were inexpensive and temperate." [26]

Theirs was a generation that could still weep openly without fear of being called effeminate, could embrace without taint of sexual deviation. They enjoyed a cult of warm, open male friendship not unlike that of the German Romantics whom they admired; and they associated manliness with high, rather priggish, moral standards, that they felt preserved them from both childishness and adult indulgences. Though few Englishmen of their social position were touched by either the bohemianism or the utopianism so prevalent on the Continent, there were not a few who would later be attracted to the monastic vows of the Tractarian Movement of the 1830s. "Having formed intimate friendships at an age when it is proper to see visions," writes David Newsome, "they developed a common resolve to impress their ideals upon the particular society into which their work was to take them." [27]

Arnold proclaimed his calling as educator to be that of the keeper of the whole person: "He must adjust the respective claims of bodily and mental exercise, of different kinds of intellectual labour; he must consider every part of his pupil's nature, physical, intellectual, and moral; regarding the cultivation of the last, however, as paramount to that of either of the others." [28] Arnold wished to turn out young men characterized by intellectual toughness, moral earnestness, and deep spiritual conviction. The feelings he wished to develop were not those of childish emotion but noble idealism. His own upbringing accustomed him to thinking in terms of precocious behavior and when he asked himself the question "Can the change from childhood to manhood be hastened in the case of boys and young men without exhausting prematurely the faculties either of body or mind?" his answer was staunchly affirmative. The object of a Rugby education was, he wrote, "if possible to form Christian men, for Christian boys I can scarcely make." [29]

The philosophy of "boys will be boys" had no place in Arnold's world, one still so close to the conditions that encouraged precocity among the young earlier in the century. "If the change from childhood to manhood can be hastened safely, it ought to be hastened; and it is a sin in everyone not to hasten it," remained his educational

[26] Quoted in Newsome, pp. 9–10.
[27] Newsome, p. 7.
[28] Newsome, p. 2; Bamford, pp. 19–26, 49–53; Mack, pp. 194–200.
[29] Quoted in Newsome, p. 51.

philosophy to the end.[30] As an admirer of tradition, Arnold did not attempt to destroy the structure of peer group. Instead, he turned the traditional hegemony of the older over the younger boys to his own advantage, purging the prefectorial system and the fagging of their violence, modifying both to fit the new, more paternal discipline of the schools. It will be remembered that in the early-nineteenth-century school, boys had virtually governed themselves, controlling their members through group pressure that tolerated an excess of bullying. When masters tampered with these rights of self-rule, they did so at their own risk, often provoking the kind of rebellion that was a frequent event in school histories throughout the first half of the nineteenth century. Nineteenth-century schoolmasters were infamous for their use of the whip, and reign by corporal punishment certainly did not end with the beginnings of reform. Nevertheless, the relationship between students and masters was both milder and more intimate. Repressive force was reduced by a system of almost fatherly supervision, aimed at preventing abuses rather than punishing them. And so it could be reported in 1864 that "the relationship between Masters and boys is closer and more friendly than it used to be. . . . Flogging, which twenty years ago was resorted to as a matter of course for the most trifling offenses, is now in general used sparingly, and applied only to serious ones. More attention is paid to religious teaching . . . and more reliance is placed on a sense of duty." [31]

The authority of the Masters, so much depreciated in the previous 100 years, was raised, by those who followed Arnold, to the point that it was possible to think of the school as a proper substitute for the family, the teachers serving as surrogate fathers. By the 1860s it could be said that the Master was *in loco parentis* in the full sense of that term. Reform had given the school complete authority over its inmates, something never dreamed of earlier when schooling was marginal to the principal place of learning, the world at large. Now, however, the school was viewed as a superior substitute, not only for the family but for life itself: "To the boarding scholar, the school is the world, the work of the world." The lessons, promotions, and privileges of the school made a greater impact on the boy than "if his world were but a part of that larger world to which his father and his mother belonged." The company of his peers is in all respects superior to that of adults, because "his father's conversation is partly on subjects that he does not yet understand, partly is removed from him

---

[30] Quoted in Musgrove, *Youth and Social Order,* p. 55.
[31] Publication/report: *Parl. Papers* XX, p. 44.

by the undefined difference caused by difference of age; but the
conversation of a boy, even if far cleverer than himself, is still within
his comprehension." [32]

Arnold himself would never have argued the case for the complete
separation of the boy from the world. True, some topics like sex were
inappropriate to youth, but his goal of making Christian scholars precluded the exclusion from schoolboy life of other concerns—social,
political, and ideological—that were necessary to the multifaceted
development of the individual. But even Arnold, in his desire to
create an environment conducive to growth, had given encouragement to the erection of barriers between the school and adult life.
In order to attract the right kind of middle-class boys, he had excluded local day scholars of poor backgrounds. Town and gown
never mixed easily after Arnold's tenure, and as the social exclusivity
of the schools became more pronounced so did the isolation of their
inmates.[33] The momentum of reform had its unintended results,
among them the transformation of the boarding school into a cloistered institution that it has remained ever since. Arnold's fatherly
supervision was transformed gradually into paternalistic surveillance.
Boys interested in the outside world, its poetry or its politics, were
permitted to experience them only at secondhand through debating
societies and other such imitations of adult life.[34] Continental schools
went a step further, entirely eliminating politics and social issues from
their curriculum. One German observer commented that in English
schools, "imitation of the life of adults in clubs and other societies,
and their observing the forms of public meetings, cannot but appear
to us as signs of a certain precocity." [35] Yet, this was not the same as
the precocity that Arnold had encouraged. Playing at politics maintained a veneer of sophistication among schoolboys, but this was no
closer to authentic political experience than juvenile war games of
the public school cadet corps were to actual war. Nothing could substitute for actual involvement with the social, economic, and political
facts of life, confrontation with which was being postponed to later
and later ages.

Reform, however liberal and enlightened, contained a fundamental
contradiction in so far as it tried to hasten the passage from childhood

---

[32] Publication/report: *Parl. Papers* IV, p. 44.

[33] Weinberg, pp. 37–38; Rupert Wilkinson, pp. 8–26.

[34] Weinberg, pp. 34–52; Rupert Wilkinson, pp. 29–32; Bamford, pp. 80–82; Wakeford, Chapter 1.

[35] Wiese, p. 48.

to adulthood by institutional means. By the 1860s, English public schools had become what Erving Goffman describes as a total institution: "a place of residence or work where a large number of like-situated individuals, cut off from the wider society for an appreciable period of time, together lead an enclosed, formally administered round of life."[36] The cloistering of the boarding school was, of course, much more complete than that of the day school, but even in France and Germany, where the boarding tradition did not prevail, there was a certain tendency for schools to extend their authority over an increasingly large part of the student's life. Continental secondary schools followed this pattern to the point that, by the end of the nineteenth century, they had hedged their students' independence to such an extent that no activity could be carried on without the school authorities' permission. Homework became tantamount to make-work, so heavy as to regulate most of a student's time outside the school hours.[37]

The cloistering of adolescents was justified in England by religion, on the Continent by appeal to culture; but in both places the tangible fears that moved both parents and schoolmasters were actually quite similar. There was, of course, the recent memory of student radicalism and schoolboy rebellion. It was not only foreign threat that English adults thought about when they organized juvenile cadet companies in the 1850s. A similar combination of nationalism and social conservatism was behind a similar flurry of juvenile marching and drilling in France after the Commune of 1871, culminating in the colorful but short-lived *bataillons scolaires* of the early 1880s.[38] When boys tired of playing at war, their elders found other games to engage and divert their energies, however. The French archconservative, Hippolyte Taine, could recommend to his countrymen the English mania for team sports on the grounds that it was socially conservative and militarily useful. They apparently took his advice, for by 1899 the *Almanach des Sports* was reporting: "*Le football* is a veritable little war, with its necessary discipline and its way of getting participants used to danger and to blows."[39]

Too young to vote, be drafted, or volunteer for the real army,

[36] Goffman, p. xiii.

[37] Wiese, pp. 23–32; Waas, pp. 87–89; Pross, pp. 87–89; Muchow, *Sexualreife und Sozialstruktur*, pp. 14–16; Bamford, pp. 80–83; Newsome, pp. 81ff; Weinberg, pp. 45–46.

[38] Eugen Weber, pp. 74–75.

[39] Quoted in Eugen Weber, p. 90.

schoolboys were not necessarily exempt from the discipline that was in store for their older brothers. But real soldiering had at least the compensations of access to the status of adulthood, and the swaggering young reserve officer of the later nineteenth century was very much a symbol of the liberties of older youth, which seemed all the more pronounced precisely because they contrasted so sharply with the straitjacket of adolescence. German university men marked the social distance between themselves and schoolboys by indulging in excessive duelling and drinking. Fraternal connections between the two levels, which had existed in the early nineteenth century, declined to a state of unimportance.[40] In England, too, the lines between school and university were more sharply drawn, though the customs and fashions of college men continued to set the style for hero-worshipping schoolboys.

Affectation of adulthood by adolescents continued, but the substance of manliness as Arnold's generation had understood it—namely, spiritual autonomy and intellectual maturity—was replaced by an emphasis on physical prowess and pure will power. This new cult of masculinity worshipped a different set of virtues. The spartan replaced the platonic, as "fraternity" came to mean shared physical rather than spiritual characteristics. Treitschke was not far wrong when he said that the Englishman's idea of civilization was soap. Arnold's successors thought goodness to be a function of good health and strong muscles. "That morning bath, which foreigners consider as young England's strangest superstition, has done as much to abolish drunkenness, as any other cause whatever," stated Charles Kingsley.[41] Simultaneously, the importance of team sports rose, and by 1880, games were compulsory in most public schools, justified largely by their alleged contribution to the training of boys from different backgrounds in a common *esprit de corps*. Edward Thring, headmaster of Uppingham and one of sport's greatest advocates, believed it to be the key to the formation of a new national elite, composed of the fittest of both the aristocracy and the middle class.[42]

> There is a very strong feeling growing up among the merchant class in England in favour of the public schools; and hundreds go to schools now who thirty years ago would not have thought of doing so. The learning to be responsible, and independent, to bear pain, to play

---

[40] Waas, pp. 98ff; Zorn, p. 329.
[41] Quoted in Newsome, p. 211.
[42] Quoted in Newsome, p. 227.

> games, to drop rank, and wealth, and home luxury, is a priceless boon.
> I think myself that it is this which has made the English such an ad-
> venturous race; and that with all their faults . . . public schools are
> the cause of this "manliness."

Sport was taking over many of the functions of the rite of passage once reserved to Latin language study, for it, too, ensured the separation of boys from the world of women during the critical transition from childhood to adulthood. There was an important social change involved in this substitution, however. The model of the earlier Latin school was the monastery; the ideal of the public school was increasingly military. Women were to be avoided by adolescents because femininity was now associated with weakness, emotion, and unreliability. So strong was the avoidance of female traits by 1860 that men no longer dared embrace in public and tears were shed only in private. A whole series of male clubs sprang up to shield men from women. Some, like the Young Men's Christian Association, founded in 1844, drew their inspiration from the temperate evangelical fellowships of the late eighteenth and early nineteenth centuries; but, for the upper classes it was more likely to be hard-drinking, hard-riding organizations that attracted them. Despite their Victorian exteriors, these upper-class fraternal groups tended to uphold a double standard with respect to social morality, including sexuality. As males, they reserved for themselves the right of access to drink, gambling, and prostitution, rationalizing these things as "natural" to men and "unnatural" to women.[43]

"God made man in His image, not in an imaginatory Virgin Mary's image," explained Charles Kingsley, one of the so-called "muscular Christians" for whom traits of sensitivity or domesticity in a man were a kind of sin against nature and society.[44] And, of course, what could better preserve the differences between the sexes than the military? —thus a partial explanation for the popularity of the rifle clubs and cadet corps in the second half of the century. Here male and national chauvinism blended neatly in a spartan model of boyhood that permitted no deviation. Boys who did not play the game or march in step were looked upon as misfits. Uniforms, whether athletic or military, underlined the growing intolerance of individuality that characterized late-nineteenth-century schooling in both England and Germany. Max Weber, looking back on the enormous impact of student

---

[43] Thomas, pp. 196–201, 215–216; Cominos, pp. 243–46; Harrison.
[44] Kingsley quoted in Newsome, p. 210.

fraternities on German life, wrote of the false understanding of freedom that these engendered:[45]

> The "academic freedom" of dueling, drinking, and class cutting stems from a time when other kinds of freedom did not exist in Germany and when only the stratum of literati and candidates for office was privileged in such liberties. The inroad, however, which these conventions have made upon the bearing of the "academically certified man" of Germany cannot be eliminated even today.

He praised the English for educating their sons to a broader definition of rights, but he might well have listened to those in England who warned of the trend toward mindless conformity that was the product of the philosophy, "boys will be boys." To George Trevelyan the results were clear:[46]

> What else can be expected, when a young man at the age his grandfather was fighting in the Peninsula or preparing to stand for a borough, is still hanging on at school, with his mind half taken up with Latin verses, and the other half divided between his score in the cricket field and his score at the pastry-cook's?

III

Increasing concern with the physical elements of boyhood brought parents and educators face to face with sexuality, the taboo subject of the earlier generation. By the 1870s the subject of "puberty" was being discussed openly in both medical books and parents' manuals; and a decade later, even the conservative Oxford Clerical Association declared for "frankness" in the catechising of its young confirmees.[47] Recognition of the sexuality of adolescence did not mean, however, a liberalization of Victorian attitudes. On the contrary, the tendency of writers was to blame parents for being too careless, allowing their sons to pick up bad habits from both peers and servants. Warned

---

[45] Max Weber, pp. 387–388.
[46] Quoted in Newsome, p. 227.
[47] Ms. source B, Mins. Oxford Clerical Assn., May 5, 1879, MS Top Oxon e 38.

Elizabeth Blackwell: "The physical growth of youth, the new powers, the various symptoms which make the transition from childhood into young man- and womanhood are often alarming to the individual. Yet this important period of life is entered upon, strange to say, as a general rule, without parental guidance." [48] If parents could not deal with it, then other institutions would. The cloistered sex-segregated schools were the best guarantee against sexual deviation, but Dr. William Acton also praised the efforts of the Young Men's Christian Association and the Volunteer Movement to impose continence: "I am convinced that much of the incontinence of the present day could be avoided by finding amusement, instruction, and recreation for the young men of large towns." [49]

Contemporaries recognized that the high age of marriage among the middle classes (29.9 years for English professional males in the period 1840–1870) represented an enormous challenge to supervision and control, not just of relations with the opposite sex but of those between boys and boys. It was admitted by Acton and others that "a schoolmaster should be alive to the excessive danger of platonic attachments that sometimes become fashionable in a school, especially between boys of very different ages." [50] As Robert Graves was to experience later, social attributes that were normal in the outside world were forfeited in favor of loyalty to the male group. Boys were forced even to abandon normal sex roles. "In English preparatory and public schools romance is necessarily homosexual," Graves noted. "The opposite sex is despised and treated as something obscene. . . . For every one born homosexual, at least ten permanent pseudo-homosexuals were made by the public school system; nine of these ten as honourable chaste and sentimental as I was." [51]

For most, the regression to this form of innocent affection was but a temporary detour on the way to adult heterosexuality. Headmaster G. H. Rendall was probably accurate in his assessment that "my boys are amorous, but seldom erotic." [52] Yet, while it is unclear whether the schools produced more than their share of adult homosexuals, almost complete isolation from the opposite sex had the effect of

---

[48] Blackwell, p. 68.

[49] Acton, p. 30.

[50] Acton, p. 47; figures on age of marriage from Banks, *Prosperity and Parenthood*, p. 48.

[51] Robert Graves, p. 19; Cominos, pp. 226–228.

[52] Robert Graves, p. 19; on Germany, see Muchow, *Sexualreife und Sozialstruktur*, pp. 52–53.

transforming the facts of genitality into a forbidden secret world, exposure to which had a traumatic effect on young asexuals like Graves. Confrontation with the effects of puberty was more unexpected and, therefore, more traumatic than today. At 17 Graves had his first real introduction to love play: "An Irish girl staying at the same pension made love to me in a way that, I see now, was really very sweet. It frightened me so much, I could have killed her." [53]

Headmasters looked upon the peer group as a means of controlling sexual delinquency, both because it was the least expensive way of extending their own control and because they, like Arnold, sensed the power of "public opinion" among the boys themselves. Problems arose from the fact that group pressures became so strongly organized that any kind of individualism was immediately taken as a sign of sexual vice. A sure sign of "self abuse" (masturbation) was physical weakness: "Muscles underdeveloped, the eye is sunken and heavy, the complexion is sallow and pusty, or covered with spots of acne, the hands are damp and cold, the skin moist." [54] How many innocents undergoing the physical change associated with adolescence, a growth spurt that was now coming earlier and more rapidly among the middle classes, must have been terrified by these symptoms of normal development? But even more telling was any failure to play the game or to march in step with the group, a sure sign of secret sin.[55]

> The boy shuns the society of others, creeps about alone, joins with repugnance in the amusements of his schoolfellows. He cannot look anyone in the face, and becomes careless in dress and uncleanly in person. His intellect becomes sluggish and enfeebled, and if his evil habits are persisted in he may end in become a drivelling idiot or a peevish valetudinarian.

Thus, what were historically-evolved social norms of a particular class became enshrined in medical and psychological literature as the "natural" attributes of adolescence. The transmutation, through institutional imperatives, of social values into natural laws suited the new materialist outlook of the middle classes in the second half of the nineteenth century. One of William Acton's correspondents, writ-

---

[53] Robert Graves, p. 36; Muchow, *Sexualreife und Sozialstruktur*, pp. 36–40.

[54] Acton, p. 16. On the growth of fear of masturbation in the early nineteenth century, see Spitz, pp. 490–527.

[55] Acton, p. 16.

ing to him concerning ways of convincing the younger generation of the dangers of incontinence, expressed the universal desire to find in science a new legitimation of old social controls: "It would be the greatest encouragement to know that physical science confirms the dictates of revelation." [56] Conformity, self-denial, and dependence— all essentially functions of the kind of upbringing that was peculiar to a particular class—had become positivistic standards of human behavior by which an upper class could assure itself of its inherent superiority to the lower orders. The fact that children of the working class were independent and resistant to institutional controls was now proof of their inferiority.

IV

However pleased the middle classes were with their invention, they were also aware of its difficulties, particularly the emotional deficits that arose out of so much investment in the artificial world of the school. "Left entirely to themselves they [adolescents] tend to disorder and triviality, and controlled too much by adults they tend to lose zest and spontaneity," wrote G. Stanley Hall. His conclusions were not unlike those Stephen Spender arrived at some 50 years later, when, reviewing English adolescence, he wrote that the schools taught "boys to take themselves seriously as functions of an institution, before they take themselves seriously as persons or individuals." [57] England's schoolboys possessed a composure and polish that surprised and delighted most foreign visitors, but beneath this surface lay considerable turmoil and self-doubt, the product of an education that gave little attention to personality and emotional development. Robert Graves, who was particularly sensitive to this deficit in his own training, wrote of how the total institution was arranged so that boys came to view themselves as possessed of no personal rights as such, but only of statuses granted to them as privileges. "A new boy had no privileges at all; a boy in his second term might wear a knitted

---

[56] Acton, p. 51.
[57] Spender, p. 235; see also Carter, pp. 209–234.

tie instead of a plain one; and a boy in his second year might wear coloured socks."[58] A sturdy individualist like Graves was able to subvert the rules of Charterhouse School and develop a personal identity apart from its hierarchy, but most of his fellow students were not so fortunate. "School life becomes reality, and home life the illusion"; and boys whose whole lives had been built around team sports and fraternity life were naturally insecure in the company of the opposite sex. Moving on to university, the army, or the professions—all still exclusively male institutions—it was understandable that they should seek to allay their anxiety about this aspect of adulthood by perpetuating schoolboy comradery well past their own years of adolescence.[59]

The most famous fictional schoolboy of the mid-century, Tom Brown, had been eager to get on with life. "If I can't be at Rugby, I want to be at work in the world, and not dawdling away three years at Oxford," he told his tutor. But in the end he accepted advice of the kind that was to become conventional by 1900: "Don't be in a hurry about finding your work in the world for yourself. You are not old enough to judge for yourself yet, but just look about you in the place you find yourself in, and try to make things a little better and honester there."[60] The gap between Arnold's generation and that of the schoolmasters who followed them can be measured here. David Newsome has summarized it best: "The worst educational feature of the earlier ideal was the tendency to make boys into men too soon; the worst feature of the other, paradoxically, was that in its efforts to achieve manliness by stressing the cardinal importance of playing games, it fell into the opposite error of failing to make boys into men at all."[61]

By century's end, schoolmasters all over Europe could congratulate themselves on the good order of their pupils. Never had the schoolboy been so at peace with the world, so accepting of his social deprivation, so apathetic toward his civil status. Although young fools might still play their pranks on a November night or dance on May mornings, middle-class boys did not ordinarily don the masks of Misrule except in a patriotic or conservative cause. Yet, beneath this surface calm many thought they detected an inner storm. The asso-

---

[58] Robert Graves, p. 45.
[59] Rupert Wilkinson, pp. 29–37, 54–63.
[60] Hughes, pp. 305–307.
[61] Newsome, p. 238.

ciation of emotional turmoil with transition from childhood, which can be traced back at least to the writings of Rousseau, had by 1900 found a prominent place in medical and psychological literature. The image of the schoolboy had shifted from trouble-maker to troubled, particularly in Germany, where the relationship of the school to the home only increased the problems of prolonged dependence.

The day-*Gymnasium* lacked those features of a total institution which distinguished the English public school. In Germany, the middle-class family retained control of social learning, the school monopolized intellectual training, and both civic and sexual education were left at dispute between them. This uneasy allocation was the subject of increasing controversy at century's end. The demographic and economic situation of the German bourgeoisie was much like that of its English counterpart, except that it placed greater emphasis on academic success because of the greater prestige conferred on formal educational attainment in that society. There appears to have been the same growing pressure on adolescents to meet parental expectations and thus justify the growing investment in education. In contrast to the English public school, however, the German *Gymnasium* was less well-equipped to deal with the phenomenon of "boyhood" that this produced. Lacking the characteristics of a total institution, it had greater difficulty in shaping youth to conform to its elite goals. There were no sports or extracurricular activities to cope with the social and emotional side-effects of prolonged dependence; and thus the school appeared to many of its inmates as an arid brain-factory, unable to meet the needs of the young. A rash of student suicides in the 1890s caused Ludwig Gurlitt to ask: "Can there be any graver charge against a school system than these frequent student suicides? Is it not grisly and horrible if a child voluntarily renounces seeing the light of the sun, voluntarily separates himself from his parents and brothers and sisters, from all the joys, hopes, and desires of his young life, because he doubts himself and no longer can bear the compulsions of school?" [62]

The family, on the other hand, was organized in an authoritarian way around its own private affairs and was also poorly equipped to deal with the larger tasks of youthful development. Sexual learning remained in a kind of no-man's land, attended to by neither parents nor schoolmasters, despite the growing anxiety about the onset of puberty. Deprived of youth's traditional agency of sexual education,

---

[62] Quoted in Fishman, p. 176.

the peer group, German middle-class boys and girls found their stage of dependency an extraordinarily lonely, disturbing experience. By 1900 this social experience was translating itself into literary expression, with the novels of Thomas Mann, Hermann Hesse, and Robert Musil exploring the inner turmoil of adolescence. Similar concerns were reflected in the work of the German and Austrian psychological schools, including, of course, Freud and his followers.[63] And their definition of the "problematic" character of adolescence was then influencing views in both England and the United States, particularly in the latter, where G. Stanley Hall published his massive *Adolescence, Its Psychology and Its Relation to Physiology, Anthropology, Sociology, Sex, Crime, Religion, and Education* in 1904. Adolescence, wrote Hall, was one of the most important blessings that civilization had bestowed; and yet its promise was also its danger. A stage of life withdrawn from adult pursuits was desirable, but it also exposed the young to idleness and depravity. "Modern life is hard, and in many respects increasingly so, on youth. Home, school, church, fail to recognize its nature and needs and, perhaps most of all, its perils." [64]

V

The problems of the adolescent were gaining public attention by 1900 because an increasingly larger minority of the population was finding itself in the demographic and economic situation that produced this new phase of life. To be sure, their numbers were still limited. In England, the richest country in Europe, those parents who could afford a secondary education for their children still amounted to only about 6% of the population in 1909; and there were only 1.5% of the age group 15–18 engaged in secondary education.[65] But there was beneath the solid middle class a growing lower-middle class who were encouraged, by the expansion of white-collar jobs in the

---

[63] Fishman, pp. 180–185; Pross, pp. 44ff.

[64] Hall, vol. 1, p. xiv.

[65] Lowndes, pp. 78–90; Halsey, *Trends*, p. 163; for Germany, Samuel and Thomas, pp. 36–54.

last quarter of the nineteenth century, to send their sons to local secondary schools in order that the sons might pick up sufficient education for qualifying as clerks, secretaries, and lower-ranking civil servants. "Parents are eager to get their sons into houses of business where they can maintain the appearance, if not the standing, of gentlemen," noted one contemporary who knew well the changing occupational pattern of London. "The City is crowded with well-educated lads, who are doing men's work for boys' wages. It is quite useless to argue with parents, and urge the propriety of sending boys to learn a trade; the idea of a lad returning from his work in the evening with dirty hands, and clad in fustian or corduroy, is quite shocking to the respectability of Peckham or Camberwell." [66] The expanding white-collar class was heard among the voices calling for a further growth of secondary education in all European countries, because, as the earlier entrepreneurial ideal of the self-made man faded, this became the only way to attain the respectability they so strongly desired.[67] In their minds, adolescence was part of that respectability; and it was due in no small part to this class that the popularity of new juvenile magazines, hobbies, and fashions expanded rapidly toward the turn of the century.

Below the lower-middle class, however, the attitude toward education and the valuation of adolescence was much less uniform, with the working classes—who still constituted the vast majority of the population—dividing roughly along the lines of the skilled versus the unskilled in the way they treated the teen years. At the very top of the working classes were the so-called "aristocracy of labour," a group of skilled, highly-paid artisans whose standard of living was similar to that of the lower-middle class. Strictly speaking, they constituted only about 15% of the English working-classes in the period 1890–1914; but we must place in a similar category another 40–45% of the proletariat who were skilled or semiskilled and whose standard of living was also above the poverty line, which in 1914 still exceeded the earnings of over 30% of the English population.[68] Among the top half of the working classes, the trend toward a family strategy somewhat like that of the middle classes was already apparent by 1900. Among the poor and the unskilled, who were still struggling against the conditions of the city slums, the same situation of high

---

[66] Quoted in Banks, *Prosperity and Parenthood,* p. 193.

[67] Musgrove, "Middle Class Families," pp. 169–178; Perkin, "Middle Class Education," pp. 122–130; Musgrove, "Middle Class Education," pp. 320–329.

[68] Hobsbawm, "Labour Aristocracy," pp. 284–285.

mortality and high fertility that had characterized practically the entire working class 50 years earlier was still in effect.

Rising wages and improved health conditions had altered skilled workers' attitudes toward their children. Many lived outside the central core of the cities and were now enjoying an average living space of three or four rooms per house.[69] Home life had been transformed, with mothers being less likely to be employed, and therefore devoting increasing amounts of time and energy to child rearing. "Family life becomes more private," Seebohm Rowntree observed, "and the women are left in the house all day whilst their husbands are at work, and largely thrown upon their own resources. . . . Character and attractive power of family life are principally dependent on her." [70] The care and attention devoted to the individual child was reflected in the extended training and education that was given to both boys and girls. Surveys before 1914 showed that skilled workers were likely to keep their children in school longer than the unskilled, and to place a value on post-school training, whether it be night education or apprenticeship. They were not so eager to rush their children to work immediately upon school-leaving; and in Oxford some artisans even allowed their children a few months to "look around" before starting them on careers.[71] In London, since the 1880s, the aristocracy of labor had been keeping their sons at school until the age of 14, some 2 or 3 years beyond the average leaving-age of the unskilled in the same period.[72] And they were proud of this distinction, for, as one contemporary reported, "no one has so important a contempt for the uneducated working man as has the educated working man." [73]

Parents on the upper reaches of the working class valued the school not only for the mobility that it offered their children but for the social control it represented. Their contempt for the uneducated extended to the undisciplined, with street arabs and lodging-house youth the targets of particular hostility.[74] Obedience on the part of children was regarded as an especially important status symbol, leading to a situation that caused Alexander Paterson to remark: "Parental discipline is, in fact, a sure sign of prosperity and respectability." [75]

---

[69] Bray, "Boy and Family," p. 11.
[70] Rowntree, *Poverty: A Study,* p. 109.
[71] Butler, p. 53.
[72] Rubinstein, pp. 8–10.
[73] Quoted in Rubinstein, p. 12.
[74] Russell, *Manchester Boys,* p. 47.
[75] Paterson, p. 16.

This same group was also the most likely to plan its leisure activities around the family, in the manner already established among the classes higher up the social scale. They were the first of the working classes to take family holidays, and it was also among their ranks that the greatest support for organized extracurricular activities for children—temperance clubs, junior friendly societies, Sunday schools—was to be found.[76] Aylward Dingle was born in the poorest section of Oxford, St. Ebbe's, but his father had pretensions to respectability and joined a series of different churches, beginning with the low-prestige Salvation Army and ascending ultimately to the Methodism as his prospects improved. The boy was shifted from one church organization to another, as these suited the father's aspirations:[77]

> At Sunday school most of the kids hated it as much as I did, but went because they had to. The "best" boys played up to their teachers and the parson, and most of them were the veriest toadies, sneaks, and liars; but they were the ones I was told I must copy. I saw little to admire in them, and tried my best to get turned out of the school; but now Father rented a pew, like Aunt Lizzie, and put sixpence in the plate every Sunday, and I couldn't get expelled.

Not all the organizations that children like Dingle were joining were as middle-class as the Methodist Sunday School. They also filled the ranks of the Secularist and Socialist Sunday schools at the turn of the century and were active in the junior ranks of the trade unions.[78] But they were an elite and they tended to monopolize the opportunities within the trades themselves, including the best apprenticeships. During the last quarter of the nineteenth century, apprenticeships of all sorts were disappearing, and the ones that were left were far too expensive for the vast majority of working-men's sons. Furthermore, the sons of the skilled had the advantage of the patronage wielded through the unions by their fathers and other kin, which gave them an additional advantage over those further down the social scale, most of whom were still unorganized. While it is true that the ability of workers to find jobs for kin was generally declining by 1900, studies at the time showed that the skilled trades were strongly self-perpetuating, producing what observers saw to be a growing gulf between the skilled and the unskilled in the decades before 1914.[79]

---

[76] Freeman, p. 130; Butler, pp. 167–181.

[77] Dingle, p. 23.

[78] Simon, pp. 48–59.

[79] Freeman, pp. 22–34; Rowntree, *Poverty: A Study*, pp. 103ff; Meachem, pp. 1343–1364.

Despite these advantages, skilled workers were not complacent about their children's chances; and from the 1890s onwards there seems to have been considerable anxiety among them, about competition for the higher-paying positions. The occasion for this was the changing character of the economy itself, which, as a result of the so-called "second industrial revolution," had drastically reduced the employment of the young in industry while at the same time increasing it in certain other areas, such as transportation, distribution, and merchandising. Increasingly, the route to highly-paid, skilled industrial work lay through technical-school training or apprenticeships, both requiring some outlay of money by the trainee. In the other sectors of the economy, however, there were by 1890 a plethora of jobs for unskilled boys from the ages 14 to 18; jobs as errand boy, street vendor, live-out domestic servant, porter, and carter's assistant, which paid as much as 7 or 8 shillings a week but usually led to no advancement as in the skilled trades. This was the category of so-called "boy labor," occupations that were absorbing an ever greater share of the teen-age labor force before 1914.[80]

Although the ultimate wage an unskilled boy could expect to earn was nowhere near that which could be expected by an apprentice once he had finished his training, the initial earnings were a great deal higher than the prevailing wages of apprentices. Furthermore, an apprentice premium or school fee meant money out of the family pocket; a job delivering for the corner shop meant more pennies in mother's budget at precisely that time in the life cycle of the working-class family when extra money to feed many mouths was most needed. Many saw this situation leading to a further decline in apprenticeship and the social control which it represented:[81]

> The master is careless, or the apprentice is idle, or the older workmen will not be troubled to show the boy his work; or if, as not infrequently happens, the boy, at fifteen or sixteen, changes his mind, begins to detest the trade he is learning, and rebels again earning 3s or 4s a week while his friend who was three standards below him in school is getting 7s or 8s as errand-boy or shop-porter, it is hard on both parties to be legally bound to each other for five or even three years longer.

Seebohm Rowntree found in his 1899 study of York that over 40% of working-class families found ends hard to meet while their chil-

---

[80] Cloete, pp. 102–135; Bray, *Boy Labour*; Tawney.
[81] Butler, p. 52.

dren were growing up. The effects of overcrowding and disease were still much as they had been earlier in the century, and the family strategy, therefore, still dictated large numbers of children, who continued, of necessity, to be treated as a form of economic and social security. As long as conditions of high mortality prevailed, their lives continued to be, as Alexander Paterson described it, "a giddy Kaleidoscope of danger, catastrophy, and unexpected windfalls." [82] The life of the unskilled remained one of cycles of want and relative abundance, depending largely on economic conditions and the size of family. Those families that were most likely to fall beneath the poverty line were those with numbers of small children not yet old enough to leave school and begin earning. Rowntree found that the worker's prospects were brightest when his children were old enough to work, but then fell again when the children left home to set up their own households. For the individual born into such a family and remaining unskilled for the rest of his life, the cycle of poverty was as depicted in Figure 4.

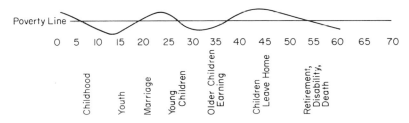

Figure 4 Cycle of poverty among the unskilled working class, 1900 [From Rowntree, *Poverty: A Study*, p. 171].

The ability of children of poverty families ever to rise above this class was severely limited by the fact that need pressed so strongly on their families precisely at that point in their lives when expenditure on schooling or apprenticeship would have facilitated movement upward. In Oxford, for example, "the traditional rate of wages for these learners or apprentices [was] an almost impossible obstacle to boys from poor families entering most of the skilled trades or the higher ranks of employment as a shop assistant." [83] This was particularly true of the eldest children, upon whom the family was most reliant for income. "By the time there are two or three of the older boys

---

[82] Paterson, p. 72; Rowntree, *Poverty: A Study*, pp. 152–172.
[83] Butler, p. 53.

at work, the family can afford to accept lower wages for the younger ones and put them to a better trade," noted one observer. Even as late as the 1930s, placement in the birth order determined whether an English working-class child would have benefit of secondary education.[84]

> It was always that way with the oldest. With big families we were waiting for them to go to work. The younger ones were better off in every way. They got the best of the education and they got the advantage of better jobs too.

Because since 1880 children under 11 had been compulsorily confined to the schoolroom (by 1918 the leaving-age had been raised to 14), the burden of earning was increasingly that of the teenaged. As late as 1914, 10% of the families in some English communities had no other source of income but their children.[85] Paterson found that in the poor districts of London, fathers earned less than 50% of the family income; and when they were disabled or laid off, the son virtually took their places in the family. Where the son earned more than the father, "he will, without comment, expect and receive two kippers for his tea, while his unemployed father will make the most of bread and butter." [86] The poor chances of boys of this sort to rise above their station was revealed in Rowntree's study of York, in which

TABLE 4

Proportions of Age Groups Living in Poverty in York, 1899

Under 1 year	33.33%
1–5	31.91%
5–15	37.58%
15–65	23.60%
Over 65	21.39%

he found that the highest proportion of the population living below the poverty level (defined at that time as families whose income was less than 22 shillings per week) were those between 5 and 15 years of age (Table 4).[87]

---

[84] Cloete, p. 106.
[85] Bowley and Burnett-Hurst, p. 111.
[86] Paterson, p. 15.
[87] Rowntree, *Poverty: A Study*, pp. 441–445.

Families were even more desperate to keep teen-aged children at home and at work than they had been in industrial Lancashire 50 years earlier, both because younger children were removed from employment by factory and school laws and because women were now less likely to be employed. Little wonder that the poverty-stricken regarded compulsory education as a threat to themselves. The long struggle of London truant officers to raise the attendance rates from 76.7% in 1872 to 88.2% in 1906 was fought mainly with the poorest classes. The most frequent reason for absence was that the child was at work; the next most important was the lack of pennies to pay the school fees or to provide shoes or a decent breakfast. Going to school often meant giving up a meal, one reason why Mrs. Besant described London parents, fined for the truancy of their children, as "gaunt, hunger pinched men and women, all, but one, decent folk, who did not want to keep their children ignorant, but sometimes there were no books, sometimes there was a baby to mind, sometimes there was not food." [88] The same class was most likely to have its younger children employed after school hours, a proportion that amounted to 25% of all London school children as late as 1910.[89] Children were pressured to leave school at the earliest possible moment, like the York lad who asked his teacher the time.[90]

> "Half past ten, my lad; but what's the matter?"
> "Please, sir, then may I go, sir? My mother said I should be fourteen at half past ten this morning, and I could leave school when I was fourteen, sir."

In all probability, then, this boy went straight into the kind of casual dead-end jobs that constituted "boy labor." He might, if he were fortunate, gravitate to higher-paying, semiskilled employment by the time he was 18 or 19, but as a report on London's poorer districts in 1909 indicated (Table 5), most must have remained at the same level they began.

The old custom of tramping in search of training was virtually dead, as the figures on emigration indicate. Contemporaries complained that boys and girls rarely looked beyond their own neighborhoods for employment, relying mainly on kin or mother's contacts with local tradesmen for their jobs.[91] The use of kin, which had been an ad-

---

[88] Quoted in Rubinstein, p. 62.
[89] Bray, *Boy Labour*, p. 153.
[90] Rowntree, *Poverty: A Study*, p. 105.
[91] Cloete, p. 108; Butler, p. 65.

TABLE 5

Age Distribution in London Occupations, 1909[a]

	Age					
	14	15	16	17	18	19
Skilled trades	11.2	14.0	16.8	17.8	18.0	16.3
Clerks	14.6	15.0	16.4	15.2	15.4	14.3
Low-skilled	28.2	32.8	34.1	33.9	32.5	34.1
Car men	.6	.2	.6	2.6	4.5	5.1
Van boys	8.2	6.6	5.2	4.9	2.8	1.2
Post office	1.4	1.4	.2	.2	.3	1.2
Errand and shopboys	30.5	22.0	18.4	15.0	12.6	10.3
General casual labor	5.3	7.0	6.7	6.9	6.4	8.7
Army		.6	.6	1.1	3.6	4.0
At sea	.2	.4	.8	1.5	2.8	3.5
Emigrants			.2	.4	.8	1.2

[a] Figures from Bray, Boy Labour, p. 145.

vantage in the Lancashire industrial towns 50 years before, was now working to the disadvantage of the poor, since jobs that could be had in this manner were often those jobs with the poorest prospects. Families could not dispense with their children's labor until the youngsters were 17 or 18; and even then, when free to leave, many simply drifted, joining the army or working on the railway as many Oxford youth did, and later returning to their homes to settle down to lives of casual, unskilled employment.[92]

Of London school-leavers studied by Reginald Bray early in the twentieth century, almost two-thirds went immediately to jobs of the casual or "dead-end" sort. Less than a third of those who left during the 1907–1908 school year took up apprenticeships leading to jobs defined as "skilled," and only 6% of the total went on to any further education, day or evening. London offered more than its share of dead-end jobs, but even in those places where the economy was more industrial than commercial or service-oriented, the story was not much different.[93] "Boys are kept to boys' work, men to men's work;

---

[92] Butler, p. 54.

[93] Bray, Boy Labour, pp. 114–118. In Oxford, about 40% of the boys leaving school in 1910–1911 were entering skilled occupations or training positions. Butler, p. 53.

there is no natural passage from one to the other," noted Bray—by which he also meant that in the great majority of cases the unskilled boy became the unskilled man, and the skilled boy the skilled man.[94] The unskilled might out-earn the skilled during their teen years, but at the age of 18 or so, this situation was reversed. Apprenticeship or schooling gave an automatic right to adult levels of remuneration at this age, but for the unskilled boy or girl there was no such guarantee. The critical turning point for the vast majority of unskilled youth came at 18, when they were compelled to ask for adult wages. At this point they might be taken on at higher rates of pay, but it was more likely that the employer would choose to let them go in favor of younger boys or girls who cost him less.[95] At this point in their lives, the high demand for unskilled labor no longer worked in their favor. Boys without skills or good references were thrown into the great pool of casual labor that was a feature of industrial capitalism at the end of the nineteenth century. There they would remain at the bottom of the social scale, perpetuating what many observers had come to fear was a semihereditary culture of poverty, a conclusion encouraged by the Social Darwinism of the period, whose advocates detected signs of moral as well as physical degeneracy among the youth belonging to the lower segments of the working class.[96]

Economic change had the effect of creating a situation which underscored two distinct turning points in the life of young workers. The first, between 12 and 14, revolved around school-leaving and was critical in determining future employment prospects. It was, according to Arnold Freeman, "a fundamental moment in the life of the individual, second only in importance to that of his physical birth. It is, indeed, the moment of his second birth into all the higher possibilities of human nature." [97] Reginald Bray, on the other hand, viewed the transition from boy's work to man's work at 17 or 18 as of no less importance, for, there, "many drop into the abyss as they essay the crossing." [98] Both were right but were talking about different segments of the working class. For the skilled, the earlier age was critical as the beginning of their technical training and as the start of a kind of adolescence, during which they would remain dependent on their parents and masters. For the unskilled, the change from

---

[94] Bray, "Youth and Industry," p. 58.
[95] Freeman, pp. 54–55.
[96] Hynes, pp. 22–23.
[97] Freeman, p. 108.
[98] Bray, "Youth and Industry," p. 61.

school to employment involved no choice on their part, no investment on the part of their parents. Many were already working, even
before they left school, and full-time employment was but one step
in a gradual realization of full independence from the home. The
critical point for the poor came toward the end of their teens, when,
to fail to attain a "man's job"—usually meaning a skilled or semiskilled position—was tantamount not only to economic poverty but
to social subordination. Thus, they would remain "lads" or "boys"
in the traditional double meaning of that term, looked down upon by
both the upper classes and the better-paid working men. (See Figure
5 for a comparison of the two groups' life cycles.)

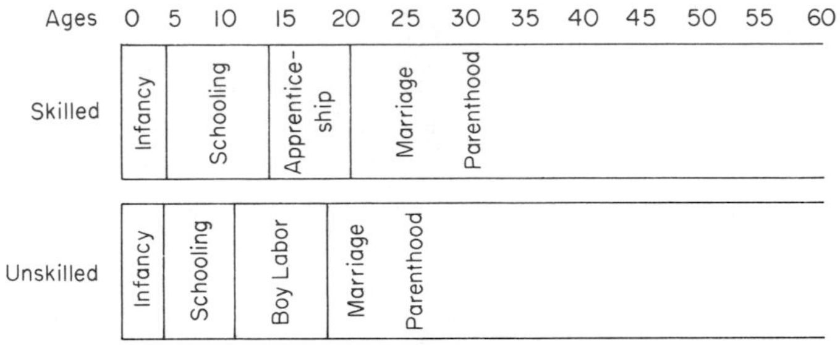

Ages	0	5	10	15	20	25	30	35	40	45	50	55	60

Skilled: Infancy | Schooling | Apprenticeship | Marriage | Parenthood

Unskilled: Infancy | Schooling | Boy Labor | Marriage | Parenthood

Figure 5   Life cycles of skilled and unskilled workers, 1900.

VI

"Father and son can seldom work together," Reginald Bray concluded after surveying several thousand families in the poorer neighborhoods of London. He found that 40% of the fathers were employed in trades and industries, as compared with only 22% of their
sons. The boys were highly concentrated in transport and other dead-
end jobs.[99] Evidence of stagnating opportunities and downward mobility was a major cause after 1900 of the skilled working-man's anxiety about the adolescent years. From it stemmed the increasing interest, shown by members of the upper levels of the working classes,

---

[99] Bray, *Boy Labour*, p. 118.

in extending the school-leaving age, providing industrial training, and generally regulating the life of the young. Their fears were also reflected in the pressures they placed on their own children to join trade and church organizations, and in the increasing strictness with which parents of that strata controlled the street life of their sons and daughters. Even before 1900, observers detected a change in the social habits of this class of youth. Their leisure pursuits were becoming detached from the traditions of the urban youth group and becoming more closely related to family pleasures. They were also becoming more commercialized, centering on the music hall, the local pub, and, as 1914 approached, on the cinema and spectator sports.[100] Much of skilled youth's activity was moving off the streets and indoors, either within the home itself or at the various youth clubs that had proliferated in the 1880s and 1890s. Among them the practice of "promenading" had virtually come to a stop by 1900, being replaced by less public forms of courtship, usually centering on paid entertainment in the cheaply furnished but comfortable public houses that by the turn of the century were rapidly replacing the rough beer shops of the early nineteenth century.[101]

A more informal peer-group structure appears to have replaced the street gang, and despite sensational reports of a rise of juvenile violence in the 1890s, there appears to be no substantial evidence to support the notion that gangs were becoming more aggressive. On the contrary, careful observers like Charles Russell found the opposite to have been the case. In Manchester, the "Scuttlers" of earlier decades had been replaced by the "Ikes," a better-dressed street idler whose distinctive mark was his bell-bottom fustian trousers and heavy buckled belt, a fashion similar to that of the London "Hooligans" of the same era. The Ikes were responsible for their share of brawls, but were less likely to defend a particular territory than were their predecessors. Furthermore, they were abandoning the calendar customs of the past, substituting the relatively new Bank Holiday for the more traditional dates of revel like November 5th or May 1st. With greater leisure and more pocket money, these lads were able to pursue more individualized forms of pleasure, leading Russell to conclude: "The Scuttlers, for better as well as for worse, had a sense of comradeship, and could, in a sort, organize themselves, as we have

[100] Stedman-Jones.

[101] Rowntree, *Poverty: A Study*, pp. 368–369; Rowntree, *Poverty and Progress*, p. 478.

seen, in gangs; but the Ike is for the most part solitary—less dangerous, therefore, to the community but more deplorable in himself." [102]

Large amounts of leisure in the teen years was still limited, however, to the higher levels of the working classes. The children of the
poorer elements worked longer hours and had less spending money
than the class above them. They contributed as much as 80% of their
earnings to their families and, thus, were not yet in a position to take
up either the entertainments or the activities which were attracting
the more prosperous working class. Holidays, camping trips, club
fees, however inexpensive, were above their means; and what fun
they had was made by themselves in the traditional manner of the
urban youth group. Living in houses of two or three rooms crowded
with large families of eight persons or more precluded the kind of
privatized family life that was developing among the more affluent
workers, as well as the bourgeoisie. [103] The street was still their major
recreation ground; territoriality was maintained and intruders,
whether they be rival gangs or adult-organized youth groups, were
bitterly contested. It was in slum neighborhoods that the church-
sponsored Boys' Brigades of the 1880s met with the greatest antagonism. [104]

> *Here comes the Boys' Brigade*
> *All smovered in marmalade*
> *A Tup'ny-'apenny pill box*
> *And 'arf a yard of braid.*

The Oxford boy, Aylward Dingle, found joining the Salvation Army
junior band no less painful: "Wherever we marched a horde of boys
from the school marched abreast of the band, yelling ribald jeers at
me. I got thumped at school on Monday, but had I refused to march
I would have been thumped more hellishly at home—so I tootled my
little horn and cursed the Army." [105]

Refusal to don a pill-box hat and march in step was proof to middle-class observers that the children of the poor suffered from a dangerous precocity. They were, said E. J. Urwick, "a species of man-
child, in whom the natural instincts of boyhood are almost over-

---

[102] Russell, *Manchester Boys*, p. 54; Paterson, 98ff; Turner, *History of Courting*,
pp. 175–190.

[103] Russell, *Manchester Boys*, p. 17; Bray, "Boy and Family," pp. 23–26.

[104] Quoted in Simon, p. 65.

[105] Dingle, p. 22.

whelmed by a feverish anxiety to become a man." [106] Their early entry into courtship and marriage separated them not only from the bourgeoisie but from the upper levels of their own class. By the age of 22, almost one-third of York's unskilled laborers were married, contrasted to less than 20% of the skilled workers.[107] As we have seen, marriage itself was but a brief transition from one state of poverty to another, with nothing like the interlude of freedom from care and want that the more privileged associated with adolescence and young adulthood. "At thirty a man has given up playing games, making love to his wife, reading books, or building castles in the air," wrote Paterson. "He is dangerously contented with his daily work." [108]

And so the cycle of poverty and despair was transmitted from one generation to the next. Arnold Freeman was right in stating that "to understand the problem of Boy Life and Labor it is essential to consider first what psychologists call 'adolescence,' " but wrong in implying that the problem stopped with the adolescents themselves.[109] In reality, the troubles of the children of the poor were deeply imbedded in the economic and demographic structure of the society. The growing tendency to treat these as psychological and, therefore, as subject to clinical rather than political or economic solution was at least as disturbing as the phenomenon itself. Poverty, and the high mortality that accompanied it, was still the single most important factor in determining the differences between the adolescent and the man-child, differences that were perhaps as great in 1900 as they would be at any time before or since.

---

[106] Urwick, "Introduction," p. xii.
[107] Rowntree, *Poverty: A Study*, p. 174.
[108] Paterson, p. 137.
[109] Freeman, p. 94.

OUR YOUNGEST LINE OF DEFENCE.

Boy Scout (to Mrs. Britannia). "FEAR NOT, GRAN'MA; NO DANGER CAN BEFALL YOU NOW. REMEMBER, I AM WITH YOU!"

The imperial mission of the Scouts attracted the attention of cartoonists from the movement's beginning. "Our Youngest Line of Defence" reproduced from *Punch*, September 1, 1909.

4

Conformity and Delinquency: The Era of Adolescence, 1900–1950

Tho discovery of adolescence belonged to the middle classes and they monopolized it until the beginning of this century. Exemption from the world of work could be allowed the children of the well-to-do, but there were grave doubts as to whether the economy could dispense with the labor of children of other classes. Then, simultaneously in almost every western country, the concept of adolescence was democratized, offered to, or rather required of, all the teenaged. Social and psychological theories of the instability and vulnerability of the age-group justified a deluge of protective legislation which, by 1914, had radically curbed its independence. As secondary education became more extensive, so, too, did the extra-curricular activities. For the first time, there were organizations devoted entirely to adolescence, the two best-known, the English Scouts and the German *Wandervogel,* founded in the first decade of the new century. Prisons and courts especially for juveniles, special employment services and welfare agencies, all were part of society's recognition of the unique status of those who were no longer children and, yet, not fully adult.

Contemporaries like Ellen Key and G. Stanley Hall celebrated the removal of the adolescent from the adult world as the crowning achievement of an enlightened civilization. Others were less sanguine, however, pointing to the incidence of juvenile mental disorders, misspent leisure, and rising crime rates as evidence of growing delinquency among the young. Even Hall, who had welcomed the discovery of this new stage of life almost apocalyptically as a grand turning point in human evolution, warned of dangers on every side. "There is not only [physical] arrest, but perversion, at every stage, and hoodlumism, juvenile crime, and secret vice seem not only to increase, but to develop earlier in every civilized land." [1] As the new century began, public expectations of youth had never been higher, yet there was probably no period since the late eighteenth century when there were more complaints about youthful misconduct. One can begin to explain the ambivalence only when one looks closely at the historical process that extended the middle-class norm of adolescence to other groups which had not previously shared that particular conception of youth. Hope and fear were partners in that enterprise; and the widespread ambivalence toward youth can be accounted for in terms of the conflicts and contradictions that arose as parents, schoolmasters, and youth leaders attempted to impose one tradition of youth upon another. The result was greater conformity on one hand and greater delinquency on the other, because the conditions conducive to adolescence were not evenly distributed among the various strata of European society. The imposition of adolescence provoked strong resistance from a sizeable part of the population, particularly the laboring poor, with the result that for most of the period 1900–1950 the lines between conformity and delinquency were drawn along what were essentially class divisions.

We dealt, in the previous chapter, with the reasons why adolescence as a stage of life was confined to the middle classes and the very highest strata of the proletariat. Forces tending to spread adolescence downward were certainly present as the twentieth century began and, as figures for secondary education show (Table 6), more and more young people were being removed from the labor market during their teen years.

These numbers reflected the raising of the school-leaving age from 14 in 1918 to 15 in 1947, but they also displayed a genuine social tendency of parents to seek further training for their children—a trend which gained considerable momentum during the 1920s, regressed somewhat during the economic hardships of the 1930s, and then boomed after the Second World War.[2]

It would seem that the concept of "adolescence" was gradually but smoothly extending beyond the classes with which it had originated to an increasingly larger part of the laboring population. How-

---

[1] Hall, vol. 1, p. xiv; Key; also Demos and Demos, pp. 632–638.
[2] Lowndes, Chapter 6; Glass, p. 392.

TABLE 6

Percentage of Age Groups in Full-Time Education
in England, 1870–1962[a]

Age	Year			
	1870	1902	1938	1962
10 years	40	100	100	100
14 years	2	9	38	100
17 years	1	2	4	15
19 years	1	1	2	7

[a] Marsh, p. 218.

ever, we should be careful not to treat figures on secondary education as representing conclusive evidence that the acceptance of adolescence was proceeding at an even pace. On the contrary, the benefits of schooling were not evenly distributed and the bulk of the growth of secondary school and university populations came mainly from *within* the ranks of the middle classes themselves, not from additional recruitment of working-class boys and girls. In England, the chief beneficiaries of the 1902 Education Act, which permitted local authorities to support secondary education out of public funds, were the middle- and lower-middle strata. Of the cohort of boys born 1910–1929, some 39% of middle-class boys were getting some kind of secondary education, while, of working-class lads born in the same decades, only 10% were staying beyond the primary grades. If we look at the same cohort's university attendance, the disparity is even more obvious. Of middle-class boys, 8.5% were reaching higher education, as compared with only 1.4% of working-class boys.[3] In Germany, where the expansion of secondary and university education had been even more rapid during the first three decades of the century, over a half of these at university were from lower-middle class backgrounds. However, only 5.8% were from the urban or rural proletariat.[4]

The reasons for these disparities, which became even more pronounced during the Depression, are not hard to find if one looks at the economic conditions of the period 1900–1950. Seebohm Rown-

[3] Figures from Glass, p. 398.
[4] Kotschnig, pp. 13, 57; Samuel and Thomas, Chapters 3, 8.

tree, who went back to York in the 1930s to see what changes in poverty had occurred in the first three decades of the century, found a distressing 31% of the population still below the poverty line.[5] The same cycles of poverty operated, and although unemployment connected with the Depression contributed heavily to the poverty figures, there was no question that the situation of the children was much the same as earlier, with some 39% of the age-group 5–15 living below the poverty line in 1931.[6] Conditions such as these did not disappear until after World War II, when affluence finally began to be distributed more evenly across English society. In his final survey, made in 1961, Rowntree could report that only 3% of the English people were living in what he considered primary poverty— and almost all of these were aged persons.

The companions of poverty—namely, overcrowded housing, disease, and high death rates—also persisted among the poor until after 1945. Infant mortality was falling from a rate of 145 per 1000 births in 1900 to 63 in 1930, and then to 30 in 1950.[7] But again, these gains were not evenly distributed and, until very recently, the life chances of the poor continued to lag behind those of the economically better-off. As one might expect, England's poorest families were forced to continue the family strategy of high fertility to make up for their losses, so that the differential of family sizes among the various classes was actually increasing in the first four decades of the twentieth century, although fertility was dropping on all levels. Among the middle classes, family size dropped steadily until after 1945, when it showed something of an upswing, particularly among the professional elites. Lower-middle-class families were contracting at an even faster rate, while skilled workers were also showing signs of wanting fewer children. The family size of unskilled workers was declining, too, but not as fast as the classes above it and, therefore, its deviation from the national average was even more pronounced by 1930 than it had been in 1900.[8] Thus, while there would ultimately be convergence in family size as the professional middle classes began to produce more children after the War, the family strategy of the poor, for most of the period 1900–1950, was still at odds with that of the rest of the society.

---

[5] Laslett, *World We Have Lost,* p. 206.
[6] Rowntree, *Poverty and Progress,* p. 156.
[7] Marsh, p. 63; Bechtel, pp. 324–330.
[8] Wrigley, *Population and History,* pp. 186–187.

The demographic and economic pressures, which had traditionally forced children of this class out to work as soon as legally possible, went on unabated at a time when other groups were seeking further education for their children. The economic conditions that encouraged "boy labor" continued into the late 1930s, when more skilled jobs finally began to become available to the young.[9] Until then, there was still the old incentive for boys to begin with unskilled jobs, to neglect further education, and to resist all attempts to curb their independence. One sign of their continuing precocity was the continuing gap between their age of marriage and that of higher strata. The middle classes continued to marry late, and while the Depression tended to retard the marriage age of the lower classes somewhat, the difference in courtship patterns remained very great until after World War II, when the middle classes began to marry at younger ages.[10]

Evidence of persistent and even growing divergencies in the life cycles of various classes indicates some of the salient peculiarities of this period. On the institutional level, the raising of school-leaving ages and the provision of extracurricular activities indicated the middle classes' belief in the universality of adolescence. However, their expectations were not fulfilled and there was even evidence of a countermovement among lower-class youth who were resistant to the pressures for conformity that were being exerted upon them. The conflict between their life cycle and that of the more privileged was most obvious at the level of the school, where early leaving contradicted the goals of teachers and youth workers. But it was also evident at other social interfaces, where the traditions of youth clashed with the officially sanctioned norms of dependence and conformity. It was no accident that what the public came to regard as juvenile delinquency became the focus of attention precisely at the time that pressures to universalize adolescence were first becoming felt; for, despite their apparent dissimilarities, the two were related. The very traits that stigmatized certain youth as delinquent—namely, precocity and independence of adult authority—were precisely the opposite of those embodied by the model adolescent. Delinquency served to delineate the central features of conformity, and *vice versa*. Historically speaking, the two were, in fact, dialectically inseparable in their origins and development; and no discussion of one is complete

---

[9] Musgrove, *Youth and Social Order*, pp. 81–87.
[10] Musgrove, *Youth and Social Order*, p. 80; Goode, pp. 40–45.

without investigation of the other. We will, therefore, begin with the pressures toward conformity that youth were experiencing at the turn of the century, returning to discuss both the emergence of juvenile delinquency at the end of the century and the manner in which both trends define the period of roughly 1900 to 1950 as a unique era in the social history of youth.

I

We have seen in the previous chapter that adolescence was a product of the elite secondary schools. Until the 1880s, the assumption that "boys will be boys" was applied mainly to the inmates of those schools. Lower-class boys were regarded almost as a race apart, hardly amenable to the same handling, and perhaps even a little dangerous if too much indulged by education or leisure. The way poet George Crabbe had viewed the educational hierarchy in the seventeenth century still held almost to the end of the nineteenth.

> To every class we have a school assigned
> Rules for all ranks and food for every mind.

And Bishop Samuel Wilberforce was still talking in the 1850s of the danger of educating the lower classes, for it "would make everyone unfit to follow the plough, or else the rest of us would have nothing to eat." [11] Children of the lower orders were simply assumed to be "hardened" in their habits by teen-age, and although there were those like Mary Carpenter, the mid-Victorian juvenile reformer, who believed that love and attention might soften even the most vicious criminal, one of her closet collaborators, Matthew Davenport Hill, still spoke of juvenile delinquents as "little stunted men," whose most irradicable trait was their precocity.[12] Early-nineteenth-century reformers tended to focus their attention on the children of the poor, as if they were a separate species whose problems bore little or no

---

[11] Quotations from Stone, "Literacy and Education," pp. 71, 95.
[12] Hill quoted in Carlebach, p. 61.

resemblance to those of respectable boys and girls, who were to be treated according to entirely different standards.[13]

By the end of the 1880s, however, these distinctions were melting into a single approach to youth which assumed that "boys will be boys," "girls will be girls," regardless of class background. The style of youth work already well-developed in the elite schools but as yet little attempted among the children of the working class, namely a combination of games and drill, was now becoming universalized. Its proponents felt that they had found in boys' physical natures that common denominator which had eluded the earlier reformers. The early-nineteenth-century evangelical approach—which had been common to Johann Wichern's *Rauhe Haus*, the French colony for wayward youth at Mettray, and Carpenter's Red Lodge for girls—was giving way to means which were less reliant on religion or the intellect and more attentive to the psychology and the biology of the adolescent.[14] Playing and marching would somehow heal the deep class-divisions of the 1880s by wiping away the artificial barriers that divided boy from boy. "Class distinctions are difficult to maintain amid the healthy rivalries of the open air, and 'footer shorts' and naked bodies make for equality," wrote one enthusiast of the new method.[15]

The physical side of humanity, so distrusted by the older generation of youth workers, was rapidly becoming an obsession with the new. Shirt sleeves replaced clerical collars, and the forbidding evangelical demeanor gave way to a more informal, comradely attitude which characterized middle-class reformers from the 1880s onwards. Those like Charles Russell felt that the decline of the urban gang offered an opportunity to substitute adult supervision for the traditional leadership of older youths.[16] They would enter into boys' own fun and thereby win over those who could not be reached by standing in the pulpit or remaining behind the teacher's desk. This was the philosophy behind the English settlement movement of the 1880s, which flooded the city slums with earnest but hearty child-savers from the universities and public schools. They wished to meet delinquent youth more on their own terms, without the interference of the formality that their predecessors had felt necessary to put be-

---

[13] See Carlebach, Chapter 3.

[14] Useful surveys of international trends in the treatment of the delinquent young are provided by Robert Mennel, Chapters 4, 6; and Joseph Hawes.

[15] Hope, p. 302.

[16] Russell, *Manchester Boys*, p. 54.

tween themselves and their charges.[17] Their example was copied in the next decade by the Hamburg pastor, Walther Classen, who used sport and similar physical activities to draw working youth to his version of the settlement house.[18]

There was a strong dose of paternalism in this new fraternity, however. Middle class child-savers never quite forgot their position, and when Oxford students founded the Oxford Working Men's and Lads' Institute in 1884, it was, as they stated, because "the more forward classes of society have the power to show those below them how to live." [19] In Germany, too, there was a renewed attempt to establish the natural leadership of the upper classes. The "new feudalism," as some critics called it, was prompted by the obvious inroads that socialism and secularism were making among the working classes at that time. The German boys' club movement benefitted from the same conservative thrust that spurred and financed its English counterpart. According to its historian, the English club movement of the 1880s was "to preserve the established order in Church and State by educating the masses in manners and morals, and up to political responsibility, which meant, of course, acquiescence." [20] In both countries, the elites assumed that national interest required deeper involvement in the life of the poor; and, since children and youth were more accessible than adults, it was they who came in for increasing attention from the clergy, businessmen, and other leaders of middle- and upper-class opinion. "The children of the poor follow where they are led," stated E. J. Urwick at the turn of the century. "Their 'betters' are their leaders, and the example of their life determines the path." [21]

Percy Manning found vicars, schoolmasters, and reforming gentlewomen to be particularly adept at turning the traditions of youth to their own purposes. But nothing could surpass the ingenuity of the new youth movements, particularly the Boy Scouts and the *Wandervogel*, in the proliferation of games and rituals, all purporting to meet the natural, i.e., the instinctual, needs of the universal boy. Much of their adult-sponsored juvenalia was comical even to the youngsters

---

[17] On settlement movement, see Eagar, pp. 184–225; Simon, pp. 69–71, 78–85.

[18] Freudenthal, pp. 309–314.

[19] Publication/report, Report of Oxford Working Men's and Lads' Institute, 1893–1894 and 1898.

[20] Eager, p. 149. For similar anxiety among Oxford clergymen, see ms. source B, Mins. Oxford Clerical Assn., November 11, 1878, MS Top Oxon e 36.

[21] Urwick, "Conclusion," p. 318.

for whom it was intended, but entertainment was not the only purpose designed by the originators. The popularity of Kipling tales and solstice ceremonies reflected a longing for simpler, more natural, forms of life by men and women becoming uneasy about their own material progress. The new model youth-movements of the turn of the century were expressions of a general cultural movement among the European middle classes that bore strong traces of antimodernism as well as antimaterialism. Mixed together with the *fin de siècle* pessimism were also more tangible fears, anxieties about the decline of religion and the threat of working-class socialism to bourgeois society. Ranging along a spectrum that ran from romantic escapism to militant political conservatism, the major nonsocialist youth movements of this period projected the anxieties of ruling elites seeking to secure their position in a world disturbed by class conflict and international crisis.

The new movements were less eager to press the young into a mold of adult conventions, more willing to treat even their most frivolous pursuits as healthy and innocent. All were marked by a certain romanticization of youth as the source of personal and societal revitalization, a sign that the century-long struggle to establish a liberal civilization had left the middle classes exhausted in terms of political methods and ideologies. They tended, therefore, to view their role as child-savers as apolitical or, rather, as being above politics and political criticism. For example, Pastor Clemens Schultz, whose boys' organization in the Hamburg district of St. Pauli attracted considerable attention by its successes with working-class youths, declared that youth work must be "independent of every political and religious party." [22] For him, as for other English and German child-savers, working with the fresh, pure impulses of the young provided an exciting alternative to the shallow soulless civilization of industrial society. Thus, on one hand, the new movements attempted in an ostensibly apolitical manner to achieve cultural revitalization through the revivification of what they believed to be the archetypical form of youth, "adolescence." On the other hand, in so far as their forms and ideologies reflected elite values, they tended to constitute a conservative force despite all disavowals of political intention.

Through games, rituals, juvenile pursuits of all kinds, the post-Victorian youth leaders had set out to free the young from the bonds

---

[22] Freudenthal, p. 311. On the cultural and social background of this mood of fear and pessimism, see Stern; Mosse; Dangerfield; and Hynes, Chapter 2.

of an urban-industrial civilization grown rigid and corrupt in their eyes by virtue of its own material progress. In the process of seeking the physical and instinctual essence of boyhood they managed, however, to separate the notion of "youth" from its earlier associations, both from morality and spiritual strength. The emphasis on the physical and psychological sides of adolescence, a trend which we saw developing among the educated elites even before the turn of the century, was ultimately to reduce this phase of life to an object of scientific observation and clinical treatment by adults. What began as an effort to allow the young to live by the rules of nature, ended in chaining them to a new conformity sanctioned by positivist social science. Furthermore, in an attempt to protect the adolescent against the decadent world of adults, the young were separated from those civil and social rights which were their only real protection against the elders. These were some of the contradictions inherent in the history of youth beginning at the turn of the century.

II

In both purpose and method the new generation of self-appointed caretakers that emerged at the turn of the century diverged sharply from their Victorian predecessors. The metaphors of religious conversion had been replaced by a language of "treatment" and "cure," borrowed directly from the sciences. The object of attention at the turn of the century was the whole child, his or her social, economic, hygienic, as well as spiritual well-being. The new century had generated a reevaluation of the potentialities of child care and education, now defined more broadly to encompass whole areas of child life which had previously been left to the control of the family or the peer group. The social ideology behind these innovations was much more aggressive, less tolerant of failure than the more laissez-faire Victorian doctrines. The new metaphors of medical pathology reflected imperatives more scientific than moral in their origins. Just as the public interest dictated the immunization of all children against certain contagious diseases, so the future of the nation required the "immunization" of the younger generation against various social maladies to which urban-industrial society was believed particularly susceptible.[23]

The voluntaristic methods of an earlier generation came in for criticism. The pioneers in the field of child care had not gone far enough; they had left too much to parents of low character and faulty understanding; their work had been too much like charity, sufficient to maintain the *status quo* but inadequate for a period of more rapid change when internal unrest and external aggression threatened national survival. Adolescence was suddenly thrown into the battle against decadence at home and threat from abroad. After all, "with its adolescents from age to age rests the destiny of the nation, the race," wrote the English social reformer, C. E. B. Russell. "By them, if by any, will great deeds be planned, high thoughts translated into action. It is for us, so far as we are able, to see what opportunity, sympathetic guidance, and worthy example are theirs." [24]

Socialists like Ellen Key liked to think of the younger generation as committed to "the work of popular education, the temperance movement, the peace movement," but by the eve of World War I it was clear that a greater segment of adolescents had been captured, symbolically at least, by the forces of nationalism and conservatism. In Germany, General Keim's militaristic *Jugendverband* was only the first of a number of defense and sport clubs which preceded the founding of the strongly conservative *Jungdeutschlandbund* in 1911, which by 1914 had 750,000 members.[25] The Boer War gave a strong boost to similar attempts in England to capture the young for national service. It hurried along the passage of the 1902 Education Act, establishing state support for secondary education. "The very existence of the Empire depends upon sea power and school power," warned Michael Sadler, who was keenly aware of Britain's inferiority to Germany in the educational field.[26]

A similar language of national preparedness was part of Lord Robert's speech to the newly-formed Oxford Scout troops in 1909: "Let the watchwords of the boys be those of the Empire Movement—responsibility, duty, sympathy, and self-expression." [27] Local scout mas-

---

[23] On the growth of the medical metaphor, see Platt, p. 35; Morrison, pp. 38–40; Bray, *Town Child*; Hall, vol. 1, pp. xiv–xviii.

[24] Russell, "Adolescence," p. 55.

[25] Kitchen, pp. 136–142.

[26] Quoted in Lowndes, p. 72.

[27] Publication/report, Oxford and Dist. Boy Scouts' Chron.

ters took it as their prime duty to "convert the growing boys of today into the useful citizens of tomorrow," a goal they shared with their German counterparts of the *Jungdeutschlandbund*.[28] All the major child-saving movements of both countries—the English National Society for the Protection of Children and the German *Pestolozzi Stiftung*, the Mothers Union and the *Deutsch-Evangelischer Frauenbund*, the Council for the Industrial Advancement of Young People and the *Herberge zur Heimat*—had incorporated some elements of the conservative formula of patriotism and social reform into their official philosophies by 1914. Ideologies of national purpose, often couched in Social Darwinist terms of racial survival, had supplanted earlier religious and moral justifications, though the latter were still very much a part of public rhetoric. Appeal to nationalist justifications for social reform were carried to such length that not even babies were exempt from the call for national revitalization. "The race marches forward on the feet of little children," proclaimed Oxford's Infant Welfare Committee in 1919.[29]

Contributing to this change was the realization that Europe had entered into an age of democracy in which no class or group could be excluded from a share of responsibility and power. In this sense, the child savers proceeded on the same principle of preemptive social control that had led Robert Lowe to remark upon passage of the 1867 suffrage act: "We must educate our masters." [30] The feeling that the education of little children was insufficient to that purpose and that the years between school-leaving and young adulthood had also to include education, was one of the strongest motives of the extra-curricular youth-movements. What the schools could not accomplish, they would attempt to achieve. The fact that the first years of the twentieth century were not socially peaceful ones for either Germany or England gave added impetus to those caretakers who saw themselves as the disinterested mediators of class conflict. State legislation in Prussia in 1911, establishing public support for voluntary youth agencies, was directly related to the industrial unrest that had begun four years earlier.[31] A similar impulse was behind the foundation of Oxford's Balliol Boys' Club. "To encourage friendship between classes, so that there shall be no barriers between classes," was the

---

[28] Ms. source B, Mins. General Committee, Report of Scouts Friends Central Committee; also Pross, p. 163; and Laqueur, Chapter 8.
[29] Ms. source G, Mins. Oxford Subcommittee, June 1919, EE 1/18.
[30] Lowndes, pp. 3–17; Simon, Chapter 2.
[31] Pross, pp. 160–162.

way the wife of the founder, Mrs. A. L. Smith, later recalled her husband's vision.[32] We know from the records of the club's debate society that the truly divisive issues then agitating society were usually kept at a distance; and when in 1910 the sensitive issue of tariff reform was debated, the leaders found to their satisfaction that "nearly all the club seem staunch Tories."[33] But more typical was the experience of a Scout: "The Scout Movement teaches you to be good citizens, and not to know anything about politics"—an apt summation of the goals of this and other middle-class-sponsored youth organizations.[34]

The social and political precedents for the new approach to youth work were set in the 1880s, when the older evangelical approach began to be replaced by a more vigorous program of drill and athletics. The first to break with tradition in England was William Smith's Boys' Brigade, founded in 1883 with the novel idea of substituting a regimen of military drill for the conventional Bible reading. "Amazing and preposterous illusion!" wrote one patron of Smith's movement. "Call these boys 'boys,' which they are, and ask them to sit up in a Sunday class and no power on earth will make them do it; but put a five penny cap on them and call them soldiers, which they are not, and you can order them about until midnight."[35] The Boys' Brigade found that by dispensing with some of the earnestness and decorum that had burdened Victorian youth organizations it could attract even members of the working class. But the idea that physical exercise was more appropriate than spiritual remained suspect until the turn of the century when many of Smith's techniques were popularized through the Boy Scout movement.

By the time of the Boer War, English public opinion, including a segment of the previously antimilitaristic working class, had swung behind the drilling and marching.[36] The nation was now aware of the need for military preparedness; and one of the heroes of the Boer campaign, General Baden-Powell, was so impressed with the potential of the Boys' Brigades that he wrote his famous *Scouting for Boys* to be used by his friend Smith. As it turned out, Baden-Powell's formulation of an outdoor life for boys, influenced by the "wood-

---

[32] Remarks made by Mrs. A. L. Smith at the opening of the Keith Rae House, November 19, 1921. Ms. source I, Balliol papers.

[33] Ms. source I, Balliol log book, January 17, 1910.

[34] Paul, p. 21.

[35] Quoted in Simon, p. 65.

[36] Price, pp. 172–176; Hynes, pp. 17–32.

craft" romanticism of the American youth leader, Ernest Thompson
Seton, was so well-received as to justify the establishment of its own
organization separate from the Brigade. With the financial support
of conservative sources and with strong backing from his former army
comrades, the General created in 1908 the vastly more popular Boy
Scout movement.[37]

It is not surprising that, from the start, Scouting had a strong nationalist orientation. "The ideology underpinning Scouting was a
combination of Baden-Powell's own personalized brand of social-
imperialism, an omnipresent social darwinism and the Edwardian
cult of national efficiency," writes one of the movement's more critical historians.[38] Two-thirds of the leadership at the national level were
high-ranking military officers, and the first Executive Committee was
closely connected with the National Service League, a conservative
organization that had been pressing for universal conscription since
1902.[39] Although Baden-Powell went to some lengths to deny that his
troops were recruiting agencies for the Territorial Army, the suspicion
lingered that the uniforms, drilling, and weekend war games were
aimed at indoctrination. Some of the more liberal members of the
movement found the influence of the National Service League too
strong for their liking and they pressed the General to move in the
internationalist direction that had been part of the original charter
of Scouting. Sir Francis Vane left the movement in protest to the
continued militarism, but it was not until after World War I that the
more democratic and pacifist elements split off to form separate
organizations. The most important of these, John Hargrave's Kibbo
Kift Kindred and Leslie Paul's Woodcraft Folk, both of which had a
strong socialist orientation, reflected the disillusionment that many
felt with the conservative bias of Baden-Powell's brand of youth
work.[40]

The politics of Scouting were not the only thing that marked the
movement as upper class. Baden-Powell prided himself on his understanding of "boy spirit," and his fertile imagination was prodigious
in its production of rituals, songs, and festivals adapted to the malle-

[37] Springhall, pp. 125–158; also Paul Wilkinson, pp. 7–23.
[38] Springhall, p. 136.
[39] Springhall, p. 135; Paul Wilkinson, p. 14. In Oxford, the Scouts were closely
linked to the conservative National Service League. See ms. source B, Mins. General Committee, September 2, 1909, Dep. d 50. For further evidence of N. S. L.
activity among young people, particularly the schools, see ms. source B, Mins. Oxford Branch N. S. L., June 19, 1908, MS Top Oxon e 228.
[40] Springhall, pp. 153–155.

able nature of the adolescent; but he had little experience with, or understanding of, the life style of the working class. Bare knees and segregation from the opposite sex might suit middle-class boys, but could hardly be expected to be immediately popular with the vast majority of working lads. Scouting chose as its model the separation of adult and youth worlds already established in the elite public schools. As a single-sex organization, it made a virtue of the postponement of access to adult roles, maintaining that premature contact with the opposite sex endangered the masculinity of boys and corrupted the domesticized femininity of girls. Even when Lady Baden-Powell created the Girl Guides in 1909, the General insisted that nature required the activities of the two be kept quite separate. Boys would be boys and girls would be girls, and the two would never meet. A fanaticism for the temperate, ascetic life ensured the isolation of youths from the normal pleasures of adulthood. The ethic of the "good deed" implied a certain carefully controlled involvement in the civic and social life of the community, but stopped well short of the encouragement of actual social or political commit ments. "Be Prepared" meant to refrain from all prematurities, for the value to the nation of its young lay in the innocence and purity that were being endangered by the alluring amusements and rapid pace of urban-industrial society.

Little wonder, then, that the Scouts, with their abundance of rules and distrust of precocity, had greater success among the middle classes than among the proletariat. A poll of adult males made in 1966 revealed that while 44% of middle-class Englishmen had been Scouts at one time or another, only 25% of working-class males had had any contact with the movement.[41] The movement proceeded under the banner of classlessness, but it was stamped indelibly with the life style and ideology of those higher on the social ladder. The movement relied for membership on the heavily middle-class areas of southern England, including some parts of London that were lower-middle class in composition. It would appear that the working-class boys that it and similar movements attracted were primarily from the skilled segment of the proletariat, particularly those with aspirations for upward mobility, lads in school, whose parents could afford the money for uniforms and fees. Scout leaders, like Oxford's Jimmy Law, found that the poorer segments of the working class simply could not afford the outlay of time and money necessary to join their movement. Law would even tell parents that he would pay

---

[41] Springhall, pp. 138–139; also Paul, p. 36.

for the uniforms, tempting the boys by promising them a bugle so
that they could join the band.[42]

That same band was jeered by boys too poor or proud to join, and
in the first few years of its existence, the Scout movement, like the
Boys' Brigade before it, had to defend itself against verbal and physical abuse when it paraded in slum neighborhoods. Some Scout leaders recognized that bare knees and hiking breeches were just not acceptable to boys who were already at work and who valued their
precocity. They broke with the adolescent model of Baden-Powell
and, after World War I, established a series of youth movements that
were mixed-sex, and self-consciously aimed at the working class.
Leslie Paul's Kibbo Kift Kindred rejected as nonsense the middle-class
notion that coeducation "softens the fibres of boys and makes girls
hoydenish," and his movement provided a vote to all its members
regardless of age.[43] A. S. Neill taught Paul to regard the separation
of youth and adults as unproductive and undemocratic. Another
ex-Scout, John Hargrave, founded the Woodcraft Folk, whose motto
"Learn by doing, teach by being" expressed an entirely different
approach to the growth process, one much more in tune with the
life cycle of the English working class.[44] By the 1930s the various
socialist youth movements had a membership of about 100,000, small
in comparison with the million plus boys and girls claimed by the
various bourgeois organizations. The Cooperative Youth Movement
and the Girls Friendly Societies did have, however, the distinction
of having a higher percentage of members over 14 than any of the
other youth movements, a tribute to their success in providing mature pursuits for the young people they did attract. The low overall
enrollments reflected the fact that neither the Labor Party nor the
powerful trade unions had taken much interest in youth mobilization.
The apathy that characterized working-class youth during the Depression hurt all the youth movements, but the socialists the more so
because of their smaller resources.[45]

---

[42] Hiscock, p. 4.

[43] Pre-war working-class youth groups included the Socialist Sunday Schools
(founded 1909), Junior Cooperative Clubs (1895), and Girls' Friendly Society (1875).
Ernest Westlake's Order of Woodcraft Chivalry was founded in 1915; John Hargrave's Kibbo Kift Kindred in 1920; and Leslie Paul's Woodcraft Folk in 1925. See
Paul, pp. 31–48; Paul Wilkinson, pp. 19ff.

[44] Paul, p. 60.

[45] Paul, p. 48; Beard, "Appendix"; publication/report, Disinherited Youth, pp.
106–118.

III

In Germany, too, old-fashioned corporate and denominational youth organizations predominated until the early twentieth century. Early evangelising efforts like Johann Wichern's *Rauhe Haus* (1833) and Adolf Kolping's *Rheinischer Gesellenbund* (1846) were directed primarily at the children of the poor. Later religious youth organizations such as the Protestant *Christlicher Verein junger Männer* (1883) and the Catholic *Quickborn* (1909) assumed a broader social constituency, but retained a strong denominational character. Various guild and trade unions sponsored activities for their younger members and, beginning in Holland in 1885, socialist youth movements spread across the continent, reaching Germany in 1904. Various party groups had also begun to organize junior sections around the turn of the century, the Catholic Center Party's *Windthorstbünde* establishing the precedent in 1895. The conservative *Jungdeutschlandbund* was founded in 1911, adding to the list of sport and military training groups supported by the various antisocialist parties and organizations. All manner of temperance organizations had also entered the field before 1900, adding to the number of groups vying for the attentions of the younger generation.[46]

Not until 1901, however, was there an organization that claimed no ulterior interest other than youth itself. In that year, the *Wandervogel* took form in a Berlin suburb under the direction of a charismatic but eccentric stenography teacher by the name of Karl Fischer. Members of Fischer's original group who could not tolerate his authoritarian personality left to form their own movements, but the various branches of the original stem all owed much to his original impulse.[47] A German counterpart of the English Boy Scouts, the *Deutscher Pfadfinderbund*, was formed in 1911 but it never gained the popularity enjoyed by the *Wandervogel*. Not so much in terms of numbers but in the way it shaped the approach to adolescence in

---

[46] Pross, pp. 469–482; Laqueur, pp. 66–73.
[47] Laqueur, especially Chapters 2–3.

Germany, it remained the most influential of the youth movements, leaving its mark on the civil as well as the social status of the young for several decades to come.

The ultimate importance of the *Wandervogel* lay not in its myriad organizational forms, but in the historical social reality that it reflected. At first glance, it would appear that it represented a tendency very different from English Scouting. The latter, so archetypically British in its disciplined compromise of middle-class utilitarianism and the sporting instinct of the aristocracy, contrasted stylistically with the *Wandervogel,* whose defiantly unconventional manners and appearance seem to reflect a revival of the youthful radicalism of the early nineteenth century. The *Wandervogel* seemed to challenge the social conventions of the German aristocracy and, initially at least, placed itself in opposition to its militarism as well. Their bizarre dress, uninhibited behavior, and reputation for sexual liberation shocked the Wilhelminian upper crust and earned for the movement a reputation for rebelliousness that contrasted sharply with the sober image of English Scouting.[48]

Yet, beneath the differences lay similarities of origin and purpose. The *Wandervogel* was also the product of middle-class concerns, though the history of the German bourgeoisie had been sufficiently different from that of the English so as to produce very different ways of handling adolescence. Relations between the middle and upper classes in Germany had been marked not by compromise but by tension. The German state and its educational institutions remained highly stratified, the aristocracy clinging to the traditional military schools, the middle classes monopolizing the day *Gymnasia*. We have seen that the socially integrative English public school produced a single model of boyhood. In contrast, the German educational system afforded no such concensus.[49]

Germany's military academies turned out models of conformity. The day *Gymnasium*, lacking the features of a total institution and distributing the important tasks of education and socialization between itself and the home, produced a troubled adolescent.[50] The prolonged, lonely social moratorium expressed itself in the kind of restless self-absorption described so well in the novels of Hesse and other contemporaries; and even before Karl Fischer began to or-

---

[48] Laqueur, pp. 25–31, 56–65.
[49] Muchow, *Sexualreife und Sozialstruktur,* pp. 27–70; on the reflection of this in literature, see Hicks, pp. 105–115.
[50] See pp. 117–118.

ganize his hiking and camping trips, the students of Germany's academic secondary schools were spilling out of the cities into the countryside in search of the freedom and companionship they could find neither at home nor in school. "The essence of the *Wandervogel* was flight from the confines of the school and city into the open world, away from academic duties and the discipline of everyday life into an atmosphere of adventure," recalled Göttingen's Frank Fischer.[51]

Although the middle classes themselves were divided in their attitude toward the self-assertion of their sons and daughters, concern for the disturbing effects of adolescence ultimately led them to support movements like the *Wandervogel* which attempted to bridge the gap between the home and the school by offering a comprehensive approach to the young. The rhetoric of generational conflict should not obscure the degree to which the *Wandervogel* was adult-sponsored and -directed from the very start.[52] Although certainly less strictly regulated than the Scouts, the movement reflected the concerns of middle-class parents at every point in its development. The paradox of youthful rebelliousness supported and encouraged by adults is more apparent than real, however, for it reflected the situation of the German middle class itself, which, caught between a militant working class on one hand and a semifeudal military and bureaucratic elite on the other, sought to create a movement that would meet the special needs of its youth while at the same time avoiding the possibly dangerous social and political consequences of their deviation from the cultural norms of the upper classes.

In its initial phases, the movement was indeed highly individualistic, even anarchical, in its antagonism toward all conventional restraints on the freedom of expression. Yet, it was also productive of its own kinds of conformity, many of which we would recognize today as typical of the life styles associated with adolescence. The movement was like the English Boy Scouts in its emphasis on small groups, though initially it relied much less on the rules and regulations that Baden-Powell felt so necessary to boyhood conduct. The intimate circles that Karl Fischer called his tribes (*Horde*) were, like the troops and dens of scouting, functional substitutes for the peer-group culture that was repressed by the German system of secondary education. Around the campfire or in the privacy of what they called their "Nests," the *Wandervogel* were encouraged to be free in the expression of their deepest emotions, safe in the knowledge that

---

[51] Frank Fischer; Rabe, pp. 109–110; Lütkens.
[52] On leadership, see Jantzen; also Freudenthal, pp. 297–305.

none of the Victorian taboos applied in the company of their peers. The comradely "Heil" had replaced the despised formalism of conventional greetings, serving also to underline the equality that went with the new-found sense of fraternity. Fischer's model was the Medieval vagabond, carefree and indifferent to all the conventions and responsibilities associated with adulthood. Bare knees and hatless heads initially shocked Wilhelminian society, but gradually the innocent pleasures of hiking and camping found acceptance among the upper classes.[53]

The comradeship of the *Wandervogel* resembled that of the earlier *Sturm und Drang* movement, except insofar as the new Romantics were younger and their modes of expression less mature than their eighteenth- and early-nineteenth-century predecessors, most of whom were socially and intellectually quite adult. As adolescents they were incapable of artistic or poetic expression of the kind that had distinguished the earlier movement, yet they retained its ascetic if not its aesthetic features. A strong temperance element existed from the start and their attitude toward sexuality was distinctly puritanical. Even the "homoeroticism" that was preached by some of its leaders was more platonic than genital and, if the *Wandervogel* were prone to any perversion, it was the neglect rather than the encouragement of heterosexual development.[54] Even after the entry of girls into the movement, there was strong resistance to mixed activities. Folk dancing was preferred because it was in the round and avoided the premature pairing-off of couples. Lederhosen and dirndle were scarcely high-fashion at the turn of the century; nevertheless they were part of the attributes of innocence that characterized *Wandervogel* circles. So naive were the relationships between the sexes that many graduates of the movement later had difficulty adjusting to the conditions of marriage.[55]

Indeed, it would be interesting to know how many other difficulties were encountered by those for whom adolescence was such an unusually drawn-out process. Movement literature dwells so heavily on the value of the social moratorium provided by *Wandervogel* culture that it is difficult if not impossible to gain a clear picture of the kinds of burdens age-segregation imposed on its members. The fact that so many lives were cut short by World War I complicates the

---

[53] Pross, pp. 75–99; Laqueur, pp. 25–31; Weidelmann, Chapter 2.

[54] Interesting discussion of homosexuality in Laqueur, pp. 56–65; and Muchow, *Sexualreife und Sozialstruktur*, pp. 30–32; Mosse, pp. 176–177.

[55] Pross, p. 129.

question of the effects of prolonged dependence. Its critics claimed that *Wandervogel* institutionalized the worse effects of self-indulgence; supporters emphasized the regenerative effects of extending the possibilities of growth beyond the age limits that civilization had previously imposed.[56] In the end, the cult of youth won this argument, for even before 1914 there were signs that the kind of vitality that the youth movement represented was becoming fashionable among the previously straightlaced members of the Wilhelminian upper classes.

Spontaneity, sensitivity, and the other spiritual qualities of *Wandervogel* culture were hardly those to attract support among the military or the bureaucracy. On the other hand, the emphasis on physical exercise and the training of the will fit well with the demands for discipline emanating from those quarters as World War I approached.[57] The German middle classes were at odds with these elites culturally, but politically they remained loyal to the patriotism enunciated by militarism. Despite its unconventional social and cultural features, the essentially apolitical stance of the movement made it an acceptable alternative to the socialist movements that were beginning to make inroads among students just before the First World War.[58] The inner freedoms that the adolescent tribes talked so much about made no mention of civil liberties; their sense of equality was confined to members of their own class and thus did not threaten the social order; and the vaunted spirit of fraternity carried sufficient patriotic conviction so as to be perfectly acceptable. It is not without significance that the *Wandervogel* enjoyed its greatest growth at a time of social and political unrest; for, to parents indoctrinated by pedagogues and psychologists to view adolescence as the critical stage of life, a movement so dedicated to the postponement of social and political choice was extremely attractive.[59] The *Wandervogel* itself was, by 1911, moving closer to movements like the *Jungdeutschlandbund*, whose scarcely disguised antisocialist partisanship had made it the most popular single youth-movement in Germany by 1914. Even though *Wandervogel* still held themselves aloof from the military style of groups like the German Boy Scouts, it was clear that, beneath the unpolitical exterior, there lay commitments that were

---

[56] Muchow, *Sexualreife und Sozialstruktur*, pp. 44–45; Mosse, pp. 171–175; Stern, pp. 266–274.

[57] Kitchen, pp. 139–142; Rabe, pp. 110–114; Laqueur, pp. 57–58.

[58] Laqueur, pp. 32–38, 41–49; Pross, p. 157.

[59] Pross, p. 162.

every bit as conservative as the more overtly partisan youth groups.[60]

The implicit middle-class orientation of the movement also made it impossible for it to achieve the classless character its founders had envisioned. Leaders continued to talk of the universal appeal of hiking and folk dancing, but the great mass of the nation's youth had little of the leisure time or pocket money required of regular members. The innocent, puritanical life style of the *Wandervogel* bore no resemblance to the experience of working-class children, who were brought up to value a quite different kind of masculinity and femininity. Little wonder that, on passing through working class districts, the hikers were greeted with jeers and even physical abuse. Campers found, as did the early Boy Scouts, that peasants were also very unlikely to welcome city boys with bare knees and strange habits.[61] Even before the socialists established their own youth organizations in 1904, it was quite clear that in style and ideology the bourgeois movements offered little that could attract many working youth.

The leadership of the *Wandervogel* nevertheless retained the pretense of classlessness and nonpartisanship. They continued to believe in the innocent functions of *Kriegsspiele* (war games) even in the face of the mounting hysteria of war preparedness. Not until war itself broke upon Europe did they abandon the pretense of innocence, and then, with a naïveté that was typical of their movement, made war a holy cause. "Nothing divides the *Wandervogel* from manhood," proclaimed the first war edition of *Der Wandervogel*. "We are not special. We wish to be considered like all the others, men in the fullest sense of that term." [62] But whatever demands the war may have made on these young recruits, it was in its peculiar way a continuation of the youth-prolonging institutions of peacetime. As Harry Pross has pointed out, the trenches provided a further moratorium on all the social and political choices that this generation felt so ill-equipped to handle. For young men like Frank Fischer, the *Wandervogel* had represented "flight from the confines of the school and the city"; now death on the battlefield was to be their ultimate escape.[63]

War deprived the organization of its leadership, and on their return from the trenches the surviving *Wandervogel* had little desire to ex-

---

[60] Pross, p. 163; Laqueur, p. 73.

[61] Gillis, "Conformity and Rebellion," pp. 256–257.

[62] Newspaper/periodical, *Der Wandervogel*, Heft 9–10, 1914.

[63] A rich source of material are the unpublished notebooks of Frank Fischer, ms. source A.

change the field grey for *lederhosen*. The youth groups spawned by the revolutionary years 1918–1919 were more political, and their membership older. Yet, the same theme of rebellion against society persisted, only this time specifically directed against the Weimar Republic, and having a much more overt rightist orientation than before. The cult of strength and joy served the *Freikorps* and other proto-Fascist movements well. The classless image of the pre-war years fell away and the successors of the *Wandervogel* emerged as strongly antisocialist. In Göttingen, for example, the remnant of the prewar *Wandervogel* membership found their way mainly into the right-wing *Jungnationaler Bund,* a pattern similar to other German communities.[64]

Yet, while the *Wandervogel* of the old style vanished, the concept of adolescence that it had created became a force of its own, both in the bourgeois youth movements of the 1920s and in the greatly expanded public youth services that were established after the war. Pedagogues and psychologists like Gustav Wyneken and Eduard Spranger, who had been influenced by the earlier movement, had in the meantime universalized the experience of pre-war middle-class youth into theories of adolescence that were now accepted, in the name of science, as universally applicable. Ironically, the most notable contribution of the *Wandervogel,* a social–historical movement associated with rebelliousness, was a new kind of conformity which was institutionalized in schools and extracurricular organizations as meeting the supposed needs of adolescents. The image of dependence and immaturity gradually became the operating principle for all state and voluntary agencies concerned with the education and care of that age-group. By 1933 the dependent status of those 14 to 18 was taken for granted; and the Nazi declaration of that year, officially requiring the association of all youth with the Hitler Youth, only completed a trend toward compulsory supervision already well under way.[65]

---

[64] Waite, pp. 207ff.
[65] Laqueur, pp. 50–55. For the evolution of the Göttingen youth organizations, see publication/report, Berichte den Jugendpfleger.

IV

Despite the obvious political differences, it is clear that socially both England and Germany were moving along the same general path toward the definition of "adolescence" as a subordinate, dependent category of the population. Coercive legislation, aimed at increasing society's control over children even when this conflicted with the interests of parents, gained considerable momentum in England after the founding of the National Society for the Prevention of Cruelty to Children in the 1880s. "Our grandfathers were great on the 'rights' of parents," argued Canon Horsley. "We have had to enforce their 'obligations,' and if necessary to destroy their 'rights' when these are made to injure the child." [66] The Prevention of Cruelty and Protection of Children Act of 1889 provided for the removal of children from homes that the courts ruled dangerous to their health and well-being, which often meant poverty households where children had to work to maintain the family income. This was a prelude to the more comprehensive Childrens Act of 1908, that provided stiffened penalties for child abuse and banned, among other things, the sale of tobacco to children under 16 and the entry into taverns by children under 14. These and subsequent legislative amendments (1933 and 1963) had the effect of eliminating "the sharp distinction between those children who come before the juvenile courts because they have committed offences and those who require care, protection or control," and were a major step toward placing all minors under the supervision of the state.[67]

The evolution of British court and penal procedures paralleled and reinforced this trend, beginning in the 1850s with the establishment of reformatory and industrial schools for offenders under 16. In 1899, imprisonment of the members of this age-group in the same facilities as adults was prohibited. Probation for young offenders was estab-

---

[66] Publication/report, Report of Oxford and County Branch, 1914.
[67] Boss, p. 15. Musgrove, "Decline of Educative Family," pp. 182–183; on Germany, see Muchow, *Sexualreife und Sozialstruktur,* pp. 18–19.

lished in 1907; and, in 1908, justices were empowered to deal in separate closed session with those under 16. The Children and Young Persons Act of 1933 extended still further the principle of special summary jurisdiction, so that young persons up to the age of 17 were, effectively, subject to a system of jurisdiction that assumed those before the court to have less than adult responsibility for their actions.[68] The traditional adversary proceeding was, therefore, eliminated in favor of a procedure in which the opinion of "experts" was substituted for the arguments of lawyers. In the name of social and psychological understanding, a system of treatment was substituted for that of justice.[69]

Originally, the arguments for the protection of the child were moral and religious in character. By 1910, however, science was increasingly invoked to justify the control and confinement of the young. Social Darwinism had alerted the educated public to the dangers of physical and mental degeneration and it was in the name of the survival of the race that compulsory physical and military training were argued. To Eugen Sandow, writing in the journal of the Children's Protection League, "scientific physical training sharpens the intellect and develops valuable moral qualities. A splendid physique is rarely accompanied by a vicious trait; it is the loafer, the weedy, the sluggard who is the bane of the school and the degenerate of after life." [70] The medical literature of the day was filled with the kind of behaviorism that proclaimed "mind and body are so interwoven that care of one implies the care of the other." [71] Henceforth, national as well as individual character would be viewed as a function of sound genes, square meals, and plenty of cold baths. Reduced to its physiological and neurological fundamentals, adolescence was obviously too important a matter to be left to parents or youth themselves. "Speaking generally, the longer children are at school and the longer they are away from the influence of their homes, the better strangers do find them," noted Dr. Eric Pritchard. "It is in my mind a very significant fact that recent statistics show that the average number of successes is greater and of failure less in our industrial and reformatory centers than in our ordinary elementary schools. That is to say, the organized and ordered discipline of industrial schools can

---

[68] Boss, pp. 19–35.
[69] Platt, pp. 142–143; Simonsohn, pp. 19–20.
[70] Newspaper/periodical, *National Health* 1 (9)(1909), p. 81.
[71] Newspaper/periodical, *National Health* 2 (15)(1910), p. 34.

make respectable citizens out of a class of children who are quite unmanageable and even anti-social in their own homes." [72]

Nowhere was the substitution of scientific judgment for common sense more noticeable than in the treatment of juvenile sexuality. This had always been a concern of child savers, but never before had it been viewed through such a deterministic perspective. Masturbation, or what the Victorians liked to call "self-abuse," had been causing increasing anxiety since the late eighteenth century. [73] Medical men and moralists (often one and the same) had attributed the most terrible consequences to it; everything from impotence to epilepsy, with melancholia and suicidal depression heading the list of symptoms of what was commonly called "masturbatory insanity." Dr. Henry Maudsley, a leading English physician, could write in 1867 that masturbation "gives rise to a particular and disagreeable form of insanity characterized by intense self-feeling and conceit." But by 1895 Dr. Maudsley had significantly modified his views, indicating a major shift in medical and moral opinion. A direct cause-and-effect relationship was no longer demonstrable; rather, both were the effect of something he called "adolescent insanity." Henceforth, both melancholy and masturbation were to be diagnosed as being due to "the process of adolescence and not to the particular vice." [74] Level of maturity rather than level of morality was the cause of the problem, after all.

It would be some time, however, before masturbation and other sexual delinquencies of youth entirely escaped the clutches of moralism. Doctors like Maudsley still referred to it as a "vice"; and even the most enlightened sex educators of that era, including G. Stanley Hall and Havelock Ellis, did not break entirely with the Victorian notion that childhood sin was the cause of adult depravity. [75] Instead, they subsumed the old cause-and-effect relationship under a new, even more deterministic psychological theory, arguing that the course of an individual's development in adolescence necessarily had consequences for his or her formation as an adult. There was something both comforting and frightening about this substitution: comforting to this "enlightened" generation of adults, who could deplore old-

---

[72] Newspaper/periodical, National Health 4 (37)(1912), p. 249.

[73] Spitz, pp. 499ff; Hare, pp. 1–25.

[74] Comfort, Anxiety Makers, pp. 76–77.

[75] Hall, vol. 1, pp. 434, 439; Ellis, pp. 20–21, 382; Edward Carpenter, pp. 102–120; Bloch, p. 690. General discussion of sexual controversy in England is provided by Samuel Hynes, Chapter 5.

fashioned punitive attitudes toward sex without having to abandon their middle-class respectability by advocating an actual change in sexual behavior; frightening to the adolescent, to whom the burden of discipline was now shifted, and whose responsibility it now was to work out a balance between what were loosely defined as the "natural instincts" of youth and the equally vague consequences of self-indulgence in the impulses of their own sexuality.[76] Little wonder that youths themselves showed greater personal confusion and anxiety under the new "law of nature" than under the previous regime of moral absolutes.

V

In England, work with youth above school age (14 in 1918) had been traditionally left to voluntary agencies. This legacy of nineteenth-century liberalism was modified in 1916 with the creation of official Juvenile Organization Committees, designed to encourage and coordinate on a voluntary basis all public and private youth work.[77] The reform had been spurred by rising rates of juvenile crime during the war and it was clear that the state would have liked to have pressed its controls further had conditions permitted.[78] But financial difficulties prevented the 1921 Education Act from imposing compulsory further education on school-leavers, and most local J.O.C. remained weak throughout the 1920s and 1930s. A census of school-leavers in the 1930s showed that only 30–40% had any contact with youth organizations; and commissions on both youthful unemployment and physical conditioning brought in reports that provided further ammunition for those who wished to strengthen

---

[76] See Cominos, pp. 241–242. Typical of the cautionary literature was Edward B. Kirk's *A Talk with Boys About Themselves,* a book which provided two sets of illustrations of the reproductive organs, one explicit and the other less so, allowing parents to tear out the first if they thought it inappropriate for their sons. For other such literature, see Blackwell; Lyttelton, *Mothers and Sons;* Lyttelton, *Training of Young.* On the German literature, see Spitz, p. 500.

[77] Brew, p. 89.

[78] Beard, pp. 139–149. Mannheim, p. 122.

controls.[79] Yet, it was not until a second war broke out that the English government moved with great energy. In November, 1939, a National Youth Committee was created, with powers and funds much greater than the earlier J.O.C. The 1944 Education Act, which made secondary education universal and raised the leaving-age to 15, strengthened the hand of the youth service by making coordination with its committees compulsory and by providing for the training of professional youth workers. But the reliance on voluntary organizations continued, and for the rest of the 1940s and the 1950s, England's youth service was plagued by public indifference and governmental austerity.[80] Of England's youth programs, 80 to 90% continued to be privately funded, and a commission reporting in 1960 found only one in three youths, aged 14 to 18, enrolled in a recognized organization.[81] By that time, however, youth workers were beginning to recognize that coercion was neither in their interests nor in those of youth. Changing concepts of youth work reflected the changing perception of adolescence itself, and an era in English social history came to an end.

The greater involvement of the state in German society reflected a political and economic history characterized by higher levels of social conflict. England's middle classes did not have to face the same kind of militant proletarian movements as did their German counterparts, a major reason why the latter supported stronger controls over the youthful part of the population. A precedent for the care and protection of juveniles was provided by the various sumptuary laws relating to apprentices, relics of the social policies of monarchical absolutism. These were turned to a new and different purpose when, in 1878, schoolboys in Prussia were forbidden the use of taverns, a favorite haunt of the semisecret drinking clubs (*Verbindungen*) that had been a part of scholastic existence for centuries. Reasons of health and morality given at the time concealed a deeper sort of anxiety, for it was clear that the ruling class was worried about the

---

[79] Ms. source I, Cole Papers, "Report on How the War is Affecting Youth Organizations in Oxford," prepared by E. Gili, September 1941, as part of social survey of Oxford. Also publication/report, City of Oxford Youth Committee, 1941, which showed 50% of those 14–20 enrolled in some organization. This was a rise of 14% over the 1938–1939 figure. See publication/report, Report of Oxford Council. Also ms. source I, Cole Papers, "Voluntary Services in Oxford," prepared by C. Craven, 1842; E. Eric Roberts; publication/report, Disinherited Youth, pp. 114ff; Brew, p. 96.
[80] Brew, pp. 92–95.
[81] Publication/report, Youth Service in England and Wales, pp. 8–12.

social and even the political results of uncontrolled activity among the nation's educated youth. No less an authority than the Prussian Minister of Interior, Friedrich Graf zu Eulenberg, contended that *Verbindungen* constituted a danger "not simply to the students and their future, but directly to family life and even to the status of their class." [82] Anxiety did not diminish with the passage of restrictive ordinances, however, and by 1899 the government was considering even more comprehensive legislation, this time covering all adolescents, workers as well as students. Apparently, control was ineffective as long as the prohibitions were not universal, a deficiency in the original legislation which was attested to by local police who encountered great difficulty in enforcing the 1878 edicts.[83]

Such extension did not come until 1915; but, in the meantime, school and university authorities had discovered new causes of concern. In Göttingen, police were keeping careful watch in 1904 on left-wing activity among students.[84] For their part, the middle classes of the town founded the *Nationalliberaler Jugend Verein,* an antisocialist organization aimed at rallying support for patriotic causes.[85] Political organization of juveniles was illegal in Germany, but despite these restrictions both the socialists and the conservatives found ways of reaching youth. The former worked through the regular Social Democratic Party, while the latter used all kinds of sport and patriotic organizations as instruments of indoctrination. The conservative effort was made a good deal easier by the Prussian youth service legislation of 1911, which authorized local officials to encourage all nonsubversive youth organizations by providing funds and facilities. Groups like the militaristic *Jungdeutschlandbund* grew enormously under this program and, prior to 1914, bodies like Göttingen's *Kriegsverein* had begun extensive programs of premilitary training for boys.[86] In 1914, only an estimated one-sixth of Berlin youth were enrolled in any recognized youth organization, but with the coming of war extensive mobilization powers strengthened the hand of Germany's youth services, granting them the right to compel premilitary

---

[82] Ms. source C, Pol. Dir., Besuch der Wirtschaften durch Schüler, Directive of Minister of Interior Eulenberg, June 1882, Fach 52 No. 8.

[83] Ms. source C, Pol. Dir., Besuch der Wirtschaften durch Schüler, Directive of Minister of Interior Eulenberg, June 1882, Fach 52 No. 8.

[84] Ms. source C, Pol. Dir., Sozialdemokratische Bewegungen unter den hiesigen Studierenden, 1904–1905, Fach 161 No. 16.

[85] Ms. source C, Pol. Dir., Nationalliberaler Jugend Verein Göttingen, 1904–1921, Fach 161 No. 20.

[86] Pross, p. 163; Laqueur, p. 72; Kitchen, pp. 129–138.

training and thus lending further prestige to the conservative organizations.[87]

Ironically, legal restrictions on the young increased at the same time that the conditions of war provided youth with a freedom and status it had not known prior to 1914. During hostilities, the pre-war trend toward the exclusion of youth from highly-paid industrial jobs was temporarily reversed. The military services, competing with one another for enlistments, offered their youth brigades (*Jugendkompagnien*) the forbidden fruits of wine, women, and song; and with fathers, teachers, and elder brothers at the front, both adolescent boys and girls enjoyed unprecedented freedom as well as greater earning power. Naturally, this new status brought the young into conflict with those authorities charged with the care and protection of the rising generation. Reaction was not slow to set in, and by 1915 there was widespread support in school and government circles for a curb on what seemed to be an epidemic of juvenile crime and misbehavior. In October of that year, sale of liquor and tobacco to youths under 17 (later lowered to 16) was forbidden under martial law. Movie theatres, dance halls, and even ice cream parlors were declared off limits; curfews were imposed, loitering prohibited, and the sale of certain categories of pulp literature banned. Ordinances fixing the levels of take-home pay for those under 18 were also instituted, but met with such strong resistance from working-class parents that they were soon abandoned. Yet, the ban on youthful assembly was extended even to courtrooms and places of civic business, thus legally quarantining adolescents from political as well as social life.[88]

The effectiveness of these decrees seems to have been limited; working youths appear to have successfully evaded all but the most repressive measures and even school boys found life a good deal freer. This only reinforced the near hysteria that arose in middle-class circles, whose fear of juvenile delinquency and degeneracy was unabated at war's end. In 1918 a new element of fear—democratic revolution—had been added to the cauldron of anxiety. New political

---

[87] Ms. source C, Ober., Jugendflege, Kriegszeit und Aufgaben der Jugendpflege, December 1914, E. 17. Publications/reports, Jahresbericht des Ortsausschusses; and Berichte den Jugendpfleger, December 11, 1915.

[88] Ms. source C, Pol. Dir., Verordnungen betreffend jugendliche Personen, 1915–1944, Fach 59 No. 12. In particular, the orders of Army Command, October 30, 1915; Ministry of Trade and Industry, February 29, 1916. Further evidence on wartime restrictions is provided by ms. source C, Felix–Klein, Militärische Verbereitung der Jugend, 1914–1918, 16 E. 3; and Brieke.

freedoms seemed to threaten the very foundations of the old order, with the result that, instead of relaxing controls, every effort was made to strengthen them. The caretaker elites were strongly resistant to any attempt to disestablish their wartime powers, and the governments of the Weimar Republic were quick to support them through further legislation. Convinced that democracy required greater rather than less discipline, the Ministries of Welfare and Education ordered reorganization of local youth authorities, with the aim of extending state control over voluntary youth organizations.[89] The brief revolutionary period 1918–1919 had thrown up a whole new set of political youth organizations on both the left and the right, and as early as December 1918 the youth service moved to defuse these movements by encouraging them to sink their differences in a common effort to provide for the needs of the younger generation. Leaving aside any mention of responsibility to the fledgling Weimar democracy, the youth workers defined their mission in unmistakably conservative terms: "The task of the youth service is to cooperate in the cultivation of happy, physically healthy, morally strong youth, filled with a sense of community and a love of home and country." [90]

By devoting itself to "depoliticization," the youth service placed itself firmly, if unwittingly, on the side of the conservative forces that were bent on maintaining a social and political status quo. In Göttingen, youth workers readily cooperated with the police in excluding Communist youth from public facilities. Throughout the 1920s they consistently showed themselves more tolerant of right-wing youth groups, with the exception of the Nazis whose activities were considered too radical by the Prussian authorities.[91] In their choice of social activities, as well as in their political orientation, the caretaker organizations betrayed a distinctly middle-class character. Their model was a modified version of prewar *Wandervogel*, only with less emphasis on freedom of individual expression. Like the earlier movement, they preferred sex segregation. Folk dancing was favored because of its group character, and premature pairing-off of young

---

[89] Ms. source C, Ober., Fürsorge für Schulentlassene Jugend, Grundlegende Erlasse betreffend Förderung der Jugendpflege in Preussen, 1920, E. 17.

[90] Ms. source C, Ober., Fürsorge für Schulentlassene Jugend, Directives of December 17, 1918, and November 22, 1919, E. 17.

[91] These relations can be traced through publication/report, Berichte den Jugendpfleger, 1915–1930; ms. source C, Pol. Dir., Die Kommunistische Jugendabteilung, 1921–1932, Fach 155 No. 4, and Jung Stahlhelm and Jungdeutschen Orden, Fach 153 No. 20 and No. 27. Also Laqueur, Chapter 16.

people was strenuously discouraged.[92] As the old religious atmosphere of German youth work was replaced by a more open, hearty
spirit, the numbers of members grew. Enrollment in youth organizations tripled in Göttingen in the years 1921–1930 and, although we
have no social breakdown of the membership, it would seem that
the vast majority of recruits were from the middle, lower-middle,
and top strata of the working classes. The latter tended to keep to
themselves in organizations sponsored by craft guilds, trade unions,
and the proletarian political parties, however. As in England, it was
only a small minority of the working classes, mostly the skilled, who
wanted much to do with adolescent-model youth movements.[93]

Schools were no more successful in meeting the needs of the new
democracy for political commitment and social equality. In 1922 the
Prussian Ministry of Education ordered a ban on the wearing of political insignia, symbolic of its effort to exclude all civic concerns from
the schools. Teachers were told that their responsibility lay in preparing students for future political choices rather than present commitments, a charge welcomed by that overwhelmingly conservative
profession. In place of party insignia, they were only too happy to
substitute distinctive school caps. Sports, scholastic journalism, and
other extracurricular activities multiplied as alternatives to the political and social activities considered dangerous by school authorities.[94]
Progressive in the sense that it encouraged closer cooperation among
students, parents, and teachers, the extension of the reach of the
school to areas previously outside academic jurisdiction also had its
conservative aspects. The more strenuously the school pursued its
charge of creating a neutral "sense of community," the more it became a socially exclusive and authoritarian institution, reinforcing the
immaturity of its inmates while at the same time segregating them
from working youth. By the mid-1920s, German schoolboys and
schoolgirls were restricted by regulations that prohibited unauthor-
ized participation even in dancing lessons. Breach of any rule could
mean forfeiture of scholarship and the foreclosure of opportunity for
further upward mobility. The middle-class parents at the *Oberlyzeum*
for Girls, anxious about the effects of radical feminism among their
daughters, readily agreed to a school rule prohibiting teachers from

---

[92] Publication/report, Bericht den Jugendpfleger, 1925.
[93] Publication/report, Bericht den Jugendpfleger, 1930. On growth of workers organizations, see Pross, pp. 87–89, 265–279.
[94] Baustedt, pp. 17–18.

addressing their students with the adult *"Sie."* [95] Such was the kind of fear that gripped the status-conscious lower-middle strata during the 1920s, thus reinforcing the demand for conformity.

The coming to power of the Nazis in 1933 threatened to radically revise the status of youth by politicizing every aspect of German life. All youth organizations except those officially sponsored by the party were banned; the school schedule was invaded by the political activities of *Hitler Jugend* and the *Bund Deutsche Madel*; and teachers found themselves contending with militant youth leaders, some of whom made life very uncomfortable for their former masters. But the new-found status and freedom of youth was short lived. It was found that the hastily organized units of the Hitler Youth took too readily to various forms of delinquent activity, including theft and assault.[96] Total involvement had brought into youth activities elements of the population, mainly lower-class, which had never taken part before. They brought with them habits and attitudes that were not easily reconciled with the concept of youthful obedience that was a part of the Nazi design. As a result, the proletarian leaders of many units were purged and the whole organization took on an aura of bourgeois respectability under the leadership of Baldur von Schirach. Conformity to middle-class norms of adolescence meant that Nazi youth organizations lost the active allegiance of many, if not the majority of, working youth. Even in the early years of the regime, the resistance of so-called "wild gangs," expressed in delinquent acts, was a major concern to the authorities. Once the war had begun and youth were less subject to direct control, the problem grew to epidemic proportions.[97]

What independence adolescents did retain was due more to the

---

[95] Evolution of rules and regulations can be traced in ms. source C, Ober., Allgemeines über Fragen der Schulzucht, 1912–1929, E. 7. Discussion in ms. source C, Ober., Minutes of Elternbeirat, October 17, 1924, A 14 A. Other discussions concerned curfews for students, prohibition on dancing and dancing lessons, drinking, etc.

[96] Ms. source C, Pol. Dir., Verordnungen betreffend jugendliche Personen, Report to the Oberpräsident, March 9, 1935, Fach 59 No. 12. Report stated that the "subleaders of the Hitler Youth are immature and not ready to take on the role of youthleader and educator." For an excellent discussion of resistance of working-class youth groups to state organization, see Horn, pp. 30–38.

[97] Pross, pp. 425–433; in November 1939, women under 16 and men under 18 were forbidden public dancing. As the war went on, the regulations on youth were further stiffened, but with little apparent effect. Ms. source C, Pol. Dir., Police Ordinance of March 9, 1940, Fach 59 No. 12. See also Schoenbaum, pp. 291ff.

full employment economy of the Third Reich than to the official policies of its youth organizations. The prohibitions on smoking, drinking, and entertainment remained in effect throughout the 1930s and
were further tightened during the Second World War. The substitution of therapeutic for judicial treatment of juvenile delinquency,
begun before 1914, was continued in Germany as in England. Children who were judged genetically deficient faced sterilization, the
ultimate in a preventative approach to social control.[98] Evidence of
rising rates of absenteeism and delinquency among young workers
also provoked the same kind of resentment from the Nazi caretakers
as it did from their English counterparts, with the result that even
after the beginning of the war, when the demand for labor and talent
rose even more rapidly, the Nazis were telling their youth workers
that "to be addressed as 'Du' is a reminder to the young that they
have no grounds for considering themselves fully adult."[99]

VI

Who, then, were the child savers who were behind the protective
legislation of the period 1900–1950? Ultimately, youth work was to
become professionalized, but prior to World War II it was still primarily the voluntary effort of upper- and middle-class men and
women, most visibly the clergy, educators, and the military, with doctors also playing a prominent role in some places. Their involvement
with the young betrayed a certain anxiety about both the nature of
society and the stake of the propertied and educated classes in it.
For the men of this strata, leadership seemed but an extension of
their roles in the economy and the social hierarchy. For the women
of this class, who in increasing numbers made child saving their per-

---

[98] Ironically, this nightmare policy was partly the outcome of a more progressive
impulse toward sexual liberation and protection of children. Ellen Key, a socialist,
had written at the beginning of the century: "This new ethic [free love] will call
no other common living of man and woman immoral, except that which gives occasion to a weak offspring. The Ten Commandments on this subject will not be
prescribed by the founders of religion, but by scientists." Key, p. 14.

[99] Ms. source C, Pol. Dir., Report of Hitler Youth Conference, December 10, 1941,
Fach 59 No. 12.

sonal crusade and even their whole purpose in life, youth work was something of a social redefinition, however. There had been lady child-savers before, but they had always remained in the background, fearing, as Mary Carpenter had, the "unsexing" of themselves by a too active participation in what was previously the male preserve of public affairs.[100] By 1900 this was changing and, in both England and Germany, lobbies like the NSPCC and *Pestolozzi Stiftung* were predominantly women's organizations. The English Mothers' Union and the German *Verein der Freundinnen junger Mädchen* made a special point of the female's unique responsibility in the field of child rearing and her natural role as the guardian of the young. The entry of women into civic affairs might disturb conservatives, but they could hardly object to a movement that maintained a strong separation between male and female roles and involved no real redistribution of power between the sexes. What Anthony Platt has pointed out for the American case was equally true for the English and German: The involvement of women "was not so much a break with the past as an affirmation of faith in traditional institutions." [101] Because this was "unpolitical" activity and eminently bourgeois in its social orientation, it presented none of the challenge to male dominance that radical feminism and suffragette movement presented. In Oxford, for example, women were prominent in the various moral vigilance societies that sprang up at the turn of the century. There they could heed the appeal of the Reverend Warden of Keble College to "organize and increase the better moral forces of public opinion," particularly with respect to children, precisely because it coincided so well with the traditional role of motherhood. Middle-class women, released by birth control from the burdens of child raising, found in the career of moral crusader a status that was responsible and at the same time respectable. It goes without saying that women much further down the social scale, still burdened with the fruits of high fertility, found the zealous visiting of their female superiors no less objectionable than the interference of male child savers such as the truant officer or the medical inspector.[102]

---

[100] J. Estlin Carpenter, p. 158.

[101] Platt, p. 98. For the philosophy of the Mothers' Union, see publication/report, Mothers' Union Report, Fourth Report. For various German groups, consult publication/report, Jahresberichte des Ortausschusses; and ms. source C, Soz. Fürsorge, Report to Bürgermeister, III M 23.

[102] Publication/report, Report of Oxford Vigilance Assn. Also ms. source B, Mins. Oxford Clerical Assn., May 9, 1882, MS Top Oxon e 85; and Inglis, pp. 195–199.

If the professional middle class and their wives formed the general staff of the war against juvenile degeneracy, its foot soldiers were the new lower-middle class, namely those groups we have come to know as white-collar. For them, the youth movements were a way of overcoming their social isolation from the solid middle class. Groups like the Boy Scouts and the *Wandervogel*, together with sports clubs and the army reserves, served to bind the two together through their common interest in patriotism. This was particularly true of elementary teachers, whose status had been rising since the turn of the century but whose standing was still uncertain until they began to demonstrate new forms of civic activism.[103] Together with ex-military men, many of whom found a place in civilian society as physical-training instructors, they contributed strongly to the leadership of the Scouts and Boys' Brigades on the local level. In Göttingen, both elementary and secondary school teachers worked closely with the community's various youth groups. Among the most active was Franz Henkel, who was a leader not only in the *Wandervogel* and gymnastic society, but also in the conservative *Kreigsverein*. By the time of the First World War, teachers in both Germany and England were strongly representative of the patriotism that was, by then, part and parcel of the child-saving movement. When the Oxford teachers proclaimed in 1916 that "it remains with the teacher and with those who help the teacher in any capacity to determine whether England shall be better or worse after the war," they were using a language almost identical to that of German youth workers.[104]

It is also interesting to speculate what the decline of the old lower-middle class, consisting of small artisans and shopkeepers, had to do with the rise of the youth movements. We know that in Oxford the old artisan class showed great concern about the younger generation. It was the craft unions of the city that were taking a strong line, *vis a vis* juvenile delinquency, in urging stricter discipline by the police and the schools.[105] Their fear of seeing their sons and daughters associated with the less reputable youth of the town seems to have had a great deal to do with this; and indeed, in Germany as well, it was those groups who occupied the border line between the middle class

---

[103] C. F. G. Masterman called them "the suburbans," and wrote: "The young men of the suburban society, especially, are being accused of a mere childish absorption in vicarious sport and trivial amusements." Masterman, p. 91.

[104] Ms. source A, Franz Henkel, *Personal Akten;* ms. source B, Mins. Church of England, February 15, 1916, MS Top Oxon e 238.

[105] Butler, p. 47.

and the proletariat who were often the most active in the new youth work. Franz Henkel, for example, was a man only one generation removed from artisan status.[106] And Göttingen's Catholic *Gesellenverein*, which had begun in 1884 as an organization for apprentices, was by the 1920s a young men's club for members of the white-collar class, a change reflecting the broader shifts that were occurring within lower-middle-class groups in the early twentieth century.[107]

It is significant that the new white-collar class came into existence at precisely the time that the new social attitudes toward youth were being generated. The mode of upward mobility of this group was no longer the time-honored ladder of the trades and private enterprise, but education, at first secondary but later at university as well. Little wonder that so much of the anxiety about the years 14 to 18 was expressed in the organizations and agencies that were patronized and staffed by the members of this class. Discipline, deferred gratification, and conformity were the keys to their success in the difficult years of inflation during the 1920s, in the Depression, and again during the period of austerity after the Second World War. Their anxiety to attain and hold the respectability generally accorded a middle-class person came to be institutionalized in the schools and youth organizations through two different channels. The first were the school teachers and youth workers themselves, many lower-middle class in origins and eager to serve bourgeois norms as a way of certifying their own status. The other way was through the parents, who were willing to fit their sons and daughters to the social and psychological demands of adolescence in order to guarantee them a step up the ladder of success. Education was, as the generally lower-middle class students of Oxford High School put it, "the only means of distinguishing us from the ignorant, the poor . . . and the incompetent." [108] The social requirements of the school, including the dependence and deprivation of civil status that were a part of adolescence, were the price they were willing to pay to establish their superiority to the working classes.

In a period when even the smaller cities like Oxford and Göttingen were losing their hometown quality, lines drawn by wealth or birth were not so obvious as they had once been. It was becoming somewhat easier to appropriate the symbols of higher status just by *appearing*, in dress, language, or demeanor, to belong to the respectable

---

[106] Ms. source A, Franz Henkel, *Personal Akten*.
[107] Ms. source C, Pol. Dir., Katholishen Gessellenverein, 1884–1934, Fach 61 No. 4.
[108] Newspaper/periodical, *Oxford High School Magazine* **9** (1)(June 1911).

strata of society, because one's background was now anonymous. Contemporaries noticed that the obvious lines of class, once so pronounced among children, were rapidly blurring. "Collars and ties are now almost as common as rags were a few years ago," noted E. J. Urwick in 1904. "The bare-footed ragamuffin of popular imagination figures still as the frontispiece to well meaning philanthropic appeals, but is no longer a common object of the streets." [109]

But the lowering of one type of barrier meant that others would be put in its place. The middle and lower-middle class were now marking the distinction between themselves and the children of the poor through the use of school uniforms, which became increasingly popular in the 1920s. To parents of the Oxford High School for Boys, who were worried about the social standing of the school, the headmaster stated: [110]

> I am sometimes told that the boys at the City School are rather mixed. It is perfectly true and I see no prospect of any move toward restricting our intake to any social class. The best boy in the last year's Sixth Form is the son of a farm labourer, but he commanded the respect and affection of everyone. A uniform dress will help boys to forget the differences of social standing and live on terms of friendly equality.

Class lines were still there, but were being redrawn along new boundaries set by the school and extracurricular activities. The uniform, the school, the club—these were the new symbols of status of the era of adolescence.

VII

We have drawn a profile of those who "democratized" the norm of adolescence. Not surprisingly, it was the same groups who were instrumental in creating another of the twentieth century's social stereotypes, namely the aggressive, antisocial image of the modern juvenile delinquent. If the model adolescent stood for everything

---

[109] Urwick, "Introduction," p. xi; similar comments in Sherwood, pp. 42–45.
[110] Ms. source D, Min. Book of Board of Govs., Headmaster's Report of October 1928.

pure and stable in a period of internal and external tension, the juvenile delinquent embodied everything to be feared and resented, making him an indispensable part of the social world of the child savers. This is not to say that they invented juvenile crime, for it had been a subject of concern throughout the nineteenth century. But the child criminals of Dickens' time had been more closely associated with a class than an age group. They had been spoken of as "little stunted men" whose misfortune it had been to miss the softening influence of a true childhood and adolescence. By the 1890s, however, delinquency was beginning to be seen not as an attribute of precocity but of immaturity. Adolescence itself was identified as a cause of delinquency and thus all children, regardless of class, were deemed vulnerable to deviance unless carefully protected.

This was an age deeply impressed by the ideas of biological determinism, and those influenced by the Italian criminologist, Lombroso, were certain that they could detect "criminal types" at a very early age. Even theorists not committed to the idea of an inherited criminal disposition were now more aware of the way nature (as opposed to environment) shaped behavior; and the English, who had always tended more toward environmental explanations, were stressing the existence of some inherited traits.[111] Their carefully balanced view was expressed by William Douglas Morrison, writing in 1896: "The results of recent research point to the conclusion that human beings are born into the world with a distinct bent of temperament and character which will always manifest itself in some form, no matter what process of training the individual is called upon to undergo. But the ultimate shape which inherited characteristics will assume is largely dependent on the sort of social conditions in which human development takes place."[112] Signs of criminality, like signs of sexual perversion, if picked up early enough could be treated and even cured, but this required constant vigilance and complete control over the age group in question, coercive measures which Morrison and his contemporaries were willing to take.

Not until the 1890s did the question of juvenile crime become generalized into the question of juvenile delinquency, a problem pertaining not just to what Mary Carpenter's generation had called the "dangerous and perishing classes," but to all youth, regardless of background. When Canon Horsley wrote his *Juvenile Crime* in 1894, he

---

[111] Radzinowicz, pp. 52–56; also Platt, pp. 18–36.
[112] Morrison, p. 121.

referred to his subject as the "great social question of the day," a conclusion seconded by the Howarth Association in the published results of its inquiry into the same subject issued in 1898. Not all contemporaries would have agreed, of course, with an analysis that placed the problems of poverty and war second to those of rowdyism and masturbation, but in the eyes of the middle classes the threat of all forms of deviance took precedence. Juvenile misconduct was no longer explicable in terms of grinding poverty, but was instead the function of rising affluence and abundant leisure. "Most juvenile offenses committed in this country arise from cupidity, and consist of offenses against property," wrote Morrison; but it was the opportunity to steal rather than need itself that was behind crime. "The strongest temptation of the ordinary juvenile is the impulse to steal; in the towns, this impulse is stimulated in every street by the interminable lines of shops and warehouses exhibiting all kinds of merchandise in half-protected state." [113]

Only a generation earlier the "ordinary juvenile" was the honest, respectable juvenile, the polar opposite of the delinquent type, which had previously been associated only with the sons and daughters of the lower classes. Authorities were now willing to admit that the children of the rich could be just as deviant as those of the poor and, thus, the images of the ordinary and the delinquent youngster were no longer linked with different classes but were considered the opposite faces of a certain age-group. All young people at adolescence were to be considered potentially delinquent, a concept much more suitable to a democratic age. Morrison wrote that "in very early life inadaptability to social surroundings usually shows itself in the shape of truancy, vagrancy, wandering habits—in short, a disposition to revert to the nomadic stage of civilization. The greater the demand made by society on the child, such as the demand of the present century that he shall regularly attend an elementary school, the more clearly the extent of this nomadic instinct is brought to life." [114] The "street arab," previously identified with the underdeveloped morality of a particular class, was now seen as the product of the emotional underdevelopment of the adolescent age-group, regardless of class. Social and economic factors were not discounted, but they were no longer the primary cause of delinquent behavior. This lay in the peculiar character of adolescence as a stage of life, whose control and

---

[113] Horsley, p. 9; Russell, "Adolescence," pp. 45–55; *Juvenile Offenders*, p. 189; Morrison, p. 28.
[114] Morrison, p. 58.

direction were absolutely critical in determining the future of the individual. To those who wrote on the subject, the threat to society posed by the existence of this huge concentration of half-tamed savages was self-evident: "There is not an hour of it [youth] but it is not trembling with destinies, not a moment of which once past, the appointed work can never be done again or the next blow be struck on cold iron." [115]

None of the classic Victorian environmental explanations of juvenile crime were entirely discounted in the literature of the 1890s, but there was a tendency to replace the moral voluntarism of the earlier era with a new psychological determinism. Fifty years before, in Dickens' time, the pernicious influence of adults had been held accountable for juvenile crime. By the 1890s it was the conduct of the child itself that was supposed to be the determinant of adult criminality. The influential American child-psychologist, G. Stanley Hall, wrote in 1904 that "criminals are like overgrown children," when only a few decades earlier it had been common to describe little artful dodgers as miniature adults.[116] With the change in the perception of the causes of crime, all forms of juvenile conduct were reexamined for their effect on adult behavior and even the most innocent actions were interpreted as foretelling terrible consequences. Hall cited evidence to the effect that "semicriminality is normal for healthy boys," adding that only the right kind of care and protection would guarantee that they would step forth from this most fateful of all ages onto the straight and narrow life.[117]

By 1914 the problem seemed bigger and more threatening than any of the earlier reformers had imagined; it now seemed that earlier goals of punishment and reform needed to be supplemented by social prevention and control. As the old legal distinctions between the criminal and the noncriminal disappeared, these were replaced by contrasts between the delinquent and nondelinquent ages of children. In the mid-nineteenth century, crime had been considered a moral disease; by the early twentieth century this proposition had been reversed, and it was assumed that immoral or antisocial behavior should be treated as a crime. The new juvenile justice system was a reflection of the change which had broadened the jurisdiction of the police and the courts to include normative behavior previously beyond the reach of the law, while at the same time redefining the

---

[115] Horsley, p. 9.
[116] Hall, vol. 1, p. 338.
[117] Hall, vol. 1, pp. 360, 404.

approach to traditional offenses so that the child before the court was
no longer afforded the protection of due process. We have here a
striking case of the "criminalization" of areas of conduct once left
to private discretion, and, at the same time, a substitution of treatment for punishment that meant that older concepts of justice were
no longer applicable. Once it was accepted that every boy and girl,
regardless of class, had in them a bit of the street arab, then these
new strategies became a matter of course. Sir Leon Radzinowicz
quotes one contemporary's perception of the change: "The classical
school exhorts men to study justice: the positivist school exhorts
justice to study men." [118]

Not surprisingly, the increasing demand for preventative controls
was also one of the prime causes for the rise in recorded instances
of delinquency. Not unexpected, either, was the fact that it was the
children of the poor who were most likely to show the "antisocial"
traits that middle-class observers found so disturbing. Compulsory
school attendance produced a prolonged struggle between the poor
and local authorities. In September 1911, after a summer of intense
adult labor unrest, youths in Hull and several other industrial cities
walked out of school, demanding "less hours and no cane." Pickets
were established, blacklegs beaten, and property damaged before
authorities could get the children back to school. Adult labor agitation provided the model for these youths and their strike, however
fruitless, could not have begun without at least the passive consent
of parents, particularly fathers. As Dr. Ormerod, the Oxford School
Medical Officer, was discovering, parents resented any kind of interference with their children. One mother told him she was glad
her daughter was about to leave school, because "she will be four-
teen then, and you won't be able to worry me." [119]

If the intention of the child savers was to show the underprivileged
how to live, the slum dwellers had some lessons of their own to
teach. One clergyman who had been active in the Oxford Men's and
Lads' Institute in the 1880s remembered: "The boys were very good
fellows, but they regarded the Institute as an opening for a permanent 'Town and Gown' conflict, and naturally began at once to
measure their strength against those who had come to civilize and
instruct them. Classes were started, but often terminated prematurely; the scholars would turn off the gas, stick pins in their teacher,

[118] Quoted from Radzinowicz, p. 56.
[119] Cited in publication/report, Oxford School Board Annual Report, 1911. A
fascinating study of the strikes is provided by Marson.

and break up the furniture." [120] And in the early days of the club founded by Balliol College students in Oxford's St. Ebbe's slum, there was further evidence of the incompatibility of the paternalistic impulse with the needs of working-class boys. From the club's beginnings in 1907, its sponsors had to tolerate a good bit of ragging, even physical threat from the boys whom the club was supposed to serve.[121]

> It required all the skill of the officer of the day to establish even tolerable discipline. The chief subject for discussion, as I remember it, was which boys should be turned out. Perhaps our decisions were colored by the knowledge that whoever was turned out would probably retaliate by throwing a stone through the window from outside during prayers.

Another of the founders, looking back on the early days, nicely summarized the sociology of all the club and settlement movements:[122]

> There was a far wider social gulf than now between undergraduate and city boy. The 'toffs' or College gentlemen appeared to lead a life of luxury and indolence. . . . There was as yet little political consciousness. Here and there a thoughtful boy was beginning to wonder, but to most the pre-1914 social order appeared both 'given' and permanent.

VIII

Altruism, when met with resistance, all too often produces bitter resentment; and it was not accidental that when annoyance at juvenile misconduct turned to aggressive hostility in the early 1890s, it was those most involved with youth that were most likely to be outspoken in favor of coercive measures. The last decades of the nineteenth century were when Oxford citizens began to complain with

---

[120] Publication/report, Report of Oxford Working Men's and Lads' Institute, 1893–1894 and 1898.

[121] Bailey, p. 10. Also, ms. source I, Balliol log book, May 1907. Used by permission of Dean Willis Bund, Balliol College, Oxford.

[122] Bailey, p. 9.

persistence about the boisterous behavior at the annual St. Giles's Fair.[123] Clergy were much concerned about Sabbath observance, urging the police to clear the streets during the morning and evening services.[124] Gambling, public solicitation by prostitutes, and even such innocent pastimes as nude bathing were coming under attack, all in the name of protecting the rising generation.[125] We find the same kind of vigilance prevailing in Göttingen a few years later, where school teachers were leading a drive against the latest threat to juvenile decency, the newly arrived picture shows.[126] It is interesting to note that the police themselves found little that could be construed as illegal or immoral in most of the entertainments.[127] This did not prevent the various vigilance and childsaving organizations from bringing pressure on national and local officials to enforce their particular code of morality, and by 1914 this had paid off in the form of ordinances and policies circumscribing the activities of the child. By then the police were more likely to pick up children for "wandering," and parents more willing to bring their children before the courts for care and protection.[128]

Crime statistics seemed to justify this vigilance, for the number of juveniles being brought before the courts for various offenses was rising in all European countries. Yet, when one looks carefully at the "crimes" for which those under 19 were being arrested, one finds that it was probably the broadening definition of "delinquency" rather than a greater disposition to crime that was the cause of the increase. A review of the Oxford Police Court records for 1870–1914 reveals a sharp increase in the number of juveniles brought before the court, but not necessarily for those offenses (including theft and crimes against persons) that would have fallen under earlier definitions of "juvenile crime." (See Figure 6.)

The feeling that indictable crimes such as larceny were increasing had some substance, but while juvenile theft showed a steady increase after 1890, it is doubtful that this alone could have accounted

---

[123] Ms. source G, Mins. Watch Committee, Report of Subcommittee on St. Giles's Fair, December 14, 1893, HH 1/6.

[124] Ms. source G. Mins. Watch Committee, October 9, 1891, HH 1/6.

[125] Ms. source G, Mins. Watch Committee, Police report of November 1, 1894, HH 1/7; agreement with University Proctors in 1891, HH 1/6.

[126] Ms. source C, Übersichte über den Besuch der Kinomatographen Theater durch Schulkinder, 1913, Lfd 24.

[127] Ms. source G, Mins. Watch Committee, Inspector's Report, December 15, 1893, HH 1/6.

[128] Publication/report: City of Oxford Constable's Report, 1900–1914.

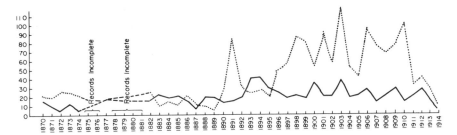

Figure 6 Indictable (represented by solid line) and nonindictable (represented by dotted line) offenses of males under 19, prosecuted in Oxford, England, 1870–1914. Indictable crimes include theft, breaking and entering, serious assaults; nonindictable crimes include gambling, malicious mischief, loitering, willful damage, begging, dangerous play, as well as so-called "care and protection" cases. [Figures from the records of the Oxford Police Court, 1870–1914.]

for the fears that ultimately generated stricter, more comprehensive law enforcement. Many of the things stolen were of little value—fruit, toys, and cigarettes destined almost certainly for personal use. There is little evidence of the organized crime or the gangs of child thieves that existed in some places earlier in the nineteenth century. However, the offenses for which boys were charged were very often those arising from or connected with traditional forms of juvenile sociability, particularly street games, gambling, and other peer-group activity. Up to 1910 most of those arrested were in groups of two or more, though most of these seem to have been informal rather than tightly-structured gangs.[129]

What this seems to indicate is that law enforcement agencies, encouraged by certain segments of the public, were engaged in a process of redefining as "delinquent" those patterns of behavior which had traditionally been tolerated by the community. They were becoming increasingly sensitized to types of social behavior—including deportment, appearance, and disposition—that in earlier decades might have been viewed as irritating but hardly dangerous to law and order. To some degree this was the product of the demands of an urban-industrial age. The increase first in horse-drawn traffic and then in motor vehicles required a regulation of the streets that had been unnecessary in a quieter era. Rough, boisterous conduct was perhaps more dangerous in an age of plate-glass show windows and delicate landscaping; yet, the court records and police minutes demonstrate that stricter enforcement was not primarily the result of

---

[129] For full discussion of the character of delinquency, see Gillis, "Emergence."

complaints by angry businessmen or anxious homeowners but of the urgings of school teachers, clergymen, and childsaving groups who liked to think of themselves as protecting youth (against itself, of course) rather than property. Like so many groups that claim the "disinterested" role of upholding public morality, their actions were characterized by a certain resentment, even hostility, towards those whom they sought to redeem.[130]

Earlier in the nineteenth century this kind of hostility would certainly have been returned in kind, but it is interesting to note how little resentment there apparently was, even in the attitudes of those older youth that were brought before the court for assault on police or willful damage to property. Just as today, these so-called "defiant" or "antisocial" crimes were more prevalent among older youth (14–18), while theft was confined largely to the younger ages. It is reasonably clear from police records, however, that the acts which were charged as disorderly were then, as now, mainly innocent assertions of independence on the part of working males attempting to cultivate the masculine prowess encouraged in young men of their class. There is little evidence of the existence of delinquent subcultures, organized around aggressive gangs, that placed themselves in permanent opposition to the dominant values of the society. For that kind of conflict, we must go back to the ritualized hostility that was organized around holiday rows and town-gown fights, a phenomenon already in decline by 1900.[131]

In the nineteenth century, aggressive hostility between children of different classes was taken for granted. One Oxford man, who could remember the bloody night in November 1867, when students armed with clubs were turned loose on a crowd of Oxford men and boys crying for cheap bread, recalled that such "cad rows" often lasted for days: "Naturally, where there was this difference in opportunity, there was a good deal of feeling between the Haves and the Have-nots." [132] Up to the end of the century, university gentlemen took delight in testing their fists against local lads, not only on those nights when battles between town and gown were customary but any time the opportunity might offer.[133] The violence was tradi-

---

[130] For this approach, I am indebted to Joseph Gusfield's discussion of status politics in *Symbolic Crusade: Status Politics and the American Temperance Movement*, Chapters 4, 7; and Platt, pp. 4–9, 77.
[131] Gillis, "Emergence."
[132] Sherwood, p. 48.
[133] Plowman, pp. 218–226.

tionally returned in kind. Margaret Fletcher, who grew up in North Oxford in the 1860s and 1870s, later recorded the peril of middle-class children passing through the poorer sections of town. "Jumping about with excitement and pointing with their fingers, they (the neighborhood children) shouted 'gentry' with such scorn and contempt as almost to imply *a la laterne!* 'Cads' called back a breathless victim sprinting for safety. . . ."[134]

Miss Fletcher found it comforting that, by the twentieth century, the cads and gentry were increasingly sharing the same classrooms; but, while school loyalties may have prevented some of the more overt manifestations of class antagonism, the change was due more to the decline of older collective norms among the working class itself. Ironically, the invention of the frightening spectre of the delinquent came at the very time when the juvenile expression of collectivity, the gang, was apparently beginning to recede. The bands that had been in possession of the streets of many poor working-class neighborhoods for most of the nineteenth century seemed to have declined after 1900, to the point, in the 1960s, that they were little more than informal cliques, less offensive than defensive in character.[135] Despite all the talk of violent gangs in the 1950s, tightly-knit hostile groups were rare in Europe. Even on the riotous night of November 6, 1959, when from 2000 to 4000 youth were on the streets of Oxford, the Chief Constable could identify only one group of 20 to 30 boys as being responsible for the extensive damage to shop windows.[136] After 1910, the earlier tendency for crime to be committed in groups tended to fall off, further evidence that behavior had become more individualized since the beginning of the century.[137]

As far as can be determined from the Oxford police and court records, the patterns of delinquency seem to have remained fairly consistent in the period 1900–1950. There is no evidence that spontaneous youth groups were hostile to adults although, when provoked by what seemed to be unjustified interference, they did tend to strike back in a way that was often interpreted by authorities as

[134] Margaret Fletcher, p. 48.
[135] Willmott, Chapter 2; Neidhardt, *Junge Generation,* p. 77.
[136] Ms. source G, Mins. Watch Committee, Special Report of Chief Constable, December 3, 1959, HH 1/32.
[137] On general decline of gang behavior in Oxford, see Gillis, "Emergence." A specific case was change in the behavior of crowds at St. Giles's Fair. See Alexander, pp. 34–37; Mays, *Young Pretenders,* pp. 28–30.

antisocial behavior. The records of truant officers, school medical people, police, and other adults likely to come into contact with the children of the poor, amply illustrate the resentments of both working youth and their parents in those instances when they believed their rights were being infringed upon.[138] Yet this kind of resistance is not so much a sign of social alienation as the simple desire to be left alone, part of the general privatization that had affected the middle class much earlier but also left its mark on the laboring poor as their conditions of life came gradually to converge with those of the upper classes.[139]

Expressions of class hostility, such as the town-gown riots of Guy Fawkes' Night, were also much rarer at the end of the century. While students and other middle-class youth had abandoned the old festive calendar for a new set of dates revolving around armistice nights and national holidays, traditions such as the First of May were now in the keeping of what Thomas Plowman described as "unkempt, bedraggled youngsters, who 'welcome in the May' with discordant cries and the shuffling of feet on our doorsteps." [140] Yet, however much the games and rituals of the poor may have irritated those like Plowman, there exists no evidence of a delinquent subculture permanently at war with respectable society. No doubt some of the violence of Misrule, finally released from traditional forms, did tend to spill out randomly and senselessly. But, while the modern delinquent's behavior may be marked by assertion of male prowess and defiance of routine, it must be remembered that these are the time-honored ways of growing up in a lower-class culture that still places great value on early maturation and independence. Most of the violence so generated is turned inward, however, and is likely to be recorded on police blotters mainly when authorities intervene in the internal affairs of the young.[141]

---

[138] Matza, "Position and Behavior Patterns," p. 195; Willmott, pp. 153–158.

[139] On the privatization of the working class, see Goldthorpe *et al.*, Chapter 4; in Oxford, Mogey; and in Germany, Neidhardt, *Junge Generation*, p. 84.

[140] Plowman, p. 86; on changing pattern of student "rags," see Porter, pp. 289–291. I have gone through the police committee minutes for Oxford for the period 1920–1960, and can find nothing comparable to the violence of nineteenth-century town-gown rows. After 1900, most Guy Fawkes Nights have been marked by minor pranks. Ms. source G, Mins. Watch Committee, HH 1/17–32.

[141] Willmott, pp. 162–167.

IX

There is no reliable social breakdown of the juvenile offenders for the period 1890–1914, but it seems likely that then, as today, those who were picked up were mostly from the working class.[142] Middle-class youth escaped the long arm of the law not because they were subject to any less strict authority, but because they were under the control of the school and university.[143] The increasingly strict rule of academe meant they were subject to other kinds of paternalism, which partly exempted them from the common law. The youth most likely to be brought before the regular courts were those young people who had no institutional affiliations aside from work. In other words, the more independent the youth, the more responsible he or she was for his or her own conduct, the more likely the stigmatization by society as a real or potential delinquent. Indeed, the very customs of the adult-centered working-class family contributed to this vulnerability, since, in the eyes of the middle classes, it deprived its children of proper care and protection by sending them into the world so early. Failing to understand, or even to tolerate, the way the working class brought up their young, the self-appointed care-takers of the younger generation viewed the "deprived" child as the potential delinquent.

This was, of course, the kind of self-fulfilling prophecy that manages to produce the deviancy it claims to abhor but which it, in fact, must have in order to sustain the ideologies and institutions that are based upon it. The attempt to legislate morality and to restrict the independence of working youth naturally resulted in conflicts between the authorities and the young, which could be interpreted as evidence of the latter's inherent tendency toward antisocial behav-

---

[142] On the problem of unrecorded delinquency, see West; and Mays, *Crime and Social Structure*, pp. 20–66.

[143] Abundant evidence on the special status of students is provided by the Proctors' Manuals in Ms. source H. I am indebted to Mr. Trevor Aston, University Archivist, for permission to consult them.

ior.[144] The sons and daughters of the poor did not adjust nearly so well as middle-class youth to the model of adolescence that schools and youth organizations presented to them. Without denying that much malicious and violent behavior characterized younger members of working class (as well as members of the middle class), a survey of historical and contemporary evidence reveals that the attitudes of the young toward their elders contains little of the aggressive resentment that is often attributed to them. Studies of intergenerational attitudes, done since 1950, have conclusively shown that the hostility that does exist emanates largely from the adults themselves, especially from middle-class probation officers, schoolmasters, and others who are the assigned guardians of youth's virtue. Musgrove, for example, found that middle-class child-savers were very much more likely to have a negative image of teen-age boys, even though there was little or no hostility turned in their direction by the youth themselves.[145]

X

It seems, therefore, that the images of the innocent adolescent and the predatory delinquent have formed an historical dialectic for most of this century. They both originated in the same period; both were largely projections of the hopes and fears of a middle strata of European society struggling to hold its own against successive waves of social and political change. The notion of a stage of life freed from all the cares and responsibilities of a troubled civilization was their escapist dream, the vision of juvenile degeneracy their recurring nightmare. In order to keep that dream alive, they imposed on the young a conformity and dependence that proved unacceptable to a significant segment of the population. Instead of accepting the independence and nonconformity of the poor as a product of economic conditions, they tended to inflate their own fears by treating a legitimate tradition of youth as punishable delinquency.

---

[144] See Horn, pp. 30–40; Gillis, "Emergence."

[145] On the hostility of adult toward the young, see Musgrove, *Youth and Social Order*, pp. 97–103; Eppel and Eppel, pp. 243–263; Friedenberg, Chapter 6.

Edgar Z. Friedenberg has noted that, since 1914, the old identification of maturity with personal autonomy has been eroded to the point that nonconformity is automatically treated as a threat to society. The delinquent, in exemplifying that independence, is met with increasing suspicion and fear. "As the conditions of life alter in such a way as to provide less scope for self-direction, autonomy itself either becomes suspect or must be redefined as a kind of considered acquiescence in the demands of group living. The persistence of the older ideal of maturity, then, becomes a source of conflict and *anomie*, burdening those who try to live up to it with additional self-doubt. Maturation itself, then becomes a source of anxiety from which the adult must seek refuge." [146]

The cult of youth, from which no western society in the twentieth century has been exempt, has been primarily the result of this historical process. The child-savers saw themselves as liberating youth and, through youth, society itself from the strictures of a highly organized industrial civilization. But their noble goal was frustrated by their own inability as adults to free themselves from a narrow class perspective. They misled themselves in thinking that the problem of the adolescent was essentially psychological, rooted in the nature of the child rather than in the nature of the society. They also ignored the fact that their own ambivalence toward youth was essentially the result of social and cultural disparities, disparities that would remain pronounced in all European countries until after World War II, when a measure of affluence would become available to a much broader section of the population. Not until the obvious inequalities of society began to diminish did the ambivalence begin to disappear and the era of adolescence itself finally begin to terminate.

---

[146] Friedenberg, pp. 284–285.

Youth showed a new face in the late 1960s and early 1970s, one not always pleasing to its elders. This scene in Madison, Wisconsin, was repeated in numerous American and European protests. Reproduced by permission of United Press International.

5

End of Adolescence: Youth in the 1950s and 1960s

The ideal of adolescence that generations of schoolmasters and youth workers had labored to perfect seemed complete in the tranquil 1950s; yet, even then, there were adults who were troubled by this, their own creation. The notion of a period of life freed from the responsibilities of adulthood was too easily distorted by the more restive members of the younger generation into the frightening image of the rebel without a cause. And if rising rates of delinquency were not enough to give second thoughts, there was also the realization that even the more benign features of adolescence, including its political passivity and social conformity, mirrored other well-known weaknesses of adult society. The likeness of model youth to organization man was pointed out by both European and American observers. At the same time that Edgar Z. Friedenberg was warning Americans that *"Homo sapiens* is undergoing a fundamental model change," Frank Musgrove and Hans Heinrich Muchow were producing discouraging reports on the loss of individualism among the young in England and Germany, respectively.[1]

Ironically, pessimism was most pronounced on the very eve of a decade in which both American and European youth would show what seemed an entirely different face to its elders. The renewal of political activism and social commitment during the 1960s seemed

---

[1] Friedenberg, p. 204; also Muchow, *Sexualreife und Sozialstruktur,* pp. 107–123; Musgrove, *Youth and Social Order,* "Introduction"; Schelsky; Marwick, p. 51; Zweig.

to terminate abruptly the long era of adolescence. In several countries the voting age was lowered, walls between school and society
were breached, and everywhere the young were reclaiming the rights
and duties of adulthood previously withheld from them. The revival
of student radicalism and bohemianism, together with an apparent
increase in various kinds of sexual experimentation, seemed, in fact,
to reverse the trend of the previous 50 years and to restore something of the social and political independence of youth that had
been a feature of the nineteenth century. Behind these movements
lay social changes that were altering the status of those youth whose
life cycles had been most accurately reflected in the institution of
adolescence, namely the upper and middle classes. Political and cultural radicalism was the outward expression of their search for new
forms to meet the needs of a changing life cycle. The 1960s were
for them, therefore, a time of reassessing old traditions and experimenting with new.

Among working-class youth, change was also evident, though perhaps not as striking if only because the norm of adolescent dependence and passivity had never been so pervasive among that group.
The rise in delinquent behavior that many observers claimed to perceive was not so much a rejection of an earlier tradition of youth as
the extension of an unbroken pattern of behavior, modified somewhat by the new standards of living of the post-World War II period.
Nevertheless, on this level of society as well, a new phase of the
social history of youth was clearly beginning. To understand the
trends manifesting themselves among the working classes and why
these differed so from those present at higher social levels, it is necessary to look at the changing demographic and economic conditions of the post-World War II period.

I

Trends toward family limitation, detected even before the beginning of the century, had continued; and, while there was some slight
increase in average family size in the 1950s, it was so small as not
to affect the overall picture of smaller families and the more careful
consideration of children's futures. The ideal of the two-child family

seemed to have percolated down to the lowest ranks of society, even though the restriction of fertility was still slightly less at the very bottom of the social order. Birth control had spread to all classes, beginning at the top and spreading downward as the century progressed. Economic conditions were also changing, as the postwar affluence eliminated the primary poverty that had been prevalent in the 1930s. Many observers thought they detected a convergence of class values during the 1950s. It appeared that the rising standard of living enjoyed by the working classes was causing their attitudes toward children to become more middle-class, while the bourgeoisie was moving in its own way toward a concept of youth that was closer to the independence and precocity earlier associated only with working-class children.[2]

For middle- and upper-class families, the period after about 1950 saw the final decline of patriarchalism.[3] One sign of the greater freedom of adolescents was the final disappearance of chaperonage; and by the 1960s there was a significant tendency for parents to place considerably greater trust in the peer group and to require less adult supervision for both their sons and daughters.[4] Freedoms previously associated with university-age youth were being rapidly appropriated by adolescents, who, having access to larger allowances and greater mobility made possible by the automobile, were gaining something of the autonomy they had lost a century or so before. While middle-class patterns tended still to segregate this age group from the world of work, this was less likely than before to be accompanied by social and sexual separation. Even in England, where sex-segregated education remained entrenched in the boarding school, there was some tendency toward more coeducation of males and females. Everywhere the walls between school and world were coming down, as new, more broadly defined types of secondary education were introduced.

The teenaged of this class were breaking out of their social isolation and nowhere was this more obvious than in their sexual behavior. Michael Schofield and Hans Heinrich Muchow have demonstrated for England and Germany, respectively, that middle-class courtship and marriage patterns were converging with those of the working strata of society. On all social levels, the tendency of the

---

[2] Marsh, p. 51; Ronald Fletcher, p. 115.
[3] For discussion of this trend throughout Europe, see Goode, pp. 17–30, 66–70.
[4] Goode, pp. 31–35; Turner, *History of Courting,* p. 69.

age of puberty and menarche to drop four months per decade had produced unprecedented levels of physical precocity. Boys, who in 1900 had reached their full growth at 23, were now fully mature at 17.[5] In both countries, working-class males and females still tended to enter sexual experience somewhat earlier than their middle-class counterparts, but this gap in precocity was much less marked than earlier. Knowledge of sex had become widespread among both groups long before puberty, and among middle-class youth there was little of the trauma of sexual awakening that was so frequent among their number 50 years earlier.[6] Thanks largely to greater access to the supportive company of peers, the adjustment to sexual maturation had lost its lonely, disturbing character.[7]

Biology was not the only determinant of this change, for it seems that schools, churches, and doctors were becoming somewhat more accepting of adolescent sexuality, however strongly moralistic might be their pronouncements on the subject. Today, the traditional anxiety is still plainly evident, but the emphasis is now as much on preventing socially undesirable consequences of early sexual experience as on condemning the act itself. Notes one perceptive schoolboy: "Before we left [school] the reverend told us not to do it; the doctor told us how not to do it; and the head told us where not to do it."[8] In any case, dating in the company of friends begins among English working youth at 13 or 14, with the middle-class youth starting only slightly later. Schofield found that middle-class adolescents were more likely to defer actual intercourse, relying longer on petting; but, again, these differences are not as pronounced as earlier. Among both classes the process of introduction to sexuality is strongly influenced by a romantic conception that tolerates intimacy only when affection is also present. Surveys show that serious monogamous dating sets in at about 17 or 18 for all social strata, and that, by that time, a third of males and a quarter of females have experienced sexual intercourse.[9] Among all groups, promiscuity is relatively rare, however. Partners in intercourse have usually known one another for some period of time and feel a strong sense of responsibility toward

---

[5] Schofield, p. 27; Comfort, *Sex in Society*, pp. 100–101.

[6] Schofield, pp. 44–45; Muchow, *Sexualreife und Sozialstruktur*, pp. 86–95.

[7] Muchow, *Sexualreife und Sozialstruktur*, pp. 92–93; Goode, pp. 31–33; Mays, *Young Pretenders*, pp. 114–124.

[8] Quoted in Schofield, p. 87.

[9] Schofield, p. 33; Willmott, pp. 54–58. For a survey of available international statistics, see Broderick, Chapters 8–9.

one another, the vast majority viewing sexual relations as a prelude to marriage.[10]

The romantic standard of "permissiveness with affection" is also reflected in the general decline of male use of prostitutes since World War I. The custom of older persons introducing the young to sex no longer holds either (if it ever did), and it would seem, if the statistics on the ages of marriage partners are any indication, that people are now more likely to be intimate with persons of their own age group. Even among the middle and upper classes, where disparities in age were once frequent, the pattern seems to be for the informal peer group to act as the central institution for introducing, encouraging, and even controlling relations between the sexes during the teen years.[11] As Geoffrey Gorer has pointed out, while moral attitudes have changed little, the locus of moral authority has shifted radically, particularly for the middle class:[12]

> Earlier generations considered that ladies needed help in guarding their chastity; the last two generations have passed the responsibility to the young people themselves. . . . We are putting a greater weight of responsibility on young girls today than they ever had to bear in the past for their own sexual conduct.

One reason why middle-class parents have relaxed control is the fact that residential and scholastic segregation of various class groups ensures that the peers will be of the same class. Class lines among the young are still so strong that persons of very different background or education are not likely to meet. In this case, the control of the young by the young has contributed to social stratification in the last two decades, a condition reflected by the fact that in 83% of English marriages, partners share either the same social background or the same level of academic achievement.[13] With respect to courtship, then, the habits of middle-class youth have moved closer to those of the working class without, however, bridging the barriers between the social groups themselves.

Age of marriage has also dropped considerably since World War II. In 1931 only 7% of English males 15–24 years of age were married. In 1951, the proportion was 12.5% and by 1957 it was 14.9%.

---

[10] Schofield, p. 75; Neidhardt, *Junge Generation*, p. 85.
[11] Goode, p. 40.
[12] Quoted in Ronald Fletcher, p. 160; also Gorer, Chapter 8.
[13] Ronald Fletcher, p. 111.

For women of the same age-bracket, the percentages for the same years were 14%, 27.2%, and 30.5%, respectively.[14] This recovery of youthful marriage is significant insofar as it demonstrates the trend toward greater autonomy. It was most marked among the middle classes, whose norm of respectability had kept the average marriage age very high until well into the present century.[15] While it is still true that young persons who are engaged in higher education postpone marriage longer than the nonstudent population, there still seems to be a convergence of class values that goes hand in hand with a society-wide redefinition of marriage. The spread of efficient means of contraception among all social groups has meant that sexual intercourse, either inside or outside of marriage, no longer necessarily means children. "Marriage has become to a considerable extent and for a large proportion of the population a method of setting up a joint home without necessarily increasing the size of family by the addition of children," writes David Marsh.[16] Marriage has been separated from inheritance even among the propertied classes, and the conditions of employment for young professional men and women have sufficiently improved since 1945, so that middle-class people can marry earlier without endangering their status, postponing children to a point later in life when they feel they can better afford them. This logical extension of the middle-class pattern of family planning has been further encouraged by the fact that many educated women wish to continue their careers after marriage. While the movement toward women's liberation has encouraged some to delay marriage or even abandon it entirely, its effect with respect to the status of youth has been, nevertheless, to increase the autonomy of young persons from the authority and control of their parents and, thus, to place them in a position more like that of the youth of the working classes.

In short, both ends of the period of middle-class adolescence have been blurred by changes relating to sexuality and marriage. The line that had once clearly separated the secondary student from the elementary school child has been erased by earlier sexual maturation and by the very fact that so many children now go on to some kind of further training, so that the profile of the once exclusive group of adolescent students is no longer as sharply defined as it once had been. At the other end of adolescence, the once-clear distinction

---

[14] Ronald Fletcher, p. 111; Musgrove, *Youth and Social Order,* pp. 80–81.
[15] Goode, pp. 41–49; Mays, *Young Pretenders,* pp. 130–138.
[16] Marsh, p. 35.

between school and university youth has also broken down for reasons that will be discussed later. In effect, adolescence, while still recognized in medical texts and psychological guides, is losing its status as a separate stage of life among the very class with whom it has been previously associated.

II

As for the laboring classes, the post-World War II period brought changes associated with the new levels of affluence that reinforced some family traditions and caused adjustments in others. Comparison of household composition in Preston in the 1850s and in Swansea in 1960 demonstrates what effect economic and demographic change has had on the general population. (See Table 7.)

TABLE 7

Percentage of Households with Kin, Lodgers, and Servants[a]

	Kin	Lodgers	Servants
Swansea 1960	10–13	<3	<3
Preston 1851	23	23	10[b]

[a] Figures from Michael Anderson, "Family, Household, and Industrial Revolution," p. 81.
[b] Includes apprentices.

The decline in servants reflects, of course, the disappearance of live-in apprenticeship. Lodgers, too, are no longer present, because working people can now afford their own houses or flats. Among the kin resident in these households, there has been a notable drop in the category of "parentless children," both because declining mortality rates have cut the number of orphans that once were accommodated by relatives and because the tradition of young people moving from the countryside to live with families in the towns has virtually terminated. Although the tendency is still for old people to live with their married children, the working-class home has largely contracted around the nuclear family.

These are changes reflecting the final extension of low mortality and low fertility to the lowest strata of society. The welfare state of the twentieth century makes it less necessary for parents to rely on children as long-term security; and higher wages have reduced their value as short-run economic assets as well. The norm of the two-child family is still alien to some working families, but the change in attitude toward family planning is obvious. A Mr. Florence told interviewers in one London survey:[17]

> Fifty years ago it was different. They had more children than they could afford. The pubs were open all day, so far as I can understand. The man would spend all his money in the pub, come home, and abuse his wife. There was no birth control in those days, I know, but even then there were ways and means not to have children if you didn't want to have them. And if the woman complained, it was hold your noise and give her another baby, and that's the finish.

The relatively new tendency among the lower orders of the working class to plan their families reflects, as Mr. Florence suggests, a new relationship between husband and wife. There is greater concern on the part of the former for his home responsibilities, including relieving his wife of some of the burdens of child care. This new companionate style is, in part, a function of the new affluence; and so is the tendency to treat all children as equal, regardless of their order of birth. The days when "younger ones were better off in every way" are over for all but the poorest families.[18] The eldest are no longer forced out to work and thus deprived of chances for further education. Studies of English working-class families show that parents have become increasingly concerned in the past two decades with planning each individual child's life chances. Like their social superiors, they tend to worry over their children's education and training, showing a strong desire that they "do well" in school.[19] There is also the concern that the children get the right things while growing up, including not only the necessities of life such as food and clothing, but what were once regarded as luxuries, entertainment and travel.

Instances where families are dependent on the earnings of their children are relatively rare now, although coresident working chil-

---

[17] Quoted in Willmott and Young, p. 20.
[18] Willmott and Young, pp. 180–85.
[19] Goldthorpe et al., pp. 130–133; on German working-class family attitudes toward education, see Neidhardt, Familie, pp. 64–67.

dren are expected to contribute part of their earnings to the family kitty to pay for room and board. Coresidency until marriage is almost universal, there being more room at home due to small families. In fact, 90% of English children in 1959 were still living at home two years after leaving school.[20] One is not surprised to find that, as the working class has become suburbanized and finds itself in more spacious surroundings, leisure time has become increasingly family-centered in the manner once confined to the better-off.[21] While parents and children spend a good deal of time together, youth, nonetheless, still enjoy a considerable freedom to come and go as they wish. Working-class parents still seem to set fewer limitations on staying out at night than do their middle-class counterparts, although they, too, are likely to make a sharp distinction between what they consider "respectable" as opposed to "rough" behavior on the part of the young. By middle-class standards they may seem permissive, but by their own norms of right and wrong they are relatively strict, putting strong pressure on their children to stay out of trouble.[22]

All this would seem to indicate a convergence of class attitudes toward youth, but there remain important differences that should not be overlooked. Working-class parents continue to expect their children to move on to work at an earlier age; and their attitude toward prolonged schooling, and the dependence that this involves, remains very different from that of the middle class. John Goldthorpe and his colleagues have concluded that working-class people continue to approach the school largely for the skills it offers and not, as with the middle class, as a source of social status or social control:[23]

> Parental concern that they [the children] should "do well" is confined to achievement within the context of working-class values and life-styles—as, for example, in becoming established in a "trade" or a "steady" job. Aspirations do not extend to levels of education or types of jobs which would result in children being taken away from their family and community in either a geographical or social sense.

Parental attitudes are an important element in the tendency of working-class youth to leave school earlier, even though wages are

---

[20] Lowndes, p. 301.
[21] Mogey, pp. 57ff, 70–75; Neidhardt, *Familie*, pp. 68–69.
[22] Goldthorpe *et al.*, 143; Mogey, pp. 70ff; Willmott, pp. 158–161.
[23] Goldthorpe *et al.*, p. 119.

not needed at home and the state pays for higher education. Worker families in both England and Germany place stronger value on technical education and regard the academic training that leads to university entrance as either a less worthy or a simply unrealistic goal. Despite the apparent equality of opportunity offered by state-financed education, there remains the suspicion—and a justifiable one—that higher learning leads to a cultural separation from the family itself, and thus the "loss" of a son or daughter.[24] Hence the tendency of many working-class parents to encourage work as opposed to school. Strong emphasis on keeping the family together, which is also reflected in the tendency of grown children to settle near their parents, finds further support in other agencies of working-class life, most notably among the peer group itself. The pressure on working-class boys by their own age mates to go along with the group and drop out of school, is reflected in the observations of one young Londoner.[25]

> The boys who didn't go to grammar school weren't particularly against you because they didn't go. But you found a big change as soon as they left school at the age of 15. You'd still got another couple of years to do and they'd started going to work, and from then on there was a difference. They went to work, they made their way in the world, and you were still at school and they thought of you as a kind of low life. They almost regarded you as a cissy.

Pressures of paternity and fraternity for solidarity and against individual mobility are based, in part, on a realistic assessment of the difficulties of rising in a society which is still so strongly stratified in terms of wealth, culture, and influence. The problems of climbing to the higher professions without aid of family wealth and connections are still very marked in both Germany and England, despite the spread of free education since 1945.[26] In Germany, working-class children make up 5% of university students; in England, their share is 25%, but still reflective of enormous inequalities. An awareness of these and a desire to maintain the collective values of family,

---

[24] On the problems of the scholarship boy and the upwardly mobile in general, see Hoggart, Chapters 7–10.

[25] Quoted in Willmott, p. 95.

[26] For international figures, see Edding, pp. 382–391; Neidhardt, *Junge Generation*, p. 38ff; Marsh, pp. 218–219.

neighborhood, and class, are responsible for the continuing differences in the life cycles of the working and middle classes.

Being less status- and career-oriented, working-class youth are more likely to chafe at the restrictive nature of the school and to be less accepting of the deferred gratification than are their middle-class peers. Their ideal is a well-paying, steady job that will permit early attainment of adult status. Correspondingly, they tend to be less loyal to institutions like the school, and more devoted to their own kind, particularly the peer group. Males, in particular, find the company of their own age-group more fulfilling than clubs or sponsored recreational activity; and where sex segregation is reinforced by work roles, the male peer group remains a primary unit of community life for the men even after they are married.[27] Ordinarily, however, the peer group rarely retains the loyalty of its members after 18 or 19, by which time they are actively engaged in courtship. Peer groups are a major social institution of those years 13–18, during which time a boy is clearly not a child and yet has not entered fully into the adult world of work or pursuit of matrimony.

The activities of such peer groups are not directed against adult institutions per se, but, in their search for recreation during after-school or after-work hours, group members often find themselves in conflict with those institutions. In this and other respects, the traditions of youth associated with the urban working-class peer group have remained very much alive in recent decades. Differences in the ways middle- and working-class youth spend leisure time reflect disparities in social and economic opportunity, and inequalities in access to higher education and desirable professions. As long as this gulf continues to exist, the function of the peer group as a supportive agency of collective and individual goals is likely to go unchallenged and, indeed, may even increase in importance as other traditional points of contact among working men, such as the work place, become increasingly depersonalized or inaccessible to those still in school. In short, the trends of the past two decades have not diminished the role of the peer group but have actually increased it.

It should be noted, however, that European peer groups remain small and loosely structured, without the authoritarian hierarchy of

---

[27] In coal mining communities, peer groups continue to remain extraordinarily strong. See Dennis et al., pp. 221–227. For less formal street corner societies, see Mogey, pp. 54ff.

American "gangs." Boys in groups do occasionally engage in collective crimes of one sort or another, most of them petty in character.
The chief purpose of their existence is social, and it is mainly in the
search for entertainment or "kicks" that misconduct occurs.[28] The
trend of juvenile delinquency is much the same as that trend noted
in the previous chapter, with the old territorially-based gangs giving
way to more mobile groups. Motorcycles and cars have been a determining factor, part of the general affluence that has encouraged
peer groups to turn their collective energies to new interests. In Liv-
erpool, for example, previously belligerent youth gangs took up
music in the early 1960s, creating a new kind of solidarity that is now
associated with "Beatlemania." Unfortunately, poorer boys, without
money for instruments or costume, were left behind by this development. They continued to manifest the aggressiveness of the old
slum groups, while the more fortunate of their peers turned to creative pursuits.[29]

Recent research indicates that the traditional distinction between
"respectable" and "rough" youth has moderated somewhat, but not
yet disappeared in either Germany or England. Large families, often
associated with low income and poor housing, continue to exist as de-
linquency-producing pockets in both countries and, not surprisingly,
it is from these that criminal careers most often develop. In an analysis of the causes of contemporary juvenile crime, which could just
as well apply to any previous century, D. J. West has written: "From
the familiar conglomeration of social handicaps (labouring class, poverty, overcrowding, immigrant, Irish Roman Catholic, bad neighborhood, poor schooling, broken home and large family) it seems futile
to single out any one as the prime factor in the development of juvenile delinquency."[30] Thus, while the level of affluence and opportunity rises generally, relative inequality remains strongly pronounced, not only between the upper and lower social strata but
within the working class itself. Despite the fact that persistent young
offenders are but a tiny minority of their total age-group, their existence remains a challenge to the optimists who perceive the past
two decades as an era of equality among Europe's young.

---

[28] See Willmott, Chapter 2; Mays, *Young Pretenders*, pp. 27–28.
[29] West, pp. 94–95; Neidhardt, *Junge Generation*, pp. 74–78.
[30] West, p. 74.

III

Life cycles have been converging, but not to the point of creating one common mold for either boyhood or girlhood. Indeed, as far as official policy toward youth is concerned, the notion of a single model of adolescence, a concept so strongly held in previous decades, has itself been giving way to greater diversity. Nowhere was this more evident than in the middle-class youth movements; and, by the mid-1960s, even the English Scouts were ready to drop "Boy" from their standard as a concession to the changing times. An official study, prompted by declining membership, justified the change on the grounds that "the older boy or youth is most anxious to be regarded as adult, and is inclined to avoid anything that causes him to be classified with an age group lower than that to which he belongs." [31] Falling numbers also encouraged the Church Lads' Brigade to reconsider its status as a drill-oriented, single-sex organization. "It would be unrealistic in the prevailing moral and social climate, to expect it to make a broad-front appeal to boys," Brigade leadership concluded.[32] In Germany as well, old-fashioned youth groups were in trouble by the end of the 1950s, not so much with youth under 14 as with the age group 14–18, as the survey of the Oxford Scouts, Table 8, illustrates.

Had it not been for the Cub membership, the movement would have been in a great deal more trouble than it was. Organizations for girls found it even more difficult to hold the attentions of members 14 and older, one of the reasons that the Oxford City Youth Committee decided as early as 1950 that the working girl could best be served by "treating her, not so much as a youth club member but as a young adult." [33] The whole approach to youth clubs was changing as churches gradually ceased to regard their facilities as recruiting grounds for new members and the old objections to mixed-sex

---

[31] Publication/report, Chief Scout's Report, p. 14.
[32] Springhall, p. 143.
[33] Ms. source E, Youth Committee, Min. Book, 1950.

TABLE 8

Membership in the Oxford Scouts, 1946–1966[a]

Year	Cub Scouts 8–11	Scouts 12–14	Scouts 15–20	Total Cubs and Scouts
1946	516	701	294	1521
1956	714	696	164	1712
1966	764	653	131	1548

[a] Census of Oxford Scout Association for the years 1920–1966 was made available to me by Mr. W. J. Willis of Oxford. The aggregate figures are my compilation.

organizations faded.[34] More informal, "open" arrangements were being experimented with as European youth workers began to adjust to the habits of the young rather than insisting that the young adjust to their standards. In 1960, Oxford's Youth Committee was willing to recommend mixed clubs "*even though* these are admittedly more difficult to run," an effort at accommodation on their part that marked a radical shift away from the institutional imperatives of earlier decades.[35]

The old fear of unsupervised activity was disappearing and a more relaxed atmosphere now characterized most youth clubs, though a certain tension between the old and new generations of youth workers was evident, as noted in the editorials that appeared in Oxford's youth newsletter:[36]

> Though many youth leaders teach the "public school" virtues of loyalty, initiative, and sense of responsibility, few encourage members of their organizations to think for themselves. So scared are we that boys and girls will become "teddified," promiscuous or communist, that we try, often unconsciously, to impose upon them our own sets of values, so that they may "fit into" our society and thus not wish to change it. Some of us therefore flag-wave with Palmerstonian abandon, others ram personally held religious beliefs down adolescent throats, while

[34] Brew, pp. 118–119. In contrast, a survey of Oxford youth taken in 1943 showed little interest and even a degree of hostility to mixed groups. Ms. source I, Cole Papers, Oxford File of the Social Reconstruction Survey, "Voluntary Services in Oxford," prepared by C. Craven.

[35] "Survey of Youth Services in Oxford," a memorandum provided me by Mr. F. S. Green, previously of the Oxford Youth Service. (Italics are mine.)

[36] Newspaper/periodical, *Contact*, July 1957.

we all preach a purely arbitrary doctrine of sexual morality as an immutable code of Divine Law. . . . Many still feel that the cinema is vaguely sinful, and that the television is the root of all evil. Antiquity spells safety, however, and the old style country dance is encouraged in many youth groups, while jiving, perhaps the true folk dance of today, is often forbidden, for it is modern and therefore dangerous.

Youth was at a transition point, and although there was much resistance to change, middle-class opinion was clearly shifting toward greater tolerance of diverse life cycles. "We deplore the habit of singling out the adolescent or 'teenager' as a separate and distinct person with a particular problem," stated the Oxford Youth Committee's 1960 report. "People of all ages have their problems, and the youth service is only one aspect of the provision by the community for its own well being." [37] Involvement in community affairs was now encouraged, though exposure to politics was still viewed with alarm. The postwar West German youth service had officially dedicated itself to the preparation of the young for participation in democracy, but, like its English counterpart, carefully avoided partisan involvement.[38] Apparently, those youths who were attracted to leadership in official organizations also shared adult apprehensions, for when the 18-year-old vote was considered at a national meeting of English youth councils in 1964 it was voted down by a considerable majority. One girl, speaking against the resolution, reflected the mood of the membership when she contended that the current Beatlemania showed youth "quite unworthy of the honour." [39]

Beatlemania was, by origin, a working-class phenomenon, and the contempt in which rock music and dance were held by many club members reflected a lingering class-consciousness on the part of those in charge. But while class differences within the youth movements remained evident, the barriers that had previously divided adult youth workers from those they sought to serve were rapidly dissipating, a trend that was reflected in the first-name basis that now prevailed in many clubs.[40] The vague mood of fear and hostility that

---

[37] "Survey of Youth Services in Oxford." Report of Committee on Age of Majority (publication/report) reported that British youth regarded themselves as adult at age 17. Wilson, p. 72.

[38] Pross, p. 455; Laqueur, pp. 216–227.

[39] Quoted in newspaper/periodical, *Contact*, May 1964. On the general tendency toward conservatism, see Musgrove, *Youth and Social Order*, pp. 19–23; Marwick, pp. 50–51; and Abrams and Little, pp. 95–110.

[40] Brew, p. 129.

had once existed was apparently disappearing, mainly because youth work was, more than ever before, a professional matter.

The position of the middle classes, particularly the white-collar groups, had stabilized in the postwar era. Pensions and tenure arrangements protected managers, teachers, and civil servants against the insecurities that had plagued that group during the first decades of the century.[41] The decline of militant working-class movements in western European countries also contributed to their peace of mind; and, as Cold War tensions abated, the need to indoctrinate the young with the values of patriotism seemed less pressing. Endowed with greater wealth and leisure than ever before, the groups from which the caretaker elites had once been recruited began to withdraw into a more self-centered private existence. By the end of the 1950s, middle-class youth movements were having trouble recruiting the volunteers that had once been at their command.[42] The fact that, since 1945, the proportion of married women at work had increased considerably may also account for the disappearance of the lady volunteer; but, for whatever reason, the middle class was leaving work with youth to the professional, a change that was bound to alter the nature of childsaving.[43]

Even those organizations that still relied on voluntary workers reflected these changes. A survey of English Scout leaders, conducted in 1966, showed that 82% had been Scouts themselves. The major reason they gave for volunteering was a sense of debt to the organization, not the moral and patriotic zeal that had moved an earlier generation. Although two-thirds were middle class and most had a very high rate of church attendance, they seemed notably lacking in missionary impulse and were clearly more interested in perpetuating an organization devoted to enjoyment than serving as agents of socialization.[44] In Germany, too, earlier purposes were at such discount that many were now worried that youth work might be suffering from a surfeit of management and a deficit of idealism.[45] There, it was clear that the ideology as well as the role of the caretaker had altered drastically, accounting, in part, for the new and more tolerant generational relations that were apparent by 1960.

---

[41] On the rise of the status of teachers, see Tropp; and Baron and Tropp, pp. 545–554. For Germany, see Samuel and Thomas, Chapter 4.

[42] Green, p. 11; also publication/report, Youth Service in England and Wales, pp. 1–7.

[43] Marsh, pp. 134–135.

[44] Publication/report, Chief Scout's Report, pp. 279–284.

[45] Pross, p. 459.

Rowdy, disruptive behavior was no less a problem than before. Indeed, during the 1950s there was growing public concern about what was termed "middle class delinquency," the misconduct of the gilded youth seeming suddenly to match that of the less fortunate in extent and destructiveness. Yet, the reaction of adults seemed less resentful and punitive, for there was less of the status anxiety that had been at the source of earlier tensions between youth workers and those placed in their charge. A greater willingness to grant older youth the status of adults reflected an important change in the self-esteem of the youth workers themselves, many of whom were now trained specialists rather than volunteers. "Offer advice when asked, and not before," was the attitude of one of the new breed; "Try to be unshockable, and not automatically critical; above all, accept young people as they are and treat them as equals."[46]

IV

The emancipation of youth from its formerly dependent status paralleled its regaining of a measure of civil equality. In part, this was due to military service required of males during the era of the Cold War. Duties must ultimately be rewarded by rights in a democratic society, and by the mid-1960s there was talk of opening access to political and civil rights to those of draft age. Introduction of the 18-year-old vote, which was accomplished in England in 1969 and in Germany in 1970, was bound to bring in its wake the abolition of various limitations on youthful drinking and entertainment. Although it is too early to tell whether restrictions on younger age groups will be progressively eliminated in the next decade, it seems clear that young people are more aware of their civil rights today than they were two decades earlier.[47]

The position of the modern adolescent has been one both of privilege and deprivation. It was inevitable that in the current period of transition these contradictions would come under criticism from

---

[46] Quoted in newspaper/periodical, *Contact*, September 1968.
[47] "Militance in High Schools"; Wildermann and Kaase; Wilson, Chapters 6, 15; Altbach and Lipset, pp. 35–95.

all points of view, and nowhere has this been more evident than with respect to the judicial and penal systems affecting juveniles. In Europe as well as America, the concept of the juvenile court has been severely challenged, both by those who feel that its functions should be assigned to social welfare agencies and those who think it provides too little protection to the child brought before the law. In Britain, a government white paper published in 1965 called for the replacement of the juvenile court by family councils based on models already existing in Scandinavian countries.[48] In Germany, similar proposals are being debated, with opinion forming along lines similar to those in Britain and America.[49] On one side are those that feel that the present courts, despite their wide discretionary powers, still "criminalize" the child and therefore inhibit the process of rehabilitation. An opposing point of view is held both by those moralists who resist any attempt to replace traditional concepts of punishment, and by civil libertarians who feel that, while a judicial proceeding may sometimes be insensitive, it at least provides the protection of law that social welfare agencies do not. The latter argue further that the juvenile court should be reformed to allow minors the same civil rights as are permitted to adults brought before the bench, thereby encouraging justice on the part of the judges and civil responsibility on the part of the young.[50] This is the position taken by the United States Supreme Court in 1967 when it ruled that "being a boy does not justify a Kangaroo court."[51] Yet, even in the United States, where the movement to restore civil rights to minors seems most advanced, the issue is still much in flux.

The way juvenile justice is reformed will have a profound effect on the treatment of youth in reformatories, training schools, foster homes, and other institutions to which they are now committed. The trend in the past 20 years has been toward the use of facilities located in the community rather than sending the offender to a distant prison or reformatory. In England about 85% of those brought before the court are dealt with in a manner that does not remove them from their families or neighborhoods.[52] Everywhere, the family and the community have regained some of the status they lost to so-called

---

[48] Boss, pp. 86–89.
[49] Simonsohn, pp. 23–28; Platt, Chapter 6; Grünhut.
[50] Boss, pp. 89–93.
[51] Platt, p. 161.
[52] Boss, p. 54.

therapeutic facilities at the beginning of the century, for the proven inefficiency of these "total institutions" in rehabilitation has encouraged experimentation with new, "open" units, located so that youth may have access to a normal round of school, jobs, and friends, within a familiar setting.[53] Younger children are rarely committed even to these community centers, but instead are returned as soon as possible to their parents or foster homes. Treatment of those over 16 had taken increasing advantage of probation devices, a trend also noticeable in the handling of adult offenders.

The decline and, in some cases, the actual closing of older juvenile institutions reflects the general desegregation of youth that has occurred over the past 20 years. This has been particularly noticeable with respect to the schools, which have retained, only with the greatest difficulty, the earlier isolation of scholastic culture. Coeducation has been extended on both the secondary and university levels; student government has begun to deal with real rather than artificial issues; and there has been a growing civil rights agitation among students at all levels, coinciding with the social and racial integration that has been forced upon elite institutions in the past 20 years.

Perhaps the most dynamic factor in this change has been what Michael Young has called the "rise of meritocracy," in and of itself an elitist phenomenon but one which has had profound implications for the traditional age-grading. One British study in the mid-1960s found that in one generation the pace of learning had been speeded up 24%.[54] And partly as a result of this renewed emphasis on precocity, the conception of prolonged adolescence has come under increasing criticism. As education has become more technical and demanding, the socialization functions once assigned to it have been de-emphasized. By 1960, even England's cloistered boarding schools were reacting to the pressure of increasing competition for university entrance by making adjustments in the model of the well-rounded gentleman. Study was replacing the so-called "character building" extracurricular activities to such an extent that it frightened those committed to the "boys will be boys" tradition. "I am not prepared to leave in this school boys who would allow preparation for university entrance to interfere with monotorial and athletic obligations. They are here to learn to live balanced and responsible lives, not to be crammed for university entrance at all costs," was

---

[53] West, pp. 267–285; Schaffstein, pp. 248–265.
[54] Lowndes, p. 313.

the response of one conservative headmaster to the trends in secondary education.[55]

Yet, most responsible educators were more ready to accept change, for at least half of the headmasters surveyed by Ian Weinberg indicated that the relationship between the closed community of the school and the wider world outside was now the most troubling problem before them.[56] The close, paternal relationships between students and teachers at both school and university level were bound to be altered by specialization and professionalization, calling into question the notion of *in loco parentis* that had for so long justified a cloistered scholastic regime. In day schools, too, academic demands were causing a reappraisal. Because upward mobility was now more than ever before dependent on achievement, sports and youth organizations could no longer be allowed to "interfere with school work to such an extent that they jeopardize these chances." [57] Of course, the same argument could be used to support the withdrawal of youth from the diverting world of adults, but during the 1960s it tended to work against rather than for age segregation, at least in those circles which most valued academic achievement for its own sake, namely the middle classes.

The academic revolution paralleled economic changes that were working to integrate the young more closely with the working world. Although there was much debate about the quality of the jobs that the postwar economy offered youth, there is little doubt that full employment meant more abundant, more secure opportunity. The problem of boy labor as it had existed since the beginning of the century virtually disappeared as increasing numbers of working youth entered training programs that led to upgraded jobs and higher wages. "The sense of being sought after in employment is perhaps more important than any other change in the actual nature of the work done, and no doubt reinforces the teenager's feeling of importance and independence," reported one British inquiry in 1960.[58] Of course, the prospects at the top and middle rungs of the technological ladder probably improved more rapidly than those at the

---

[55] Weinberg, p. 183. On the German schools in the same period, see Neidhardt, *Junge Generation*, pp. 34–37, 41–43; and Dahrendorf, pp. 312–329.

[56] Weinberg, p. 188.

[57] Comment of headmaster, quoted from newspaper periodical, *Contact*, July 1961; also Weinberg, pp. 190–191. On pressures at the university level, see Halsey.

[58] Publication/report, Youth Service in England and Wales, p. 24; Neidhardt, *Junge Generation*, pp. 50–51; Musgrove, *Youth and Social Order*, pp. 82–85.

very bottom, leaving a legacy of inequality that some observers believed would lead to an ultimate rebellion of the "losers" against the
unattainable achievement standards of bourgeois society.[59] Nevertheless, the trend up through the 1960s seemed to be toward greater
job satisfaction and general contentment among the vast majority of
working youth, with those lower on the economic scale being even
more accepting than those at the top.[60] This was, in part, a reflection
of the unprecedented prosperity of teenage workers, whose gross
wages had risen fourfold between 1938 and 1960. Studies showed
that youthful spending increased 100% in the same period, raising
the age-group's share of the consumer market to about 5% of the
total.[61]

Affluence worked in contradictory ways, however, encouraging
youth to compete for adult status economically, while at the same
time making it profitable for adults to produce fashions and entertainment specifically designed to appeal to younger age groups.
Some observers thought they detected the exploitation of the young
by commercial interests, and there were those who criticized the new
consumerism as a diversion of youthful energies from more worthy
causes. Yet, there is no evidence that the young have become so
attached to the accoutrements of the so-called "youth culture" as
to isolate them from other, more fundamental, social and civil interests. To date, there exist no countercultures capable of sustaining
themselves apart from adult institutions and values; and since adults
are so deeply involved in the music and fashions of the young, these
too seem to unite rather than separate the generations.[62]

Nowhere in Europe or America is there very much evidence of a
severe "generation gap," despite the student and worker upheavals
of the 1960s and 1970s. Studies of "young rebels" indicate that, while
there is a certain degree of child–parent tension, the major thrust of
youthful discontent is directed not at family but outward, at social,
political, and academic institutions that are only indirectly identified
with the older generation. Young people and their parents are more

---

[59] Publication/report, Youth Service in England and Wales, pp. 26–27; Willmott,
p. 165; Fyvel; and for general survey, see Bordua.

[60] Musgrove, Youth and Social Order, pp. 17–19; Neidhardt, Junge Generation,
p. 55.

[61] Publication/report, Youth Service in England and Wales, p. 23; Musgrove,
Youth and Social Order, p. 84; Neidhardt, Junge Generation, p. 55.

[62] Neidhardt, Junge Generation, pp. 64, 87–88, 91–93; Willmott, pp. 155, 179–
180; and Schwartz and Marten, p. 458.

likely to be united than divided on basic political and social issues, tensions arising over means rather than ends, a reflection of the normal pace of historical change rather than any intrafamilial disruption or severe hostility between groups on the basis of age alone. In many contemporary situations, the confrontation between young and old is actually conflict between persons of differing class position —students versus police, young workers versus employers. Therefore, we must be careful not to mistake these events as evidence of deep generational divisions.[63]

V

The political and social movements that were attracting the young in the 1960s displayed a general tendency to integrate youth with the adult world, to propel them into roles and concerns that called for an advanced level of autonomy and maturity. This was true not only of the young French workers who, in 1968, pushed their older comrades to strike, but also of those middle-class students who actively participated in political movements during the same period. Even students who expressed their discontents by dropping out and joining in various apolitical countercultural movements were demonstrating a maturity that had been rarer among previous middle-class generations. The sects, communes, and bohemias of the past two decades recall many features of their nineteenth-century predecessors. Some have perpetuated the authoritarian family motif, declaring themselves "children" and submitting to surrogate "fathers" and "mothers." Extremes of masochism and sadism, reminiscent of an earlier age, have gained widespread attention in the press and television media. But while it is possible, as Lewis S. Feuer has demonstrated, to find Oedipal themes reminiscent of the early nine-

---

[63] On the myth of the generation gap, see Musgrove, *Youth and Social Order,* pp. 80–81; Neidhardt, *Familie,* pp. 31–39, 44–50; Goode, pp. 79–81; Baumert, pp. 1–14; Himmelweit, pp. 179–190; Metraux, pp. 204–228; Adelson; Abrams, pp. 175–190.

teenth century in student movements today, these should not obscure the relative maturity of the contemporary seekers who become involved, usually for short periods, in one or another of the political or countercultural phenomena of our time.[64] It should be noted that the extreme authoritarianism of early nineteenth-century communalism is largely absent; and furthermore, that these young people seem much more at ease with their own sexuality, far less concerned with questions of masculinity and femininity, most of which they have already resolved in early teenage. The current insistence on "do your own thing" is not conducive to building permanent utopia, and the life expectancy of most communes and sects is relatively short by nineteenth-century standards. On the other hand, their experimental nature is taken for granted, youth using them to facilitate their own personal growth, submitting to collective demands only to the degree that these do not interfere with an already strongly developed sense of autonomy, privacy, and self-direction. Even while in revolt against bourgeois society, communalists continue to reflect middle-class values through their strong insistence on individuality.[65]

This is but one more indication of the obsolescence of adolescence, for the sons and daughters of the middle classes are now entering into social and sexual maturity at a point in their lives that was unthinkable a generation ago. "Emancipation without pathos," Hans Heinrich Muchow has called it, a stage of life no longer burdened by emotional or sexual turmoil. By 15 or 16, middle-class youths have developed a psychological stability that was rare in earlier generations of this strata. Having put personal tasks of development behind them by the time they reach the later stages of secondary education or the first years of university, they are able to cope with social and political questions that their forerunners gladly left to adult authority. Thus the tendency of both radicalism and bohemianism of recent decades to involve younger age groups than ever before. The traditional distinction between the conforming school boy and the radical university student breaks down as the older adolescent becomes indistinguishable from what Kenneth

---

[64] Feuer, Chapters 1, 8–9. In contrast, see Keniston, *Young Radicals*. It is those youth who were uninvolved in any kind of movement whose adolescence, including dependence and sexual immaturity, is most drawn out. Keniston, *Uncommitted*. Unfortunately there are no comparable studies of committed and uncommitted European youth.

[65] This historical contrast of American communes is based on Kanter.

Keniston has identified as "post-modern" youth.[66] "Just as making a later stage of adolescence available to large numbers of children was an achievement of industrial society, so a post-adolescent stage of youth is beginning to be made available by post-industrial society," he writes.[67] (See Figure 7.) The pioneers at this new social

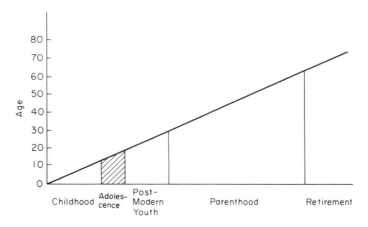

Figure 7   Phases of life in post-industrial society.

frontier are, of course, the privileged children of the educated and well-to-do, who, by virtue of their academic attainments, experience a delay of full economic independence because of graduate training into their mid- and even late twenties. Having already "developed a sense of *inner identity;* they have demonstrated a capacity for *work, love,* and *play*" long before they have entered into this student status, however; and, thus, in contrast to earlier generations whose entry into the world of work was also infinitely postponed, they are already fully adult in every sense but the economic—namely sexual, intellectual, political.[68] They remain "young" only in the sense that as students they are not yet tied down to the discipline of the work-a-day world and, therefore, have greater opportunity for the kind of social

---

[66] Muchow, *Sexualreife und Sozialstruktur,* p. 49; Neidhardt, *Junge Generation,* pp. 84–85, 89–94; Schofield, pp. 234–235. This is reflected in the psychological literature on adolescence, which places less and less emphasis on the crisis character of that age; Muuss, pp. 49–55, 177–185.

[67] Keniston, *Young Radicals,* p. 264.

[68] Keniston, *Young Radicals,* p. 260. Similar class base is found in Germany and England. Neidhardt, *Junge Generation,* pp. 78–84; Crouch.

experimentation and political activism that has distinguished their generation from previous ones.

VI

As the group most affected by the long era of adolescence that preceded the 1960s, it is not surprising that middle-class youth have been the ones most involved in the changes which have altered the conditions of dependence and conformity characterizing the earlier period. They have been in the forefront of the New Left radicalism and countercultural activity of recent decades, movements of liberation and protest that have had little apparent attraction for working youth of similar age groups. If the sons and daughters of the working classes have been less involved, it is at least partly because they have long been in possession of the autonomy and maturity for which those movements have been clamoring. They have tended to be detached from, even hostile toward, the more radical forms of middle-class emancipation, including bohemianism and feminism, precisely because their trajectory of social change, while seeming to coincide with that of bourgeois youth, has been very different in origins and direction.

While there has been some evidence of convergence of the life cycles and life styles of different classes in the past two decades, it is too early to tell whether the traditional differences in youth cultures are really diminishing. Educational opportunity has reduced the gap to some degree, but the prolongation of education, and the new forms of "post-modern youth" that this has produced, remain primarly middle-class in composition and characteristic. It seems safe to predict that as long as social and economic disparities continue, pronounced differences in class cultures of youth will persist as before. Middle-class and working-class youth will continue to make their own history in divergent ways, strongly affected by the striking differences in status, culture, and economic opportunity that continue to characterize all western societies. Therein lies the key to the origins and sustaining force behind the various traditions of youth that we have traced over the past two centuries, as well as clues to the future of those traditions in the second half of the twentieth century.

Postscript

A decade ago a reader interested in age relations would have passed the history section of the bookstore or library to seek his or her subject in the sociology, psychology, or anthropology collections. Today, the history shelves resemble Gail Sheehy's *Passages*, stocked with studies of every stage of life from birth to death.[1] An examination of the publication dates reveals a steady progression of historical interest, beginning with childhood and extending to old age. Philippe Ariès's *Centuries of Childhood* first became available in English in 1965; the new histories of youth began to appear in the early 1970s, followed by works on retirement and death.[2] This development might appear to be as predictable as Sheehy's passages, but, if the truth be known, historical circumstances rather than scholarly logic determined the sequence. Historians did not discover youth until that age group forced its way into the public consciousness in the 1960s; and, now that everyone is concerned with the elderly, their history is also being written.

Youth no longer occupies the place in our awareness it did just a few years ago. There will be many reading this edition who will have no personal recollections of the events of 1968–1969 and may even wonder whether youth as a subject is not somewhat dated. It is true that many of the psychological and sociological studies of youth culture written in the late 1960s are now mainly of interest as reflections of that particular moment. History is less prone to this kind of obsolescence, however, for it

---

[1] Sheehy.

[2] On youth, see Kett, *Rites of Passage* and U. Herrmann *et al.*; on old age, see Stearns and Fischer. For current bibliography, see Esler.

emphasizes the changing nature of age relations, their variety and essential unpredictability. Efforts by social scientists to assign a specific "nature" to youth fail to concede that the young insist on having a say in their own formation, which is the same thing as saying that they have a hand in making their own history. This was perhaps more evident in the turbulent 1960s than it is today; yet the history of the young is a good deal more continuous than our perception of it. It runs deeper than the surface events—rock concerts, drug use, teenage pregnancies—that receive the most public attention. Today, when contemporary youth appears so inert, it takes an even greater effort of historical imagination to identify the dynamic elements. There is a very real danger that as youth's presence diminishes its past will be forgotten. Efforts are already under way to rescind many of the rights that were extended to young people during the 1960s. Governments are having second thoughts about the lower age of majority, and student political participation is no longer welcomed. Revival of 1950s styles represents a similar tendency. Those adult agencies whose claims over the young were challenged during the 1960s are only too happy to forget that part of the past. They would prefer, as would those social sciences that attribute to the young certain immutable characteristics, to place youth outside history, returning them to the status of passive subjects rather than active agents of change. Under these circumstances, there is a compelling reason to restate the case for a history of the young.

I

This study is the product of a particular historical moment: 1968. That was a year of dramatic upheaval; and the role of the young in the events of Southeast Asia, Europe, and the United States had made an impression which, although I was not fully aware of it at the time, would shape my work in numerous important ways. I had long been interested in generational conflicts among nineteenth-century intellectuals, but during a year of research at Oxford in 1969–1970 the question of other groups, including peasants and urban workers, began to interest me as well. By the time I left Europe, I had accumulated considerable material on virtually all segments of German and British society, not only at moments of social upheaval but in everyday life as well.

Much of my research was unsystematic, guided by no formal theoretical perspective. Professional historical training in the United States during the 1950s and early 1960s was staunchly empirical and, with a few exceptions, concerned mainly with politics. We left theory to the social scientists, who, in turn, confined themselves mainly to the present, using history only as "examples" to prove their sweeping generalizations. Like many historians, I was much in awe of well-funded, mightily influential sociologists and political scientists. We read their books and generously contributed our "data" at their conferences, thus making ourselves as useful as possible. For those of us who were beginning to be interested in social history there were as yet very few alternatives. For the most part, the study of social groups had been left to sociology, the dominant social science of the post-World-War-II period. In Britain, social history was beginning to establish an independent existence, but only on the margins of academic life among such groups as the History Workshop. There were other new beginnings, notably in the seminars of E. P. Thompson, Asa Briggs, and Eric Hobsbawm; but, as a field, the history of society was just beginning to separate itself from its long association with economic history. The political history of youth was already part of German historiography, but social history had almost no existence in that country. As for the librarians and archivists of both England and Germany, their reaction to my topic was polite but one of total incomprehension.

I was fortunate, therefore, upon returning to Princeton in 1970, to participate in a discussion group at the Institute for Advanced Study that included Charles Tilly and Edward Shorter. It was there that I first ventured, in rough form, my ideas concerning the possibility of constructing a history of age relations. Tilly and Shorter generously suggested that their series, Studies in Social Discontinuity, might provide a format; and so began the construction of this book.

Since the writing and publication of this book, there has been a virtual revolution in American and European historiography. When I began, there was little in my own discipline to guide me. Today, social history as a field of study is a well established part of graduate training that is supported by numerous journals, frequent conferences, and institutes. Earlier, however, it was the social sciences, particularly sociology and psychology, that virtually monopolized the study of age groups. Although this book owes much to them, it also represents a break with the ahistorical premises that previously had been dominant and which had come to pervade even historical work itself. *Youth and History* should be read as an extended argument against the structural-functionalism that dominated so much of Western social thought until quite recently. Because its assumptions have so powerfully influenced the "new" social history, I must also contest much of the work done in that field. Because the origins and character of these differences may not be apparent to the general reader, it may be useful to begin discussing these differences as I, myself, first became aware of them.

II

Sociology, psychology, and anthropology, each with its own corpus of empirical studies and elaborate theoretical constructions, were bound to exercise a powerful influence over the newborn social history. Anthropology was particularly attractive to historians of preindustrial societies, whereas psychology was of obvious use to biographers. Sociology, however, was the only discipline that offered a comprehensive theory of social change, and therefore its early influence was greater than the others. I was initially attracted to sociology because in its most influential form, modernization theory, it seemed to provide an explanation of the emergence of modern youth cultures. Modernization, defined as a uniform process of change from agrarian to industrial society, posited certain changes in the life-cycle, including the development of a distinct stage of life between childhood and adulthood corresponding to what is today described as adolescence. Preindustrial forms of life and work were organized around family and local community. Modernization separated family and work, and created a gulf between the worlds of childhood and adulthood which was bridged both by formal educational institutions and by new forms of youth culture that developed alongside universal schooling. "The period of youth in our society is one of considerable strain and insecurity," explained Talcott Parsons. "Above all it means turning one's back on the security both of status and of emotional attachment which is engaged in the family of orientation. . . . There is reason to believe that the youth culture has important positive functions in easing the transition from the security of childhood in the family of orientation to that of full adult in marriage and occupational status."[3]

Parsons and other modernization theorists devoted remarkably little attention to class, ethnic, or gender differences. They wrote of a singular youth culture, whose uniformity reflected the universalistic values of what

---

[3] Parsons, "Age and Sex in the Social Structure of the United States," p. 101.

they perceived to be a tightly integrated society without significant class, ethnic, or sexual divisions. According to the functionalist explanation, which accounted for the new stage of life, adolescence itself was the axis on which individual and social progress turned. It was the point in the life-cycle when particularistic identities were dissolved and universalistic habits and values assimilated. It was the time in the life of the individual when he or she was least encumbered by the legacies of class, ethnicity, and gender, most capable of casting off the past and embracing the future. Beyond the innocence of childhood and prior to the rigidity of adulthood, adolescence facilitated change without threatening societal consensus, though a certain amount of tension was evident. Modern youth was often delinquent—even somewhat rebellious—but this was acceptable, even desirable, as long as it did not accentuate inherited social cleavages. The generation gap was viewed as a desirable alternative to class, ethnic, and sexual conflict. Young people were perceived as the one group capable of transcending outmoded identities, unburdening themselves of history and its legacies. At the beginning of the 1960s, Parsons could confidently state that if youth had its discontents, these arose more from excessive expectations for the future than from any sense of past injustices. Youth's "general orientation appears to be, not a basic alienation but an eagerness to learn, to accept high orders of responsibility and to 'fit,' not in the sense of passive conformity, but in the sense of their readiness to work within the system, rather than in basic opposition to it."[4]

Today, it is much easier to see that despite its pretensions to universal applicability, modernization theory was a rationalization of a particular course of development peculiar to North America and Western Europe in the 1950s and 1960s.[5] It was a contribution to the ideological struggles of the period, a counter argument to revolutionary theories, notably Marxism, which threatened the domestic and international status quo. Generations replaced classes in the explanation of social exchange, except that youth, unlike class, supposedly had no history of its own apart from the institutions responsible for its formation. The young were assumed to be readily malleable creatures. Vast sums were spent on their education, and an unprecedented effort at "consumer education" was mounted for their benefit. Rapid changes in ideas and taste were encouraged as necessary to the success of the growth economy, but at the same time certain limits were established. Some forms of youthful nonconformity were more acceptable than others. The juvenilia of the college campus was tolerated, even encouraged, but political and social activism were considered abnormal in adolescence. Heterosexuality was normal; homosexuality was

---

[4] Parsons, "Youth in the Context of American Society," p. 140.
[5] Gouldner; Tipps.

not. Science lent its prestige to the sanctioning of certain selected forms of social behavior, thereby underlining the boundaries between acceptable and unacceptable behavior. Perceiving modern society as a tightly organized, rational structure without significant class, sex, or ethnic divisions, modernization theorists could find no place for youth cultures that did not conform to the established norm. The behavior of sexually active girls, ghetto youth, and school dropouts posed a serious challenge to their claim that modernity had overcome the disparities of sex, class, and race supposedly characteristic only of "traditional" or "underdeveloped" societies; but this behavior was stigmatized as irrational or, in the language of the time, "dysfunctional," and youth exhibiting such behavior were referred to those correctional institutions assigned to the task of reforming the deviant. Thus, youth's role was defined for it. The plurality of youth cultures, and the history thereof, was ignored. Deprived of a past, youth became the prisoner of the present, subject to those agencies that claimed the young as their clients.

III

The assumptions of modernization theory, and of structural-functionalism generally, were already being contradicted by the time I began my investigation of the history of youth. The challenge to the notion of a rationally integrated, classless society increased in direct proportion to the internal conflicts that were beginning to appear in all Western societies in the late 1960s. Despite its claim to be a theory of change, modernization theory offered no explanation, apart from irrational deviancy, of the variety of rebellious youth cultures that were by then visible everywhere. It had particular difficulty assimilating the growth of student radicalism—the emergence of the Hippies, Provos, Mods, and Black Panthers—to its notion of a consensual youth culture. Lines of class and race fractured that notion; and the women's movement underlined the disparity of sex. While much of the debate over youth in the 1970s continued to use terms such as "youth culture" and "generation gap," the ideological character of these concepts became increasingly apparent. Most of all, however, it was the refusal of the young to act out their assigned roles that finally toppled the assumptions on which modernization theory was based. It had failed to appreciate the will and ability of the young to shape their own destinies according to the values of the class, gender, and ethnic cultures of which they were a part. The upheavals of 1968–1969 had confirmed the ability of the young to make their own history, but of equal importance to this study was the way in which working youth refused to follow the lead of student radicals. Like Humpty Dumpty, the concept of a uniform youth culture shattered, never to be put together again.

The focus of this book was strongly influenced by the class fissures that appeared in the upheavals of 1968–1969. Had I come to the subject in the mid-1970s, sexual divisions would certainly have received much greater attention, but at the time feminism had not yet raised those issues, which would have been relevant to this kind of study. Perhaps if the Marxist tradition of history had been stronger in the United States, the fact of class would never have required rehabilitation. However, it has been necessary to reassert the factor of class in the history of youth, just as it has been useful for Marxist historians to consider the way age relations affect the articulation of class in any time or place. Yet, the impulse to explore the diversity and autonomy of youth cultures owed more to events than to any theory. I found the diversity of contemporary youth cultures to be rooted in a rich, complicated experience of earlier generations, whose evocative, intractable history challenged at every turn the imposition of abstract theories of social development.

Instead of finding the history of youth to be one of gradual convergence around certain norms, I found the opposite. Prior to the industrial revolution, youth cultures paralleled the communal, trade, and corporate variations typical of that society. During the nineteenth century, these had been reconstituted into a series of class cultures which, despite enormous pressures toward conformity exerted by the institutions of state and society, resisted assimilation. The late nineteenth-century "discovery of adolescence" and its ardent sponsorship by middle-class reformers and social scientists had also failed to produce a uniform youth culture. Sex as well as class and ethnic differences persisted, mainly ignored, often repressed, but nevertheless active, perpetuating traditions of youth that had a continuous existence over several generations.

Despite twentieth-century efforts to define and contain youthful activity even more rigorously, these traditions retained their vigor. They developed and flourished not simply as mindless reactions to dominant social norms but as creative, active vehicles of youth's self-development and expression. This was true not only of those articulate middle-class youth cultures whose continuous existence can be traced back to the eighteenth century but also of the groups of young working people whose particular cultural forms have even deeper roots in the past. Whereas each has its own particular traditions, none are static or unchanging. They have shown a remarkable ability to adapt to change as well as to resist adult efforts to suppress them. Often they are presumed dead, only to reemerge at a later date in a slightly different form to meet the needs of their particular constituency. Even the most powerful assimilative institutions of the contemporary age—the factory, school, and military services—have failed to dislodge them from their place in the lives of each new generation. After more than a century of intensive effort to create a single, uniform youth culture, the variety, expressing the existing divisions within Western society, is striking. One cannot help but be struck by the refusal of the young in both past and present to accept the roles assigned to them by the theorists. Both structural-functionalist sociology and excessively economistic versions of Marxism have failed to appreciate the way in which the young confront and act on the historical circumstances in which they find themselves, and especially how past experience affects each moment in this dialectical process.

IV

My emphasis on the way historical experience shapes consciousness owes much to the work of E. P. Thompson, whose insistence on the active, conscious elements in the formation of the nineteenth-century English working class is directly relevant to the history of other groups, including youth.[6] Like class, youth cultures are influenced by economic and social circumstances, but they are not the product of material conditions alone. Members of a particular class, and the youth cultures within that class, perceive and act on the basis of collective historical experience as this is interpreted and articulated in terms of their immediate circumstances. Historical experience provides the tools with which each generation hammers out its orientation toward the world. In turn, each fresh historical experience requires a rethinking of the old values and often a radical change of orientation. Thus, for example, the culture of the journeymen's associations, which had served young craftsmen so well during the period between the decline of guild production and the rise of the modern factory system, underwent radical transformation in the early nineteenth century. It was reshaped around the

---

[6] Thompson, *Making of the English Working Class*, and, most recently, *Poverty of Theory and Other Essays*.

broader solidarities of the new working class, without entirely losing its original form or function.

Layer upon layer of youth cultures have been laid down over the centuries. We should not be surprised to find a variety of youth cultures within a particular locality or even within a particular class. Broadly speaking, there are what might be called middle-class and working-class youth cultures, but the variety within each can be explained historically. Where ethnic and gender identities add further dimensions to an already complex situation, we should also seek to analyze these in terms of historical experiences that have caused various groups to perceive and act in particular ways. Categorizing them into normal and deviant subcultures does violence to both the present and the past by obscuring the way in which the present variety of youth cultures has developed historically and how each serves to express authentic, though conflicting, interests and values.

The term "tradition" seems most appropriate to describe the youth cultures that have evolved over time. By tradition I do not mean something static or unyielding to change, but rather an experientially based set of values that permit youth to perceive and act on the world. Young people are makers as well as receivers of tradition. Each generation redefines its traditions to meet its particular needs. The traditions of youth can also be described as subcultures, distinct from but also linked with particular adult cultures. Just as class cultures have been constantly changing with each successive stage in the perpetual evolution of capitalist society, so both middle-class and proletarian traditions of youth have changed with them. Younger members of a particular class experience the world in ways different from the way their elders experience it, but both share a common heritage. The popular notion of "generation gap" ignores this totally and should be used only with great caution. There are, of course, different generations, whose placement in the overall historical process causes them to view the world in contrasting, sometimes conflicting, ways; but there is also enormous continuity within a particular class, gender, or ethnic group that binds together the generations in common outlook and behavior. As this book demonstrates, conflicts that seem to be generational are often in reality conflicts of class or race rather than age. The concept of "generation gap" should therefore be used not to obscure but to elucidate other fundamental cleavages evident in Western social development.

The essential continuity of generations within class, sex, and ethnic groups is borne out by recent American studies that have underlined the solidarity within these groups. Research sponsored by the Centre for Contemporary Cultural Studies at the University of Birmingham in England has come to a similar conclusion.[7] Fieldwork has revealed a diversity of youth

---

[7] Recent Centre for Contemporary Cultural Studies include Hall and Jefferson; Mungham and Pearson. Following a similar approach are Blake; Robins and Cohen.

subcultures, each clearly associated with a particular class and often with a specific locale. Whether it be the West Indian "rude boys" of South London or the "paki bashers" of the decaying cotton towns of England's north country, the evidence of generational continuity is clear. Investigation of the historical genesis of particular attitudes and styles of behavior has scarcely begun, but when this is completed it will almost certainly show deeply rooted traditions, reaching both into the British past and to those places of origin from which immigrant populations draw their social and cultural resources.

But whereas recent work has confirmed the existence of distinctive subcultures, it has also reinforced the findings of this study concerning the protean nature of youth—not only its ability to appropriate new styles of dress and music but also its capacity to resist attempts to inculcate standardized patterns of consumption. In the 1950s, London working-class boys with office jobs and money to spend copied the Edwardian clothing styles fashionable among the metropolitan upper classes. The latter, finding imitation a threat to their status, promptly abandoned the fashion. Adapted to a different class, the Edwardian style became markedly more flamboyant as the new Teddy Boy culture developed. This subculture ultimately underwent several modifications, but as economic conditions worsened in the 1960s, the pretense of upper-class style disappeared and London's proletarian youth adopted expressly working-class dress: heavy boots, braces, and the close-cropped hair that gave this group the name "Skinheads." Expressive of growing class differences in London at the time, the evolution of the Teds to the Skinheads illustrates the kind of change, often consciously adopted, by which the young attempt to deal with their particular historical circumstances.

Although the Birmingham researchers have not traced those changes back beyond the 1950s, their findings are consistent with my own. While I have not always been able to illustrate the genesis of earlier youth cultures in the detail they deserve, I believe that, with additional historical effort, such a reconstruction is possible for every major youth tradition, whether it be Chicago street gang life, the bohemianism of the Parisian left bank, or the nearly invisible networks of sisterhood that developed among young educated women during the Victorian era. Each generation alters its particular tradition to suit the times; a tradition may even skip a generation, but the points of connection are clear enough.

V

The notion of a uniform youth culture is no longer tenable. The harsher economic conditions of the 1970s and 1980s have completed the process of destroying the illusion of a classless, affluent society projected by the proponents of modernization theory. The divisions of class, sex, and race have been laid bare, and we are entering a period in which the old ways of treating society as a seamless, integrated system will no longer suffice. Both history and sociology have had to take into account groups that previously had been given little or no serious attention but which now, largely through their own efforts, have made themselves visible both socially and politically. The new interest in the history of blacks, immigrants, and Native Americans is part of this process. There has also been a renaissance in the history of both American and European labor, a field which now extends well beyond the conventional studies of trade unions and socialist parties to probe the work and lives of the workers themselves. The history of women is also being investigated with an intensity and at a depth unprecedented in modern historiography.

None of this would have been possible without the exploitation of new kinds of historical sources. The documentation that historians have previously used, namely the record left behind by the literate elites, does not readily yield the lives of the greater part of the population. To fill this gap, historians have learned to use a variety of sources that was previously neglected. The parish register and census schedule have, through the application of family reconstitution techniques, permitted the exploration of the demographic history of both adults and children. And over the past decade, historians have also learned to "read" the ritual and symbol of nonliterate popular cultures so as to give voice and place in history to those excluded from the written record. Our grasp of the mentalities of the past has been enormously expanded partly by the reexamination of existing documents, such as the inquisitorial records from which Emmanuel Le Roy Ladurie had constructed the collective life of Montaillou.[8] Natalie Z. Davis and E. P. Thompson have demonstrated how evidence of ritual behavior can be interrogated so as to reveal the values as well as the behavior of the past.[9] Davis's studies of the European traditions of *charivari* open a window on a world previously closed to historians. The illiterate, and more especially the young and the female, become accessible to us in moments of popular justice, festival, and recreation. Thompson has

---

[8] Le Roy Ladurie, *Montaillou.*
[9] N. S. Davis, *Society and Culture in Early Modern France;* Thompson, "Rough Music"; Le Roy Ladurie, *Carnival in Romans.*

studied the English custom of "rough music" with similar precision and results. While all such popular customs follow a particular form, their variations can be revealing. The mockery of an old man marrying a young bride or the effigy burning of a notorious wife beater can reveal much about values of the young and the old, and how these have changed over time.

Our ability to learn from such evidence owes much to anthropology, which has long been more sensitive to nonliterate modes of expression and more imaginative in the interpretation of cultural forms. Exploration of peasant and working-class cultures requires the appropriation of material long familiar to folklorists and ethnographers, but as yet little used by historians. Songs, proverbs, the artifacts of costume, dance, and ritual behavior of all kinds are awaiting historical treatment; and future historians of youth would do well to consult the methods of Matti Sarmela whose masterful use of folklore material in reconstructing the early history of Finnish youth cultures is a model of what can be accomplished.[10] The Scandinavians and the French have made much more use of folklore than have Anglo-American scholars, though this appears to be changing. Coventry's festive calendar and the modes of popular participation in it provided Charles Phythian-Adams with a major means of exploring the age relations in that particular city.[11] The pageants and customs of other communities await similar treatment.

Folklore offers immense possibilities to the historian of popular culture, though much of the evidence must be reworked before it can be used effectively. Folklorists themselves have been interested primarily in the enduring elements of culture and have given very little attention to the changing nature of ritual and custom. Their notion of the "folk" is rooted in place but not in time. The recurrence of certain ritual forms, the repetition of proverb and song, suggests to them the existence of a static, unreflective mentality. The structuralist school of anthropology also talks of mentalities as if they are immutable. Their efforts to locate "deep structures" in popular culture pays virtually no attention to change over time or the ways in which people create, use, and reshape custom according to historical circumstances. Matti Sarmela's work is unique in the way in which he is able to locate and explain the origins of Finnish folk culture in a historically precise manner.

The most effective use of folklore and antiquarian materials has been by historians such as E. P. Thompson, Robert Malcolmson, and Natalie Davis, who are conscious of the pitfalls of structuralism.[12] It is not the custom

---

[10] Sarmela.

[11] Phythian-Adams, *Desolation of a City;* and his *Local History and Folklore.*

[12] Malcolmson; Thompson, "Folklore, Anthropology, and Social History"; and Thomas, "History and Anthropology."

itself but the usage that fascinates them. Careful reconstruction of the occasion, participants, and functions of popular sports in the eighteenth and early nineteenth centuries allows Malcolmson to probe deeply into the ways the uses of leisure were altered by changes in class relations during that period. The same materials could be interrogated for evidence of changing age relations or sex roles, both of which are reflected in the history of sport. Whole areas of the past—recreation, festival, custom, entertainment—once regarded as ephemeral now move to the center of historical attention. In the eighteenth century, the Englishman's right to play football on the common land was the focus of bitter struggle, a reflection of, but also a factor in, the formation of modern proletarian class consciousness. Closer to our own time, the same sport remains one of the major terrains of social confrontation, though the issue is no longer one of land rights. Studies of contemporary football hooliganism in Britain suggest the ways in which behavior that might otherwise be interpreted as mindless can reveal much about class and generational attitudes.[13]

Sport provides only one of the many emerging possibilities for access to the history of popular cultures, including youth cultures. Since this book was written several other lines of approach have opened up, indicating enormous possibilities for further research. Restored to the context of their original performance, popular dance, drama, and song offer the historian rich evidence about a variety of attitudes, ranging from sexuality to politics. Recently the possibilities for locating performers and audience historically have begun to be realized. Martha Vicinus has shown in her history of industrial songs how much broadside and ballad can illuminate the political and social conditions of the nineteenth-century urban working class.[14] Recent work on the bawdy ballads current among the farm servants of northeast Scotland in the late nineteenth century has revealed aspects of rural sexual practices inaccessible through other sources.[15] In a similar manner, Lawrence Levine has studied the history of Afro-American folk music as a means of reconstructing the development of black culture in the United States. His use of proverb, tale, and joke as historical source provides an inspiration for those who would probe the deeper meaning of popular cultures.[16]

To date, the artifacts of youth culture have received very little attention. My own use of popular custom, dance, and song merely points in the direction of the possibilities. Contemporary youth cultures have received considerable attention, but much of it is superficial and totally lacking in historical depth. In our own time, the subject of popular culture is com-

---

[13] P. Marsh *et al.*
[14] Vicinus.
[15] Camerson.
[16] Levine.

plicated by the intervention of commercialism and the difficulty of establishing with precision the relationship between the production of culture and its uses by the mass audience. Abstracted from the people who participate in it, modern forms of youth culture are of no more interest to the social historian than those accounts of rural folk culture that neglect to locate the performance in precise time and place. Yet, the sources for a careful reconstruction of popular cultures are available and, with the assistance of more sophisticated methods, it should be possible to trace the history of modern music and dance to its origins. Without a clearer understanding of the genesis of popular cultures in both past and present, the history of youth must remain incomplete.

VI

Developments in several fields have contributed to our deepening understanding of age relations, but none have had as significant an impact as historical demography. Computer-aided surveys of parish and census records have unearthed a wealth of information that is of great significance to the history of all age groups; and we can now reconstruct with some confidence the composition, size, and extension of families over a long period of time. Not only is it possible to compare family structure at different points in time, but cycles in the development of particular families are now known in considerable detail. Most recently, research has moved beyond the family cycle to the individual life course, enabling us to understand families in the past as dynamic, expanding, and contracting, constantly reconstituting themselves as their members move through different stages of their own life-cycles.[17]

Values as well as structures change over time, and within the past decade there has been increasing attention given to the way feelings and ideas affect family life. Lawrence Stone's massive history of upper-class British families is principally concerned with the subjective and the ideological, showing the way changing ideas have affected behavior, including relations between generations.[18] To date, much less has been done with the consciousness of groups lower on the social scale, people who left no written

---

[17] Hareven.
[18] Stone, *The Family, Sex and Marriage in England, 1500–1800.*

record of their feelings about family and age relations. The absence of written source material has reinforced the tendency to treat their behavior as strongly conditioned by material factors. Stone himself concludes that whereas the patricians consciously shaped their family life, the poor had virtually no ability (or desire) to do likewise.

Historical demographers may be pardoned for thinking that the facts of birth, death, and marriage determine family relations, but historians familiar with the evidence from the popular cultures of the past should know that the poor and the illiterate hold their own very strong views on these matters.[19] The folklore of birth, death, and marriage provides abundant evidence of popular values. Much of popular song is directly concerned with the personal and moral issues that arise from sexual and age relations. At the time that this book was written, the exploration of these sources of popular values had, however, scarcely begun. As a result, I too may have overestimated the determining power of demographic and economic factors. Today I am much more skeptical about explanations of age relations that are derived from purely demographic data. Although the research of the past decade has enormously expanded our knowledge of the formal structure of families, the timing and sequencing of life-cycles, and other information derived from parish and census records, many of these studies continue to ignore the importance of volitional factors in shaping the definition of family life and age relations.[20] The assumptions of structural-functionalism have persisted longer among historical demographers than among other practitioners of the new social history. Whereas their approach to age groups has become increasingly more sophisticated, it has also become more abstract and distanced from the way life was actually experienced by those involved. The demographers' study of statistically constructed "cohorts" proceeds on quite different assumptions than the more traditional study of self-defined "generations," though the two are easily confused.[21] Until the two are brought together, neither can be complete.[22]

While my own work has benefited greatly from the findings of demographers, I remain disappointed with the tendency as well as the result of their historical efforts. Any approach to age relations that ignores the role of culture is bound to be deceptive as well as incomplete. So too are the studies that ignore the "politics" of social relations. Just as we must not think of societies as predetermined systems, so too it is dangerous to assume a unity of family interests and values without prior investigation of all the family constituents. The notion of "family strategy," often employed by

---

[19] Gillis, "Affective Individualism and the English Poor."

[20] Katz and Davey.

[21] Uhlenberg.

[22] Spitzer; for useful additional bibliography, consult Esler.

historians as well as sociologists, obscures the divergence of interests by age and gender; and it would therefore seem best to approach all social relations, in as well as outside the family, as contested territory, subject to perpetual negotiation if not outright conflict. The structure of social relations is affected by many factors, some material, others ideological, but all embedded in a particular time and place.

The dynamics that result in a particular configuration of age relations are not always easily researched. As the chapter on the emergence of the modern forms of adolescence indicates, they are generated at every level of social interaction—within families, among groups, and at the level of national and even international politics. Economics, law, and demography set the limits within which age relations are contested and formulated, but they do not determine those relations in any rigid, predetermined manner. Not every industrial urban society will experience age in the same manner. And even if universal schooling and military service do impose a certain uniformity of age groups across the spectrum of developed societies, these are not experienced in the same way in each and every one. What the French understand as youth is not precisely the same as the German experience of the same years. Different class, gender, and ethnic groups will be found defining age in different ways. As this book demonstrates time and again, the young do not passively accept the "roles" assigned them by the elders, whether these be school masters of social theorists. Taking their lead, we too should emancipate ourselves from those predetermined notions of social relations that fetter the historical imagination.

VII

One field in which this has been accomplished is women's history. The study of gender, once so subject to biological as well as sociological determinism, now provides a model for other areas of social history. This book profited greatly from the pioneering efforts in women's history, studies which made sexual relations fully accessible to historical treatment for the first time. The product of a global feminist movement, the study of women is perhaps the most important new development in American and European historiography, for it not only adds to the knowledge of a group previously largely excluded from the historical domain but also radically alters our perception of a host of questions, age relations among them. At the time this book was written, I was only just beginning to be aware of the importance of these developments, a fact reflected in its exclusively male focus. The reader should be warned that the history of male youth is not generalizable to females. To do so not only distorts the history of women, but, by fostering the myth of unisex youth cultures, falsifies the history of men as well.

Female youth deserve treatment on their own terms; the recent work by Joan Scott and Louise Tilly on the participation of women in the family and work force suggests that there is now a basic foundation for such an enterprise.[23] I would ask, however, that before such a project is entered into, the limitations of a single-sex study be considered. Historically, it has been the interaction of men and women that has shaped the social and cultural definitions of both masculinity and femininity. My own study suffers from insufficient attention to this vital point. Learning from this, future studies should take into account the dialectic of male and female youth cultures, the ways in which gender affects age, and vice-versa.[24]

Women have been the most aggressive of all groups in taking hold of their own history and making themselves visible in the past as well as in the present. Now others are beginning to emulate their initiative. Since this book was written, homosexuality has emerged as a subject of historical interest, mainly at the insistence of members of the gay community who are determined to provide themselves with an accurate picture of homosexuality in the past.[25] This, too, has important implications for the history of age relations, some of which are touched on in the later chapters of this book. A fuller understanding of both heterosexual and homosexual relations would be of enormous benefit, for these have always been of decisive importance in the structuring of relations between age groups.

Because youth cultures are strongly affected by locality, the recent revival of local history is also of enormous importance. In some cases this has been promoted by professional historians' interest in using particular communities as case studies of general trends, but there is also a renaissance in people's interest in their own past. Everywhere communities are collecting and publishing their own accounts. Ordinary men and women are articulating their view of the past, one that is often at odds with much of the history that has been written about them.[26]

The people's history movement has been closely associated with the

---

[23] Louise Tilly and Joan Scott.

[24] For new history of the male gender, see Stearns, *Be a Man!*

[25] Weeks. Also see the special issue on sexuality of the *Radical History Review* **20** (1979).

[26] *The History Workshop Journal* provides a useful introduction to the results of the people's history movement in Britain. For the background to one important element, see *Local Publishing and Local Culture*.

emergence of oral history as one of the major innovations of the past decade. Drawing on techniques long in use among historians of nonliterate societies, oral historians have become increasingly sophisticated in their approach to the accounts that can be provided by persons of all ages. There now exist many oral history archives, composed of taped reminiscences and transcripts, some drawn from noted figures but others concentrating on ordinary men and women. In Scandinavia, the cooperation of ethnographers and historians has made possible oral history projects on an impressive scale. The archives organized by Paul and Thea Thompson at Essex University in England have already generated a number of notable studies, in which the history of childhood and youth has a prominent place.[27]

As yet no project using the resources of oral history has concentrated exclusively on the history of youth or of generations. What might be possible is suggested by the work of Peter Loewenberg and Peter Merkl, historians interested in the social formation of the Nazi movement, who have approached their subject in terms of generations.[28] Using the autobiographies of Nazis available in German archives, they have constructed a portrait of social, political, and psychological development beginning with the childhood experiences of these men. Their conclusions about the unique psychological character of the generation that had experienced the disruption and deprivation of World War I as children is highly suggestive and could be confirmed by a systematic reconstruction of the life histories of larger numbers of persons. In the same way, Glen Elder's study of the generation of the American depression could serve as a model for historical research on the effects of other epochal events.[29]

We also need to know much more about how age interacts with particular modes of production, research best done on a local or regional level using a comparative method. Youth cultures in mining areas, where work is rigidly sex segregated, are quite different from those in commercial cities, where boys and girls work alongside one another, but little is known about the origins of this variation.[30] Studies taking into account local and ethnic variations in popular culture would also be enormously useful, for we must know much more about the values of the older generation before we can fully understand that of the young.

The greatest danger lies in the tendency toward specialization so apparent in every field of historical endeavor. Recent studies of retirement and aging have only reinforced earlier tendencies to separate the history of youth

---

[27] An excellent introduction to the field is provided by Paul Thompson.
[28] Merkl; Loewenberg.
[29] Elder.
[30] Dennis *et al.*

from the history of other age groups. The recent emphasis on the study of individual life cycles or "life courses" is a useful corrective but not the entire solution to this problem. Studied in isolation from the larger social and political context, the individual life cycle becomes an abstraction, empty of the collective experience of those passages which should be the chief concern of the social historian. Often the phases of life are accepted as given, psychologically rather than historically determined. As in Gail Sheehy's overly determinist account of contemporary life phases, the individual becomes a mere passenger on a journey through life in which the schedule of events seems prearranged or, in Sheehy's terms, "predictable." Such accounts ignore not only the variety and mutability of life but also the element of human agency as such.

VIII

Clearly there is much to be gained from an imaginative use of new methods and sources, but it is well to keep in mind that energetic empiricism alone did not account for the enormous extension of the range and depth of historical studies in the past decade. The kind of revolution within the historical discipline that has taken place came about only when its practitioners were forced to look at their subject in new ways and ask new questions requiring alternative means of research. Until the late 1960s, history had allowed the social sciences to monopolize the study of youth in a quite ahistorical manner. Only when youth itself began to shake the ideological foundations of this artificial division of labor did historians begin to recognize the opportunity and responsibility of studying groups that had previously been outside their chosen jurisdiction. Only when the young, the poor, and the female began to make their own history in a visible, public manner was the right of these groups to be represented in the past also recognized. Looking back on this remarkable period, I am more aware now than I was then of how much social history owes to that unique historical moment.

The current revolution in history is by no means complete, however. In the world economic crisis that is presently upon us, other equally important shifts in perspective are bound to occur. It is too early to predict what direction the next decade of historical research will take, but one can be relatively safe in assuming that, as the present conditions alter, so too will our perception of the past. At the same time, we should be aware of how easily a subject like age relations can slip out of historical focus. There is abundant evidence that this is already beginning to occur. Society's priorities have shifted considerably. Investment in education is declining; reintroduction of military service is possible; and the young themselves seem apathetic and inert. Only by being attentive to these changes, by ceaselessly resisting a return to elitist conceptions of the past, can the focus be maintained. Prior to the 1960s, historians were bemoaning the declining public interest in the past. History's position of cultural importance had been forfeited by allowing the study of the greater part of humanity to be monopolized by other disciplines. The historical renaissance of the past decade has rectified that to a very large degree, but this progress will be difficult to maintain in the present circumstances. Should history once again lose touch with the past made by the poor, by women, by people of all ages, the loss will be not only its own but humanity's.

January 1981

Bibliography

I. Manuscript Sources

A. Archiv der deutschen Jugendbewegung. Burg Ludwigstein, Witzenhausen.

Frank Fischer, unpublished notebooks.
Franz Henkel, personal papers.

B. Bodleian Library, Department of Western MSS. Oxford University.

Manning Collection on Folklore. MS Top Oxon d 190–191, 199–200.
Minutes of Church of England Association of Managers and Teachers, 1873–1918. MS Top Oxon e 236.
Minutes of the General Committee of the Oxford Boy Scouts Association. Dep. 50–60.
Minutes of the Oxford Branch of the National Service League, 1908–1915. MS Top Oxon e 277, 228.
Minutes of the Oxford Clerical Association, 1851–1895. MS Top Oxon e 22–39, 84–87.
Oxford Police Records, 1829–1869. MS Top Oxon b 129–162.
Oxford University Boy Scout Club, 1919–1942. MS Top Oxon d 328/1,2.

C. Gottingen Stadtarchiv.

Felix-Klein Gymnasium
Jugendamt
Oberlyzeum
Polizei Direktion
Soziale Fürsorge

D. Oxford City Library, Manuscript Collections.

Minute Book of the Board of Governors, Oxford High School, 1878–1932.
Oxford School Board Attendance Committee, 1879–1909.
Oxford School Board Minute Books, 1879–1903.
St. Frideswide's Boys National School Log Books, 1872–1956.

E. Oxford Education Department, departmental files.

City of Oxford Education Committee Minute Books, 1903–1963.
City of Oxford School Attendance Subcommittee, 1910–1960.
Youth Committee General Purposes Subcommittee, 1946–1960.

F. Oxford Court House, Police Court Records.

Oxford Police Court Records, 1870–1930.

G. Oxford Town Hall Muniments.

Minutes of the Oxford Subcommittee on Infant Welfare. EE 1/18.
Minutes of the Watch and Ward Committee, 1836–1966. HH 1/1–32.

H. Oxford University Archives.

Proctors' Manuals. WPY 7 (18–21); and WPY 7 (3–6).

I. Private Collections.

Balliol Boys' Club, papers and log books. In the possession of Dr. Willis Bund, Dean of
    Balliol College, Oxford.
G. D. H. Cole Papers. Nuffield College Library, Oxford.
Oxford Scout Association, membership census for 1920–1966. In the possession of Mr. W.
    J. Willis, Oxford.
St. Barnabas School, log books. In the possession of Headmaster of St. Barnabas School.
Young Men's Christian Association, Oxford Branch records. In the possession of Mr. DelNevo,
    Secretary.

II. Official Publications and Reports

Berichte den Jugendpfleger Göttingen, 1914–1930. Göttingen City Library.
The Chief Scout's Advance Party Report, London, 1966. Bodleian Library.
City of Oxford Chief Constable's Annual Report, 1897–1960. Oxford City Library.
City of Oxford Chief Constable's Annual Report, 1897–1960. Oxford City Library.
City of Oxford Youth Committee Report, 1941, 1944, 1966. Oxford City Library.
Disinherited Youth: A Report on the 18+ Age Group, Edinburgh, 1943. Bodleian Library.
Jahresbericht des Ortsausschusses für weibliche Jugendpflege, Göttingen, 1914–1917. Göttingen
    City Library.
Mothers' Union Journal, 1893–1896. Oxford City Library.
Mothers' Union Report, Oxford Branch, 1891–1910. Oxford City Library.
Oxford and District Boy Scouts' Chronicle, I, November 1909. Oxford City Library.
Oxford School Board Annual Report, 1873–1927. Oxford City Library.
Parliamentary Papers XX–XXI (1864), "Report of Her Majesty's Commissioners Appointed to
    Inquire into Revenue and Management of Certain Colleges and Schools."
Parliamentary Papers I–V (1868), Schools Inquiry Commission.
Report of the Committee on the Age of Majority, 1967. Bodleian Library.
Report of the Oxford and County Branch of the National Society for the Prevention of Cruelty
    to Children, 1899–1919. Headquarters Library.

Report of the Oxford Council of Social Service, 1938–1939. Oxford City Library.
Report of the Oxford Vigilance Association, 1888. Oxford City Library.
Report of the Oxford Working Men's and Lads' Institute, 1884–1915. Oxford City Library.
The Youth Service in England and Wales: Report of the Committee Appointed by the Minister of Education. London, 1960. Bodleian Library.

III. Newspapers and Periodicals

Contact: City of Oxford Community Center and Youth Services Newspaper, 1956–1969. Oxford City Library.
National Health, 1908–1924.
Oxford High School Magazine, 1903–1970. Oxford City Library.
Der Wandervogel, Zeitschrift des Bundes für Jugendwanderungen, 1909–1914. Burg Ludwigstein.

IV. Books and Articles

Abrams, Philip. "Rites de Passage: The Conflict of Generations in Industrial Society." Journal of Contemporary History 5(1) (1970):175–90.
———, and Little, Alan. "The Young Voter in British Politics." British Journal of Sociology 14(2) (1962):95–110.
Acton, William. Functions and Disorders of the Reproductive Organs in Childhood, Youth, Adult Age, and Advanced Life. 6th ed. London, 1875.
Adelson, Joseph. "What Generation Gap?" New York Times Magazine, 12 January 1970.
Alexander, Sally. St. Giles's Fair, 1830–1914: Popular Culture and the Industrial Revolution in 19th Century Oxford. Oxford, 1969.
Altbach, Philip, and Lipset, Seymour M. Students in Revolt. Boston: Beacon, 1969.
Anderson, Eugene N. et al., Eds. Europe in the Nineteenth Century. Vol. 1. Indianapolis: Bobbs & Merrill, 1961.
Anderson, Michael. "Household Structure and the Industrial Revolution: Mid-Nineteenth Century Preston in Comparative Perspective." In Household and Family in Past Time, edited by Peter Laslett. Cambridge Univ. Press, 1972.
———. "Family, Household and the Industrial Revolution." In Sociology of the Family, edited by Michael Anderson. London: Penguin Books, 1971.
———. Family Structure in Nineteenth Century Lancashire. Cambridge Univ. Press, 1972.
Arensberg, C. M., and Kimball, S. T. Family and Community in Ireland. 2d ed. Cambridge, Massachusetts: Harvard Univ. Press, 1968.
Ariès, Philippe. Centuries of Childhood: A Social History of Family Life. New York: Vintage Books, 1965.
Avery, Gillian. Nineteenth Century Children: Heroes and Heroines in English Children's Stories, 1780–1900. London, 1965.
Bailey, Cyril. A Short History of the Balliol Boys' Club. Oxford, 1950.
Bamford, T. W. Rise of the Public Schools. London, 1967.
Banks, J. A. "Population Change and the Victorian City." Victorian Studies 11 (1968):280–94.
———. Prosperity and Parenthood: A Study of Family Planning among the Victorian Middle Classes. London: Routledge & Kegan Paul, 1954.
Barber, C. L. Shakespeare's Festive Comedy. Princeton: Princeton Univ. Press, 1959.
Baron, George, and Tropp, Asher. "Teachers in England and America." In Education, Economy and Society, edited by A. H. Halsey et al. New York, 1961.

Baumert, Gerhard. "Einige Beobachtungen zur Wandlungen der Familien Stellung des Kindes in Deutschland." In *Recherches sur la famille*, vol 2, edited by Nels Anderson, pp. 1–14. Göttingen, 1957.

Baustaedt, Karl. *Festschrift zum 60. Jahrigen Gestehen der Felix-Klein Oberschule zu Göttingen*, 1950.

Beard, P. F. "Voluntary Youth Organizations." In *Nuffield College Social Reconstruction Survey*. London, 1945.

Bechtel, Heinrich. *Wirtschafts und Sozialgeschichte Deutschlands*. Munich, 1967.

Beerbohm, Max. "A Morris for May Day." *Harper's Monthly Magazine*, October 1907.

Berkner, Lutz K. "The Stem Family and the Developmental Cycle of the Peasant Household: An Eighteenth Century Austrian Example." *American Historical Review* 77(2) (April 1972):398–418.

Blackwell, Elizabeth. *Counsel to Parents on the Moral Education of their Children in Relation to Sex*. 2d ed. London, 1879.

Blake, Mike. *The Sociology of Youth Culture and Youth Subcultures*. London: Routledge & Kegan Paul, 1980.

Bloch, Iwan. *The Sexual Life of Our Time and Its Relation to Modern Times*. London, 1908.

Blum, Jerome. "The Internal Structure and Polity of the European Village Community from the Fifteenth to the Nineteenth Century." *Journal of Modern History* **47**(4) (Dec. 1971):541–76.

Bongert, Yvonne. "Délinquance juvénile et responsabilitié penale du mineur au XVIIIᵉ Siecle." In *Crimes et criminalité en France sous L'Ancien Regime*. Paris: Librairie Armand Colin, 1971.

Booth, Charles. *Life and Labour of the People in London*. Vol. 3. London, 1902.

Bordua, David J. "Delinquent Subcultures: Sociological Interpretations of Gang Behavior." *Annals of the American Academy of Political and Social Science* **338** (1961).

Born, Stephan. *Erinnerungen eines Achtundvierzigers*. Leipzig, 1898.

Boss, Peter. *Social Policy and the Young Delinquent*. London: Routledge & Kegan Paul, 1967.

Bowley, A. L., and Burnett-Hurst, A. R. *Livelihood and Poverty*. London, 1915.

Brailsford, Dennis. *Sport and Society, Elizabeth to Anne*. London: Routledge & Kegan Paul, 1969.

Braun, Rudolf. *Industrialisierung und Volksleben*. Erlenbach-Zürich, 1960.

Bray, Reginald. "The Boy and the Family." In *Studies of Boy Life in Our Cities*, edited by E. J. Urwick. London, 1904.

———. *Boy Labour and Apprenticeship*. London, 1911.

———. *The Town Child*. London, 1907.

———. "Youth and Industry." In *Converging Views of Social Reform*. London, 1913.

Brew, A. MacAlister. *Youth and Youth Groups*. 2d ed. London, 1968.

Brieke, Ernst. "Die Geschichte der Göttingen Jugendwehr." *Göttingen Nachrichten*, no. 271 (20 November 1937).

Broderick, C. B. *Kinder und Jugendsexualität*. Reinbek bei Hamburg: Rowohlt Verlag, 1970.

Brunner, Otto. "Das 'ganze Haus' und die alteuropäische 'Ökonomik.' " In *Neue Wege der Sozialgeschichte*. Göttingen, 1956.

Brunschwig, Henri. *La Crise de l'état preussien et la genèse de la mentalité romantique*. Paris, 1947.

Butler, C. Violet. *Social Conditions in Oxford*. London, 1914.

Cameron, David K. *The Ballad and the Plough*. London: Futura, 1978.

Carden, Maren Lockwood. *Oneida: Utopian Community to Modern Corporation*. Baltimore: Johns Hopkins Press, 1969.

Carlebach, Julius. *Caring for Children in Trouble*. London: Routledge and Kegan Paul, 1970.

Carpenter, Edward. *Love's Coming of Age*. London, 1903.

Carpenter, J. Estlin. *The Life and Work of Mary Carpenter.* London, 1879.
Carter, Lady Violet Bonham. "Childhood and Education." In *The Character of England,* edited by E. Barker, pp. 209–34. Oxford, 1947.
Chambers, J. D. *Population, Economy, and Society in Pre-Industrial England.* Edited by W. A. Armstrong. Oxford: Oxford Univ. Press, 1972.
Charlton, D. G. *Secular Religions in France, 1815–70.* London, 1963.
Chevalier, Louis. *Laboring Classes and Dangerous Classes in Paris during the First Half of the Nineteenth Century.* New York: Howard Fertig, 1973.
Cloete, J. R. "The Boy and His Work." In *Studies in Boy Life in Our Cities,* edited by E. J. Urwick. London, 1904.
Comfort, Alex. *The Anxiety Makers.* New York: Dell, 1969.
————. *Sex in Society.* London: Penguin, 1966.
Cominos, Peter T. "Late-Victorian Sexual Respectability and the Social System." *International Review of Social History* **8** (1963):18–48, 216–250.
Coornaert, Emile. *Le Compagnonnages en France.* Paris, 1966.
Crouch, Colin. *The Student Revolt.* London: The Bodley Head, 1970.
Crozier, Dorothy. "Kinship and Occupational Succession." *Sociological Review* **13** (1965):15–43.
Dahrendorf, Ralf. *Society and Democracy in Germany.* New York: Doubleday, 1967.
Dangerfield, George. *The Strange Death of Liberal England.* New York, 1961.
Darnton, Robert. "The High Enlightenment and the Low-Life Literature in Prerevolutionary France." *Past & Present,* no. 51 (May 1971): 81–115.
Darton, F. J. Harvey. *Children's Books in England: Five Centuries of Social Life.* Cambridge, England, 1958.
Davis, Kingsley. "Adolescence and the Social Structure." *Annals of the American Academy of Political and Social Science* **236** (1944):31–47.
Davis, Natalie Z. "The Reasons of Misrule: Youth Groups and Charivaris in Sixteenth Century France." *Past & Present,* (50) (February 1971):41–75.
————. *Society and Culture in Early Modern France.* Stanford: Stanford Univ. Press, 1975.
————. "A Trade Union in Sixteenth Century France." *Economic History Review* **20** (1966):48–69.
Demos, John. *A Little Commonwealth: Family Life in the Plymouth Colony.* New York: Oxford Univ. Press, 1970.
————, and Demos, Virginia. "Adolescence in Historical Perspective." *Journal of Marriage and the Family* **31**(4) (1969):632–8.
de Musset, Alfred. "Confessions of a Child of the Century." In *Romanticism,* edited by John B. Halsted. New York: Harper, 1969.
de Sauvigny, Guillaume de Bertier. *The Bourbon Restoration.* Translated by Lynn M. Case. Philadelphia: Univ. of Pennsylvania Press, 1966.
Dennis, Norman; Henriques, Fernando; and Slaughter, Clifford. *Coal is Our Life.* London: Tavistock, 1965.
Dingle, Aylward. *A Modern Sinbad.* London, 1933.
Dorwart, Reinhold A. *The Prussian Welfare State before 1740.* Cambridge, Massachusetts: Harvard Univ. Press, 1971.
Eager, W. McG. *Making Men: The History of Boys' Clubs and Related Movements in Great Britain.* London, 1953.
Edding, F. "Relativer Schulbesuch und Abschlussquoten in internationalen Vergleich." In *Jugend in der modernen Gesellschaft,* edited by Ludwig von Friedeburg. Köln–Berlin: Kiepenheuer & Witsch, 1965.
Eisenstadt, S. N. *From Generation to Generation: Age Groups and Social Structure.* New York: The Free Press, 1966.

――――. *Modernization: Protest and Change.* Englewood Cliffs, N.J.: Prentice-Hall, 1966.

Eisenstein, Elizabeth. *The First Professional Revolutionist: Filippo Michele Buonarroti.* Cambridge, Massachusetts: Harvard Univ. Press, 1959.

Elder, Glenn H. *Children of the Depression.* Chicago: Chicago Univ. Press, 1974.

Eliade, Mircea. *Rites and Symbols of Initiation.* New York: Harper, 1965.

Ellis, Havelock. *Studies in the Psychology of Sex.* Vol. 4. Philadelphia, 1911.

Eppel, E. M., and Eppel, M. "Connotations of Morality." *British Journal of Sociology* **12** (1962):243–63.

Epstein, Klaus. *Genesis of German Conservatism.* Princeton: Princeton Univ. Press, 1966.

Esler, Anthony. "Generational Studies: A Basic Bibliography." Unpublished manuscript, 1979.

Feuer, Lewis S. *The Conflict of Generations: The Character and Significance of Student Movements.* New York: Basic Books, 1969.

Fischer, David H. *Growing Old in America.* New York: Oxford Univ. Press, 1978.

Fischer, Frank. *Wandern und Schauen.* 1913.

Fischer, Wolfram. "Soziale Unterschichten im Zeitalter der Frühindustrialisierung." *International Review of Social History* **8** (1963):415–35.

Fishman, Sterling. "Suicide, Sex and the Discovery of the German Adolescent." *History of Education Quarterly* **10** (1970):170–188.

Fletcher, Margaret. *O' Call Back Yesterday.* Oxford, 1939.

Fletcher, Ronald. *Family and Marriage in Britain.* London: Penguin Books, 1962.

Fourier, Charles. *Harmonium Man: The Writings of Charles Fourier.* Edited by Mark Poster. Garden City, N.Y.: Doubleday, 1971.

Frankenberg, R. *Communities in Britain.* London: Penguin Books, 1966.

Freeman, Arnold. *Boy Life and Labour.* London, 1914.

Freudenthal, Herbert. *Vereine in Hamburg.* Hamburg, 1968.

Friedenberg, Edgar Z. *The Vanishing Adolescent.* New York: Dell, 1959.

Friedenthal, Richard. *Goethe, His Life and Times.* New York: World, 1965.

Fyvel, J. R. *The Insecure Offender.* London, 1963.

Gaustad, Edwin S. *The Great Awakening in New England.* 2d ed. Gloucester, 1965.

George, M. Dorothy. *London in the Eighteenth Century.* New York: Harper, 1964.

Gilbert, C. "When Did a Man in the Renaissance Grow Old?" *Studies in the Renaissance* **14** (1967):7–32.

Gillis, John R. "Affective Individualism and the English Poor." *Journal of Interdisciplinary History* **9** (1979):121–128.

――――. "Conformity and Rebellion: Contrasting Styles of English and German Youth, 1900–1933." *History of Education Quarterly* **13** (Fall 1973):249–260.

――――. "The Emergence of Modern Juvenile Delinquency in England, 1890–1914." *Past and Present* **67** (1975): 96–126.

――――. *Prussian Bureaucracy in Crisis, 1840–60: The Origins of an Administrative Ethos.* Stanford: Stanford Univ. Press, 1971.

――――. "Youth and History: Progress and Prospect." *Journal of Social History* **7** (2) (Winter 1973).

Glass, David V. "Education and Social Change in Modern England." In *Education, Economy, and Society,* edited by A. H. Halsey et al. London, 1961.

Gluckman, Max. "Les Rites de Passage." In *Essays on the Ritual of Social Relations,* edited by M. Gluckman. Manchester, 1962.

Goffman, Erving. *Asylums.* Garden City, N.Y.: Doubleday, 1961.

Goldthorpe, J. H. et al. *The Affluent Worker in the Class Structure.* Cambridge: Cambridge Univ. Press, 1969.

Gollin, Gillian. *Moravians in Two Worlds.* New York: Columbia Univ. Press, 1967.

Goode, William J. *World Revolution and Family Patterns.* New York: The Free Press, 1970.

Goodwin, A., Ed. *The European Nobility in the 18th Century.* New York, 1967.
Gorer, Goeffrey. *Exploring English Character.* London: The Cresset Press, 1955.
Gottlieb, David et al. *The Emergence of Youth Societies: A Cross Cultural Approach.* New York, 1966.
Gouldner, Alvin. *The Coming Crisis of Western Sociology.* New York: Basic Books, 1970.
Gown and Town Rows at Oxford and Their Historical Significance." *Dublin University Magazine* **71** (April 1868).
Graff, Harvey J. "Patterns of Dependence and Child Development in a Mid-19th Century City: Sample from Boston 1860." *History of Education Quarterly* **13** (2) (Summer 1972):129–144.
Graña, Cesar. *Bohemian versus Bourgeois: French Society and the French Man of Letters in the Nineteenth Century.* New York: Basic Books, 1964.
Graves, Robert. *Goodbye to All That.* Garden City, N.Y.: Doubleday, 1957.
Graves, T. S. "Some Pre-Mohock Clansmen." *Studies in Philology* **20** (1923):395–421.
Green, F. S. "Youth and Community Center Services: Some Facts, Figures and Reflections." September 1963. Mimeographed paper in possession of author.
Greven, Philip J. "Youth, Maturity, and Religious Conversion: A Note on the Ages of Converts in Andover, Mass., 1711–1749." *Essex Institute Historical Collections* **58**(2) (April 1972): 119–134.
Grünhut, Max. *Penal Reform: A Comparative Study.* 2d ed. Montclair, N.J.: Patterson Smith, 1972.
Gusfield, Joseph. *Symbolic Crusade: Status Politics and the American Temperance Movement.* Urbana, Ill.: Univ. of Illinois Press, 1963.
Habakkuk, H. J. "Marriage Settlements in the Eighteenth Century." *Transactions of the Royal Historical Society,* Fourth Series, **32** (1950):15–30.
Hajnal, John. "European Marriage Patterns in Perspective." In *Population in History,* edited by D. V. Glass and D. E. C. Eversley. London, 1965.
Hall, G. Stanley, *Adolescence: Its Psychology, and Its Relations to Physiology, Anthropology, Sociology, Sex Crime, Religion, and Education.* Vol. 1. New York, 1904. Vol. 2. 2d ed. New York, 1969.
Hall, Stewart, and Jefferson, Tony, eds. *Resistance through Rituals: Youth Subcultures in Post-War Britain.* London: Hutchinson, 1976.
Halsey, A. H. "The Changing Function of Universities in Advanced Industrial Societies." *Harvard Educational Review* **30** (1960):119–27.
———, Ed. *Trends in British Society since 1900: A Guide to Changing Social Structure in Britain.* New York: Macmillan, 1972.
Hammond, J. L., and Hammond, Barbara. *The Village Labourer, 1760–1832.* New York: Harper, 1970.
Hans, Nicholas. *New Trends in Education in the Eighteenth Century,* 2d ed. London: Routledge & Kegan Paul, 1966.
Hare, E. H. "Masturbational Insanity: The History of an Ideal." *Journal of Mental Science* **108** (1962).
Hareven, Tomara, ed. *Transitions: The Family and Life Course in Historical Perspective.* New York: Academic, 1978.
Harrison, Brian. "Underneath the Victorians." *Victorian Studies* **10**(3) (1967):239–62.
Hawes, Joseph. *Children in Urban Society.* New York: Oxford Univ. Press, 1969.
Henriques, Fernando. *Prostitution and Society.* Vol. 3. London: MacGibbon & Kee, 1968.
Herlihy, David. "Vieillir à Florence au Quattrocentro." *Annales Economies Societes Civilisations* **24**(6) (November–December 1969): 1338–1352.
Herrmann, Ulrich, Renftle, S., Roth, S. *Bibliographie zur Geschiche der Kindheit, Jugend, und Familie.* Munich, 1980.

Hewitt, Margaret. *Wives and Mothers in Victorian Industry.* London, 1958.

Hicks, W. R. *The School in English and German Fiction.* London, 1933.

Hill, Christopher. *The World Turned Upside Down: Radical Ideas During the English Revolution.* New York: Viking, 1972.

Himmelweit, Hilda. "Social and Class Differences in Parent–Child Relations in England." In *Recherches sur la famille,* vol. 2, edited by Nels Anderson, pp. 179–90. Göttingen, 1957.

Hiscock, Eric. *Last Boat to Folly Bridge,* London, 1970.

Hobsbawm, Eric J. *The Age of Revolution.* New York: Mentor, 1962.

————. "The Labour Aristocracy in the Nineteenth Century." In *Labouring Men,* pp. 272–315. New York: Basic Books, 1964.

————. "The Ritual of Social Movements." In *Primitive Rebels.* New York: Norton, 1965.

————. "The Tramping Artisan." In *Labouring Men,* pp. 34–65. New York: Basic Books, 1964.

————, and Rudé, George. *Captain Swing.* New York: Pantheon Press, 1970.

Hoggart, Richard. *The Uses of Literacy.* London, 1957.

Holborn, Hajo. *A History of Modern Germany.* Vol. 2. New York: Alfred Knopf, 1964.

Hole, Christina. *English Folklore.* London, 1940.

————. *English Sports and Pastimes.* London, 1949.

Hollingsworth, T. H. *The Demography of the British Peerage.* Supplement to *Population Studies* **18**(2) (November 1964).

Hope, Arthur M. "Breaking down of Caste." *Problems of Boy Life,* edited by J. H. Whitehouse. London, 1912.

Horn, Daniel. "Youth Resistance in the Third Reich: A Social Portrait." *Journal of Social History* **7**(1) (1973):28–43.

Hornstein, Walter, *Jugend in ihrer Zeit.* Hamburg, 1966.

Horsley, John. *Juvenile Crime. Its Causes and Remedies: The Great Social Question of the Day.* London, 1894.

Hughes, Thomas. *Tom Brown's School Days.* New York: St. Martin's, 1967.

Hunt, David. *Parents and Children in History: Psychology of Family Life in Early Modern France.* New York: Basic Books, 1970.

Hynes, Samuel. *The Edwardian Turn of Mind.* Princeton: Princeton Univ. Press, 1968.

Inglis, K. S. *Churches and the Working Classes in Victorian England.* London, 1963.

Jantzen, Walter. "Die soziologische Herkunft der Führungsschichte der deutschen Jugendbewegung, 1900–33." In *Führungsschichte und Eliteproblem.* Frankfurt a.M., 1957.

Jones, Louis C. *The Clubs of the Georgian Rakes.* New York, 1942.

Juvenile Offenders: An Inquiry Instituted by the Howard Association. London, 1889.

Kanter, Rosabeth Moss. *Commitment and Community: Communes and Utopias in Sociological Perspective.* Cambridge, Massachusetts: Harvard Univ. Press, 1972.

Katz, Michael, and Davey, Ian. "Youth and Early Industrialization in a Canadian City." In *Turning Points,* edited by J. Demos and S. Boocock. Chicago: University of Chicago, 1978.

Keniston, Kenneth. "Psychological Development and Historical Change." *Journal of Interdisciplinary History* **2**(2) (Fall 1971):329–345.

————. *The Uncommitted: Alienated Youth in American Society.* New York: Dell, 1960.

————. *Young Radicals: Notes on Committed Youth.* New York, 1968.

Kett, Joseph. "Adolescence and Youth in Nineteenth Century America." *Journal of Interdisciplinary History* **2**(2) (Fall 1971):283–298.

————. *Rites of Passage: Adolescence in America 1790 to Present.* New York: Basic Books, 1977.

Key, Ellen. *The Century of the Child.* London, 1909.

Kirk, Edward B. *A Talk with Boys About Themselves.* London, 1905.

Kitchen, Martin. *The German Officer Corps, 1890–1914*. Oxford: Clarendon Press, 1968.
Knoop, D., and Jones, G. P. *The Genesis of Freemasonry*. Manchester, 1947.
Kotschnig, Walter M. *Unemployment in the Learned Professions*. London, 1937.
Laqueur, Walter Z. *Young Germany: A History of the German Youth Movement*. New York: Basic Books, 1962.
Laslett, Peter. "Age of Menarche in Europe since the 18th Century." *Journal of Interdisciplinary History* **2**(2) (Fall 1971):221–236.
———. *The World We Have Lost*. New York: Charles Scribner's Sons, 1965.
Lees, Lynn. "Irish Slum Communities in Nineteenth Century London." In *Nineteenth Century Cities*, edited by S. Thernstrom and R. Sennett. New Haven: Yale Univ. Press, 1970.
Lefebvre, Georges. *The Thermidorians*. New York: Vintage, 1966.
Le Roy Ladurie, E. *Carnival in Romans*. New York: Braziller, 1979.
———. *Montaillou*. New York: Braziller, 1978.
Levine, Lawrence. *Black Culture and Black Consciousness*. New York: Oxford Univ. Press, 1977.
Local Publishing and Local Culture: An Account of the Work of Centerprise Publishing Project, 1972–77. London: Centerprise, 1977.
Loewenberg, Peter. "The Psychohistorical Origins of the Nazi Youth Cohort." *American Historical Review* **76** (1971);1457–1502.
Lowndes, G. A. L. *The Silent Revolution: An Account of the Expansion of Public Education in England & Wales, 1895–1965*. 2d ed. London: Oxford Univ. Press, 1969.
Lütkens, Charlotte. *Die deutsche Jugend*. Frankfurt a.M., 1925.
Lyttelton, Edward. *Mothers and Sons, or Problems in the Home Training of Boys*. London, 1892.
———. *Training of the Young in the Laws of Sex*. London, 1900.
MacFarlane, Alan. *The Family Life of Ralph Josselin*. Cambridge: Cambridge Univ. Press, 1970.
Mack, E. C. *The Public Schools and British Opinion, 1780–1860*. London, 1938.
Malcolmson, Robert. *Popular Recreations in English Society 1700–1850*. Cambridge: Cambridge Univ. Press, 1977.
Mannheim, Hermann. *War and Crime*. London, 1941.
Manning, Percy. "Some Oxfordshire Seasonal Festivals." *Folk Lore* **8** (December 1897).
Manuel, Frank. *Prophets of Paris*. New York: Harper, 1962.
Marsh, D. C. *Changing Social Structure of England and Wales, 1871–1961*. London: Routledge & Kegan Paul, 1965.
Marsh, Peter, Rosser, E., and Hane, R. *The Rules of Disorder*. London: 1978.
Marson, Dave. *Children's Strikes in 1911*. Oxford, n.d.
Marwick, Arthur. "Youth in Britain, 1920–1970." *Journal of Contemporary History* **5**(1) (1970): 37–51.
Marx, Karl, and Engels, Friedrich. *The Communist Manifesto*. New York: Appleton, 1955.
Masterman, C. F. G. *The Condition of England*. London, 1909.
Mathiez, Albert. *After Robespierre: The Thermidorian Reaction*. New York: Grosset, 1965.
Matza, David. "Position and Behavior Patterns of Youth." *Handbook of Modern Sociology*, edited by E. Favis. Chicago, 1964.
———. "The Subterranean Traditions of Youth." *Annals of the American Academy of Political and Social Science* **228** (1961):102–118.
Mayhew, Henry. *German Life and Manners as Seen in Saxony at the Present Day*. Vol. I. London, 1864.
———. *London Labour and the London Poor*. Vol. I. London, 1861.
Mays, John Barron. *Crime and the Social Structure*. London: Faber & Faber, 1967.
———. *The Young Pretenders*. London: Michael Joseph, 1965.

Mazoyer, L. "Catégories d'âge et groupes social. Les jeunes generations francaises de 1830." *Annales d'historie économique et sociale* **10** (1938):385–423.

Meachem, Standish. "The Sense of an Impending Clash: English Working Class Unrest before the First World War." *American Historical Review* **77**(5) (December 1972):1343–1364.

Mennel, Robert. *Thornes & Thistles: Juvenile Delinquents in the United States.* Hanover, N.H.: New England Universities Press, 1972.

Merkl, Peter, *Political Violence under the Swastika: 581 Early Nazis.* Princeton: Princeton Univ. Press, 1975.

Metraux, Rhoda. "Parents and Children: An Analysis of Contemporary German Child-Care and Youth-Guidance Literature." *Childhood in Contemporary Cultures,* edited by M. Mead and M. Wolfenstein. Chicago: Univ. of Chicago Press, 1967.

"Militance in High Schools Worries London Officials." *New York Times,* 18 May 1972.

Mill, John Stuart. "Spirit of the Age." In *Essays in Politics and Culture,* edited by Gertrude Himmelfarb. Garden City, N.Y.: Doubleday, 1963.

Milson, Fred. *Youth in a Changing Society.* London: Routledge & Kegan Paul, 1972.

Mingay, C. E. *English Landed Society in the Eighteenth Century.* London: Routledge & Kegan Paul, 1963.

Mogey, John M. *Family and Neighborhood: Two Studies in Oxford.* Oxford: Oxford Univ. Press, 1966.

Möller, Helmut. *Die kleinbürgerliche Familie im 18. Jahrhundert. Verhalten und Gruppen Kultur.* Berlin, 1969.

Moller, Herbert. "Youth as a Force in the Modern World." *Comparative Studies in Society and History* **10** (1968):237–260.

Montague, Lily H. "The Girl in the Background." In *Studies of Boy Life in Our Cities,* edited by E. J. Urwick. London, 1904.

Morley, John. *Death, Heaven, and the Victorians.* Pittsburg: Univ. of Pittsburg Press, 1971.

Morrison, William Douglas. *Juvenile Offenders.* London, 1896.

Mosse, George L. *Crisis of German Ideology.* New York, 1964.

Muchow, Hans Heinrich. *Jugend und Zeitgeist: Morphologie der Kulturpubertät.* Reinbek bei Hamburg: Rohwolt Verlag, 1962.

—————. *Sexualreife und Sozialstruktur der Jugend.* Reinbek bei Hamburg: Rohwolt, 1959.

Mungham, G. and Pearson, G., eds. *Working Class Youth Culture.* London: Routledge & Kegan Paul, 1976.

Musgrove, F. "The Decline of the Educative Family." *Universities Quarterly* **14** (1960):377–404.

—————. "Middle Class Education and Employment in the Nineteenth Century: A Rejoinder." *Economic History Review* **14** (1961):320–29.

—————. "Middle Class Families and the Schools 1780–1880." *Sociological Review* **7** (1959):169–178.

—————. *Youth and the Social Order.* London: Routledge & Kegan Paul, 1965.

Muuss, R. *Theories of Adolescence.* 2d ed. New York: Random House, 1968.

Myrdal, Alva. *Nation and Family.* Cambridge, Massachusetts: Harvard Univ. Press, 1969.

Neidhardt, Friedhelm. *Die Familie in Deutschland.* Opladen: Leske Vevlag, 1966.

—————. *Die junge Generation.* Opladen: Leske Verlag, 1970.

Newsome, David. *Godliness and Goodlearning.* London: John Murray, 1961.

Noyes, Paul. *Organization and Revolution: Working Class Associations in the German Revolutions of 1848/9.* Princeton Univ. Press, 1966.

O'Boyle, Lenore. "The Problem of an Excess of Educated Men in Western Europe, 1800–1850." *Journal of Modern History* **42**(4) (1970):471–495.

Ong, Walter J. "Latin Language Study as a Renaissance Puberty Rite." In *Rhetoric, Romance and Technology,* edited by W. J. Ong. Ithaca, N.Y.: Cornell Univ. Press, 1971.

Ozouf, Mona. "Symboles et fonction des ages dans les fêtes de L'Époche Révolutionnaire." *Annales historiques de la Révolution Francais,* no. 202 (October-December 1970):569–593.

Pantin, J. "Report of the Keeper of the Archives, 1964–5." Supplement no. 4. *University Gazette* **46** (March 1966). Oxford University.

Parry, Albert. *Garrets and Pretenders. A History of Bohemianism in America.* New York, 1933.

Parsons, Talcott. "Age and Sex in the Social Structure." *Essays in Sociology.* Glencoe, Ill. The Free Press, 1949.

———. "Youth in the Context of American Society." In *The Challenge of Youth,* edited by E. Erikson. Garden City, N.Y.: Doubleday, 1965.

Paterson, Alexander. *Across the Bridges.* London, 1912.

Paul, Leslie. *The Republic of Children.* London, 1938.

Pelles, Geraldine. *Art, Artists and Society.* Englewood Cliffs, N.J.: Prentice-Hall, 1963.

Perkin, H. J. "Middle Class Education and Employment: A Critical Note." *Economic History Review* **14** (1961):122–30.

———. *The Origins of Modern English Society, 1780–1880.* London: Routledge & Kegan Paul, 1969.

Phythian-Adams, Charles, *Desolation of a City: Coventry and the Urban Crisis of the Late Middle Ages.* Cambridge: Cambridge Univ. Press, 1979.

———. *Local History and Folklore.* London: Bedford Square Press, 1975.

Pinchbeck, Ivy, and Hewitt, Margaret. *Children in English Society.* Vol. 1. London: Routledge & Kegan Paul, 1969.

Pinkney, David. *The French Revolution of 1830.* Princeton: Princeton Univ. Press, 1972.

Platt, Anthony E. *The Child Savers: The Invention of Delinquency.* Chicago: Univ. of Chicago Press, 1969.

Plowman, Thomas F. *In the Days of Victoria.* London, 1918.

Porter, Enid. *Cambridgeshire Customs and Folklore.* London, 1969.

Price, Richard. *An Imperial War and the British Working Class.* London: Routledge & Kegan Paul, 1972.

Pross, Harry. *Jugend, Eros, Politik.* Berlin–Munich–Vienna, 1964.

Rabe, Hanns-Berd. "Der Wandervogel in Osnabrück: Bild einer Jugend von 1907–1920." *Osnabrücker Mitteilungen* **70** (1961):109–154.

Radzinowicz, Leon. *Ideology and Crime: A Study of Crime in its Social and Historical Context.* London, 1966.

Reader, W. J. *Professional Men: The Rise of the Professional Classes in Nineteenth Century England.* New York: Basic Books, 1966.

Redford, Arthur. *Labour Migration in England.* Manchester: Manchester Univ. Press, 1964.

"Reports of the Riot of November 1867." Oxford City Library, Clipping Collection, P 942571.

Ringer, Fritz. *The Decline of the German Mandarins.* Cambridge, Massachusetts: Harvard Univ. Press, 1969.

Roberts, E. Eric. "The Service of Youth." *Oxford Monthly* **17** (November 1940).

Roberts, J. M. *The Myth of the Secret Societies.* London, 1972.

Robins, D., and Cohen, P. *Knuckle Sandwich: Growing Up in the Working Class City.* Harmondsworth: Penguin, 1978.

Roessler, Wilhelm. *Die Enstehung des modernen Erziehungswesens in Deutschland.* Stuttgart, 1961.

Rowntree, B. Seebohm. *Poverty and Progress: A Second Social Survey of York.* London, 1931.

———. *Poverty: A Study of Town Life.* London, 1914.

Rubenstein, David. *School Attendance in London, 1870–1904: A Social History.* New York, 1972.

Russell, Charles E. B. "Adolescence." In *Converging Views of Social Reform.* London, 1913.

———. *Manchester Boys, Sketches of Manchester Lads at Work and Play.* Manchester, 1905.

Samuel, R. H., and Thomas, R. Hinton. *Education and Society in Modern Germany.* London, 1949.

Sarmela, Matti. *Reciprocity Systems of the Rural Society in the Finnish-Karelian Cultural Area, with Special Reference to Social Intercourse of the Youth.* Folklore Fellows Communication, No. 207, Helsinki, 1969.

Schaffstein, Friedrich. "Die Bemessung der Jugendhilfe: Erfahrung und Folerungen." In *Jugendkrimimalität, Strafjustiz und Sozialpädagogik,* pp. 248–265. Frankfurt a.M., 1969.

Schelsky, Helmut. *Die skeptische Generation.* Düsseldorf–Köln, 1957.

Schenk, H. G. *The Mind of the European Romantics.* New York: Doubleday, 1969.

Schieder, Wolfgang. *Anfänge der deutschen Arbeiterbewegung.* Stuttgart: Ernst Klett Verlag, 1963.

Schochet, Gordon. "Patriarchalism, Politics and Mass Attitudes in Stuart England." *The Historical Journal* **12**(3) (1969):413–441.

Schoenbaum, David. *Hitler's Social Revolution: Class and Status in Nazi Germany, 1933–1939.* Garden City, N.Y.: Doubleday, 1967.

Schofield, Michael. *The Sexual Behavior of Young People.* London: Penguin Books, 1968.

Schulze, Friedrich, and Ssymank, Paul. *Das deutsche Studententum.* Munich, 1932.

Schwartz, Gary, and Marten, Don. "The Language of Adolescence: An Anthropological Approach to Youth Culture." *American Journal of Sociology* **72** (1967):453–468.

Schwartz, Paul. *Die Gelehrtenschulen Preussens unter dem Oberschulkollegium (1787–1806) und das Arbiturientenexamen.* Vol. 1. Berlin, 1910. Vol. 2. Berlin, 1911.

Sheehy, Gail. *Passages: Predictable Crises in Adult Life.* New York: Dutton, 1976.

Sherwood, W. E. *Oxford Yesterday.* Oxford, 1927.

Shorter, Edward. "Illegitimacy, Sexual Revolution and Social Change in Modern Europe." *Journal of Interdisciplinary History* **2**(2) (Fall 1971):329–345.

Simon, Brian. *Education and the Labour Movement, 1870–1920.* London: Lawrence & Wishart, 1965.

Simonsohn, Gerthold. "Vom Strafrecht zur Jugendhilfe. Ein Geschichtlicher Überblick." In *Jugendkriminalität, Strafjustiz und Sozialpädagogik,* edited by Gerthold Simonsohn. Frankfurt a.M., 1969.

Slicher van Bath, B. H. *The Agrarian History of Western Europe, 500–1840.* London: E. Arnold, 1963.

Smelser, Neil, *Social Change in the Industrial Revolution: An Application of Theory to the Lancashire Cotton Industry, 1770–1840.* Chicago: Univ. of Chicago Press, 1959.

Spamer, Adolf. "Sitte und Brauch." In *Handbuch der deutschen Volkskunde,* edited by Wilhelm Pressler. Vol. 2. Potsdam, 1935.

Spender, Stephen. "The English Adolescent." *Harvard Education Review* **18** (1948):229–240.

Spitz, Rene A. "Authority and Masturbation." *The Psychoanalytic Quarterly* **21** (1952):490–527.

Spitzer, Alan B. "The Historical Problem of Generations." *American Historical Review* **78** (1973):1353–1385.

Springhall, J. O. "The Boy Scouts, Class and Militarism in Relation to British Youth Movements, 1908–1930." *International Review of Social History* **17** (1972):3–23.

Stadelmann, Rudolf, and Fischer, Wolfram. *Die Bildungswelt des deutschen Handwerkers um 1800.* Berlin, 1955.

Stearns, Peter. *Be a Man! Males in Modern Society.* New York: Holmes & Meier, 1979.

———. *Old Age in European Society.* New York: Holmes & Meier, 1976.

Stedman-Jones, Gareth. "Some Problems in Reconstructing the Culture and Attitudes of the Poor in Mid- and Late Victorian London." Paper given at Labor History Conference, Rutgers University, April 1973. Appears in *Journal of Social History,* Spring 1974.

Stephan, G. *Die hausliche Erziehung in Deutschland während des achtzehnten Jahrhunderts.* Wiesbaden, 1891.

Stern, Fritz. *Politics of Cultural Despair.* Garden City, N.Y.: Doubleday, 1965.

Stone, Lawrence, *The Family, Sex and Marriage in England 1500–1800.* New York: Harper & Row, 1977.

————. "Literacy and Education in England, 1640–1900." *Past & Present* **42** (February 1969):69–139.

————. "Marriage among the English Nobility in the 16th and 17th Centuries." *Comparative Studies in Society and History* **3** (1960):182–206.

————. "The Size and Composition of the Oxford Student Body, 1580–1910." Unpublished paper, 1972.

————. "Social Mobility in England, 1500–1700." *Past & Present*, no. 33 (April 1966):16–55.

"Survey of Youth Services in Oxford." September 1960. Unpublished manuscript in possession of F. S. Green.

Talmon, Jacob. *Political Messianism: The Romantic Phase.* New York: Praeger, 1960.

Tanner, J. M. "Sequences, Tempo and Individual Variation in the Growth and Development of Boys and Girls Aged Twelve to Sixteen." *Daedalus* (Fall 1971).

Tawney, R. H. "Economics of Boy Labour." In *Problems of Boy Life*, edited by J. H. Whitehouse. London, 1912.

Thirsk, Joan. "Younger Sons in the Seventeenth Century." *History* **54**(182) (1969):358–377.

Thomas, Keith. "The Double Standard." *Journal of the History of Ideas* **20** (1959): 195–216.

————. "History and Anthropology." *Past and Present* **24** (1963): 3–24.

Thompson, Edward P. "Folklore, Anthropology, and Social History." *Indian Historical Review* **2** (1978):247 266.

————. *The Making of the English Working Class.* New York: Pantheon Books, 1958.

————. "The Moral Economy of the Crowd in Eighteenth Century England." *Past & Present*, no. 50 (February 1971): 76–136.

————. *Poverty of Theory and Other Essays.* London: Merlin, 1978.

————. " 'Rough Music': Le Charvari anglais." *Annales Economies Sociétés Civilisation* **27**(2) (March–April 1972):285–312.

Thompson, F. L. M. *English Landed Society in the Nineteenth Century.* London: Routledge & Kegan Paul, 1963.

Thompson, Paul. *The Voice of the Past: Oral History.* New York: Oxford Univ. Press, 1978.

Tilly, Charles. "Population and Pedagogy in France." *History of Education Quarterly* **13** (Summer 1973):113–128.

————, and Tilly, Richard. "Agenda of European Economic History." *Journal of Economic History* **21**(1) (March 1971): 184–198.

Tilly, Louise, and Scott, Joan W. *Women, Work, and Family* New York: Holt, Rinehart & Winston, 1978.

Tilly, Richard. "Popular Disorders in Nineteenth Century Germany: A Preliminary Survey." *Journal of Social History* **4**(1) (Fall 1970): 1–40.

Tipps, Dean C. "Modernization Theory and the Comparative Study of Societies: A Critical Perspective." *Comparative Studies in Society and History* **15** (1973):199–226.

Tobias, J. J. *Crime and Industrial Society in the Nineteenth Century.* New York: Schocken Books, 1967.

Tranter, N. L. "Population and Social Structure in a Bedfordshire Parish: The Cardington List of Inhabitants, 1782." *Population Studies* **21** (1967):261–282.

Trollope, Frances. *Paris and the Parisians in 1835.* New York, 1836.

Tropp, Asher, *The School Teachers.* London, 1957.

Turner, E. S. *Boys Will Be Boys.* Rev. ed. London, 1957.

————. *A History of Courting.* London, 1954.

Uhlenberg, Peter. "Changing Configurations of the Life Course." In *Transitions*, edited by T. Hareven. New York: Academic, 1978.

Urwick, E. J. "Conclusion." In *Studies of Boy Life in Our Cities*, edited by E. J. Urwick. London, 1904.

————. "Introduction." In *Studies of Boy Life in Our Cities*, edited by E. J. Urwick. London, 1904.

Vann, Richard T. "Nurture and Conversion in the Early Quaker Family." *Journal of Marriage and the Family* **31**(4) (1969):639–643.

Viatte, August. *Les Sources occultes du romanticisme, 1770–1820.* Vol. 1. Paris, 1928.

Vicinus, Martha. *The Industrial Muse: A Study of Nineteenth Century British Working Class Literature.* London: Croom Helm, 1974.

von Klöden, Friedrich. *The Self-Made Man.* 2 vols. London. 1876.

Waas, Oskar. *Die Pennalie: Ein Beitrag zu ihrer Geschichte.* Graz, 1967.

Waite, Robert L. *Vanguard of Nazism: The Free Corps Movement in Postwar Germany, 1918–23.* New York: Norton, 1969.

Wakeford, John. *The Cloistered Elite: A Sociological Analysis of the English Public Boarding School.* London: Macmillan, 1969.

Walker, Mack. *German Home Towns: Community, State, and General Estate, 1648–1871.* Ithaca, N. Y.: Cornell Univ. Press, 1971.

Walsh, John. "Origins of the Evangelical Revival." In *Essays in Modern Church History.* New York, 1966.

Weber, Anna. *The Growth of Cities in the Nineteenth Century.* 2d ed. Ithaca, N. Y.: Cornell Univ. Press, 1963.

Weber, Eugen. "Gymnastics and Sports in Fin-de-Siècle France: Opium of the Classes?" *American Historical Review* **76**(1) (February 1971):70–98.

Weber, Max. *From Max Weber: Essays in Sociology.* New York: Oxford, 1958.

Weeks, Jeffery. *Coming Out. Homosexual Politics in Britain from the Nineteenth Century to the Present.* London, 1977.

Wiedelmann, Karl. *Bund und Gruppe als Lebenformen deutschen Jugend.* Munich, 1945.

Weinberg, Ian. *The English Public Schools: The Sociology of Elite Education.* New York: Atherton Press, 1967.

Welsford, Enid. *The Fool: His Social and Literary History.* London, 1935.

Wentzcke, Paul. *Geschichte der deutschen Burschenschaft.* Vol. 1. Heidelberg, 1919.

West, D. J. *The Young Offender.* London: Penguin Books, 1968.

Wiese, Leopold. *German Letters on English Education.* London, 1854.

Wikman, K. Robert. *Die Einleitung der Ehe.* Abo, 1937.

Wildermann, R., and Kaase, M. "Die unruhige Generation." In *Eine Untersuchung zu Politik und Demokratie in der Bundesrepublik.* 2 vols. Mannheim, 1968.

Wilkinson, Paul. "English Youth Movement, 1908–1930." *Journal of Contemporary History* **4**(1969):7–23.

Wilkinson, Rupert. *The Prefects: British Leadership and the Public School Tradition.* London: Oxford Press, 1964.

Williams, David. *The Rebecca Riots: A Study in Agrarian Discontent.* Cardiff, Wales, 1955.

Willmott, Peter. *Adolescent Boys in East London.* London: Penguin Books, 1969.

———, and Young, Michael. *Family and Kinship in East London.* London: Penguin Books, 1957.

Wilson, Bryan. *Youth Culture and the Universities.* London, 1970.

Wrigley, E. A. *Population and History.* London: World Univ. Library, 1969.

———. "A Simple Model of London's Importance in Changing English Society and Economy, 1650–1750." *Past & Present,* no. (37) (July 1967):47–65.

Zorn, Wolfgang, "Hochschule und höhere Schule in der deutschen Sozialgeschichte der Neuzeit." In *Spiegel der Geschichte,* edited by K. Repgen. Münster, 1964.

Zweig, Fredynand. *The Student in the Age of Anxiety.* London: Heineman, 1963.

Index